IN AFRICA

One Morning's Bag

IN AFRICA
Hunting Adventures in the Big Game Country

BY

JOHN T. McCUTCHEON

Cartoonist of the Chicago Tribune

ILLUSTRATED WITH PHOTOGRAPHS AND CARTOONS BY THE AUTHOR

TO THOSE ADVENTUROUS SOULS WHO
RESENT THE RESTRAINT OF THE BEATEN PATH
THESE OBSERVATIONS OF AN AMATEUR
ARE DEDICATED

PREFATORY NOTE

This collection of African stories has no pretentious purpose. It is merely the record of a most delightful hunting trip into those fascinating regions along the Equator, where one may still have "thrilling adventures" and live in a story-book atmosphere, where the "roar of the lion" and the "crack of the rifle" are part of the every-day life, and where in a few months one may store up enough material to keep the memory pleasantly occupied all the rest of a lifetime. The stories are descriptive of a four-and-a-half months' trip in the big game country and pretend to no more serious purpose than merely to relate the experiences of a self-confessed amateur under such conditions.

JOHN T. McCUTCHEON

August, 1910

CHAPTER I
THE PREPARATION FOR DEPARTURE. EXPERIENCES WITH WILLING FRIENDS AND ADVISERS

EVER since I can remember, almost, I have cherished a modest ambition to hunt lions and elephants. At an early age, or, to be more exact, at about that age which finds most boys wondering whether they would rather be Indian fighters or sailors, I ran across a copy of Stanley's *Through the Dark Continent*. It was full of fascinating adventures. I thrilled at the accounts which spoke in terms of easy familiarity of "express" rifles and "elephant" guns, and in my vivid but misguided imagination, I pictured an elephant gun as a sort of cannon—a huge, unwieldy arquebus—that fired a ponderous shell. The old woodcuts of daring hunters and charging lions inspired me with unrest and longing—the longing to bid the farm farewell and start down the road for Africa. Africa! What a picture it conjured up in my fancy! Then, as even now, it symbolized a world of adventurous possibilities; and in my boyhood fancy, it lay away off there—somewhere—vaguely—beyond mountains and deserts and oceans, a vast, mysterious, unknown land, that swarmed with inviting dangers and alluring romance.

One by one my other youthful ambitions have been laid away. I have given up hope of ever being an Indian fighter out on the plains, because the pesky redskins have long since ceased to need my strong right arm to quell them. I also have yielded up my ambition to be a sailor, or rather, that branch of the profession in which I hoped to specialize—piracy—because, for some regretful reason, piracy has lost much of its charm in these days of great liners. There is no treasure to search for any more, and the golden age of the splendid clipper ships, with their immense spread of canvas, has given way to the unromantic age of the grimy steamer, about which there is so little to appeal to the imagination. Consequently, lion hunting is about the only thing left—except wars, and they are few and far between.

And so, after suffering this "lion-hunting" ambition to lie fallow for many years, I at last reached a day when it seemed possible to realize it. The chance came in a curiously unexpected way. Mr. Akeley, a man famed in African hunting exploits, was to deliver a talk before a little club to which I belonged. I went, and as a result of my thrilled interest in every word he said, I met him and talked with him and finally was asked to join a new African expedition that he had in prospect. With the party were to be Mrs. Akeley, with a record of fourteen months in the big game country, and Mr. Stephenson, a hunter with many years of experience in the wild places of the United States, Canada and Mexico. My hunting experience had been chiefly gained in my library, but for some strange reason, it did not seem incongruous that I should begin my real hunting in a lion and elephant country.

Getting Ready for Lion Shooting

I had all the prowess of a Tartarin, and during the five months that elapsed before I actually set forth, I went about my daily work with a mind half dazed with the delicious consciousness that I was soon to become a lion hunter. I feared that modern methods might have taken away much of the old-time romance of the sport, but I felt certain that there was still to be something left in the way of excitement and adventure.

The succeeding pages of this book contain the chronicle of the nine delightful months that followed my departure from America.

In the middle of August Mr. Stephenson and I arrived in London. Mr. Akeley had ordered most of our equipment by letter, but there still remained many things to be done, and for a week or more we were busy from morning till night.

It is amazing how much stuff is required to outfit a party of four people for an African shooting expedition of several months' duration. First in importance come the rifles, then the tents and camp equipment, then the clothes and boots, then the medical supplies, and finally the food. Perhaps the food might be put first in importance, but just now, after a hearty dinner, it seems to be the least important detail.

Many men outfitting for an African campaign among wild animals secure their outfits in London. It is there, in modest little shops, that one gets the weapons that are known to sportsmen from one end of the world to the other—weapons designed expressly for the requirements of African shooting, and which have long stood the test of hard, practical service. For two days we haunted these famous gun-makers' shops, and for two days I made a magnificent attempt to look learnedly at things about which I knew little.

Practising in the Museum

At last, after many hours of gun shopping, attended by the constant click of a taxicab meter, I assembled such an imposing arsenal that I was nervous whenever I thought about it. With such a battery it was a foregone conclusion that something, or somebody, was likely to get hurt. I hoped that it would be something, and not somebody.

The old-time "elephant gun" which shot an enormous ball and a staggering charge of black powder has given way to the modern double-barreled rifle, with its steel bullet and cordite powder. It is not half so heavy or clumsy as the old timers, but its power and penetration are tremendous. The largest of this modern type is the .650 cordite—that is, it shoots a bullet six hundred and fifty thousandths of an inch in diameter, and has a frightful recoil. This weapon is prohibitive on account of its recoil, and few, if any, sportsmen now care to carry one. The most popular type is the .450 and .475 cordite double-barreled ejector, hammerless rifles, and these are the ones that every elephant hunter should have.

We started out with the definite purpose of getting three .450s—one for Mr. Akeley, one for Mr. Stephenson, and one for myself; also three nine-millimeter (.375) Mannlichers and two .256 Mannlichers. What we really got were three .475 cordites, two nine-millimeter Mannlichers, one eight-millimeter Mauser, and two .256 Mannlichers. We were switched off the .450s because a government regulation forbids the use of that caliber in Uganda, although it is permitted in British East Africa, and so we played safe by getting the .475s. This rifle is a heavy gun that carries a bullet large enough to jolt a fixed star and recoil enough to put one's starboard shoulder in the hospital for a day or so. Theoretically, the sportsman uses this weapon in close quarters, and with a bullet placed according to expert advice sees the charging lion, rhino or elephant turn a back somersault on his way to kingdom come. It has a tremendous impact and will usually stop an animal even if the bullet does not kill it. The bullets of a smaller rifle may kill the animal, but not stop it at once. An elephant or lion, with a small bullet in its heart, may still charge for fifty or one hundred yards before it falls. Hence the necessity for a rifle that will shock as well as penetrate.

Advice from a Cheerful Stranger

Several experienced African lion hunters strongly advise taking a "paradox," which in their parlance is affectionately called a "cripple-stopper." It looks like what one would suppose an elephant gun to look like. Its weight is staggering, and it shoots a solid ball, backed up by a fearful charge of cordite. They use it under the following conditions: Suppose that a big animal has been wounded and not instantly killed. It at once assumes the aggressive, and is savage beyond belief. The pain of the wound infuriates it and its one object in life is to get at the man who shot it. It charges in a well-nigh irresistible rush, and no ordinary bullet can stop it unless placed in one or two small vital spots. Under the circumstances the hunter may not be able to hold his rifle steady enough to hit these aforesaid spots. That is when the paradox comes in. The hunter points it in a general way in the direction of the oncoming beast, pulls the trigger and hopes for the best. The paradox bullet hits with the force of a sledge hammer, and stuns everything within a quarter of a mile, and the hunter turns several back somersaults from the recoil and fades into bruised unconsciousness.

We decided not to get the paradox, preferring to trust to hitting the small vital spots rather than transport the weapon by hand through long tropical marches.

The nine-millimeter rifles were said to be large enough for nearly all purposes, but not reassuring in extremely close quarters. The .256 Mannlichers are splendid for long range shooting, as they carry a small bore bullet and have enormous penetrating power.

The presumption, therefore, was that we should first shoot the lion at long range with the .256, then at a shorter range with the nine-millimeter, then at close range with the .475 cordite, and then perhaps fervently wish that we had the paradox or a balloon.

After getting our arsenal, we then had to get the cartridges, all done up in tin boxes of a weight not exceeding sixty pounds, that being the limit of weight which the African porter is expected to carry. There were several thousand rounds of ammunition, but this did not mean that several thousand lions were to be killed. Allowing for a fair percentage of misses, we calculated, if lucky, to get one or two lions.

After getting our rifles and ammunition under satisfactory headway, we then saw that our seventy-two "chop" boxes of food were sure to be ready in time to catch our steamer at Southampton.

And yet these preliminary details did not half conclude our shopping preliminaries in London. There were camping rugs, blankets, cork mattresses, pillows and pillow cases, bed bags, towels, lanterns, mosquito boots, whetstones, hunting and skinning knives, khaki helmets, pocket tapes to measure trophies, Pasteur anti-venomous serum, hypodermic syringes, chairs, tables, cots, puttees, sweaters, raincoats, Jaeger flannels, socks and pajamas, cholera belts, Burberry hunting clothes, and lots of other little odds and ends that seemed to be necessary.

The clothes were put up in air-proof tin uniform cases, small enough to be easily carried by a porter and secure enough to keep out the millions of ants that were expected to seek habitation in them.

Part of the Equipment

Most of our equipment, especially the food supplies, had been ordered by letter, and these we found to be practically ready. The remaining necessities, guns, ammunition, camera supplies, medical supplies, clothes, helmets, and so on, we assembled after two days of prodigious hustling. There was nothing then to be done except to hope that all our mountainous mass of equipment would be safely installed on the steamer for Mombasa. This steamer, the *Adolph Woermann*, sailed from Hamburg on the fourteenth of August, was due at Southampton on the eighteenth and at Naples on the thirtieth. To avoid transporting the hundred cases of supplies overland to Naples, it was necessary to get them to Southampton on the eighteenth. It was a close shave, for only by sending them down by passenger train on that morning were they able to reach Southampton. Fortunately our hopes were fulfilled, and at last we received word that they were on board and were careening down toward Naples, where we expected to join them on the thirtieth.

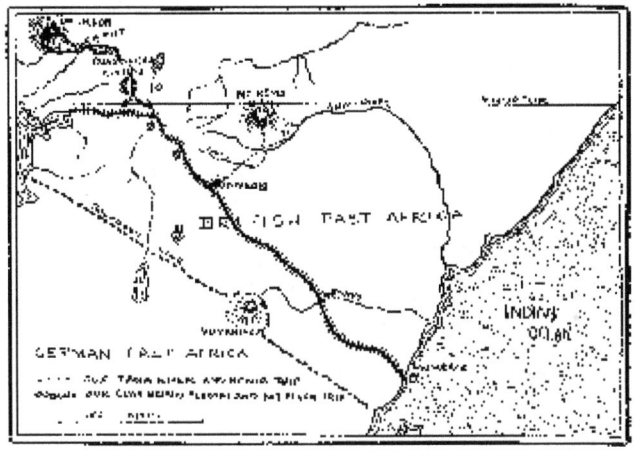

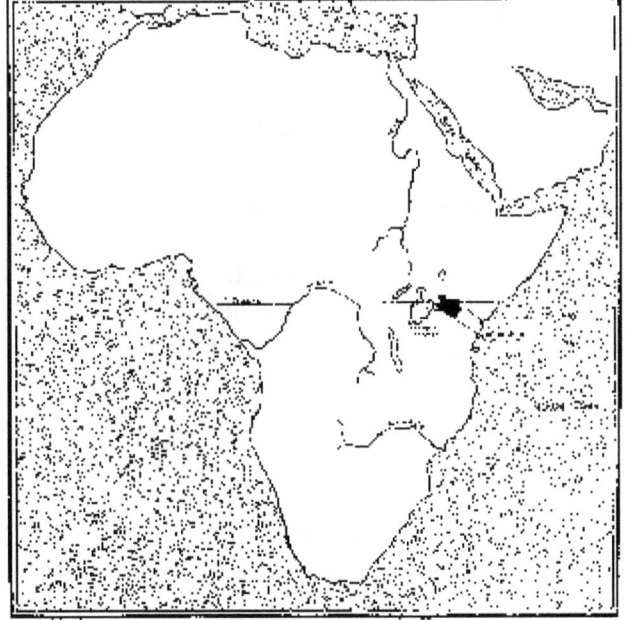

After disposing of this important preliminary, we then had time to visit the zoo at South Kensington and the British museum of natural history, where we carefully studied many of the animals that we hoped to meet later under less formal conditions. We picked out the vital spots, as seen from all angles, and nothing then remained to be done but to get down to British East Africa with our rifles and see whether we could hit those vital spots.

Studying the Lion's Vital Spots

Mr. Akeley had an elaborate moving picture machine and we planned to get some excellent pictures of charging animals. The lion, rhino or other subject was to be allowed to charge within a few feet of the camera and then with a crack of our trusty rifles he was supposed to stop. We seemed safe in assuming, even without exaggeration, that this would be exciting.

It was at least that.

At last we said farewell to London, a one-sided ceremony, stopped at Rheims to see the aviators, joined the Akeleys at Paris, and after touching a few of the high spots in Europe, arrived in Naples in ample time to catch our boat for Mombasa.

CHAPTER II
THE FIRST HALF OF THE VOYAGE. FROM NAPLES TO THE RED SEA, WITH A FEW SIDE LIGHTS ON INDIAN OCEAN TRAVEL

LION hunting had not been fraught with any great hardships or dangers up to this time. The Mediterranean was as smooth as a millpond, the Suez Canal was free from any tempestuous rolling, and the Red Sea was placid and hot. After some days we were in the Indian Ocean, plowing lazily along and counting the hours until we reached Mombasa. Perhaps after that the life of a lion hunter would be less tranquil and calm.

The *Adolph Woermann* was a six-thousand-three-hundred-ton ship, three years old, and so heavily laden with guns and ammunition and steel rails for the Tanga Railway that it would hardly roll in a hurricane. There were about sixty first-class passengers on board and a fair number in the second class. These passengers represented a dozen or so different nationalities, and were bound for all sorts of places in East, Central, and South Africa. Some were government officials going out to their stations, some were army officers, some were professional hunters, and some were private hunters going out "for" to shoot.

There were also a number of women on board and some children. I don't know how many children there were, but in the early morning there seemed to be a great number.

These Indian Ocean steamers are usually filled with an interesting lot of passengers. At first you may only speculate as to who and what they are and whither they are bound, but as the days go by you get acquainted with many of them and find out who nearly everybody is and all about him. On this steamer there were several interesting people. First in station and importance was Sir Percy Girouard, the newly appointed governor of British East Africa, who was going out to Nairobi to take his position. Sir Percy is a splendid type of man, only about forty-two years old, but with a career that has been filled with brilliant achievements. He was born in Canada and was knighted in 1900. He looks as Colonel Roosevelt looked ten years ago, and, in spite of a firm, definite personality of great strength, is also courteous and kindly. He has recently been the governor of northern Nigeria, and before that time served in South Africa and the Soudan. It was of him that Lord Kitchener said "the Soudan Railway would never have been built without his services."

The new governor was accompanied by two staff officers, one a Scotchman and the other an Irishman, and both of them with the clean, healthy look of the young British army officer. There would be a big reception at Mombasa, no doubt, with bands a-playing and fireworks popping, when the ship arrived with the new executive.

"Crossing the Line" Ceremonies

Mr. Stephenson, Mr. and Mrs. Akeley and Mr. McCutcheon.
Courtesy of Boyce Balloonagraph Expedition

There were also several officials with high-sounding titles who were going out to their stations in German East Africa. These gentlemen were mostly accompanied by wives and babies and between them they imparted a spirited scene of domesticity to the life on shipboard. The effect of a man wheeling a baby carriage about the deck was to make one think of some peaceful place far from the deck of a steamer.

Before and After Outfitting

Little Tim was the life of the ship. He was a little boy aged eighteen months, who began life at Sombra, in Nyassaland, British Central Africa. Just now he was returning from England with his father and mother. Little Tim had curly hair, looked something like a brownie, and was brimming over with energy and curiosity every moment that he was awake. If left alone five minutes he was quite likely to try to climb up the rigging. Consequently he was never left alone, and the decks were constantly echoing with a fond mother's voice begging him not to "do that," or to "come right here, Tim." One of Tim's chief diversions was to divest himself of all but his two nearest articles of wear and sit in the scuppers with the water turned on. A crowd of passengers was usually grouped around him and watched his manœuvers with intense interest. He was probably photographed a hundred times and envied by everybody on board. It was so fearfully hot in the Red Sea that to be seated in running water with almost no clothes on seemed about the nicest possible way to pass the time.

Little Tim

There was a professional elephant hunter on board. He was a quiet, reserved sort of man, pleasant, and not at all bloodthirsty in appearance. He had spent twenty years shooting in Africa, and had killed three hundred elephants. On his last trip, during which he spent nearly four years in the Congo, he secured about two and one-half tons of ivory. This great quantity of tusks, worth nearly five dollars a pound, brought him over twenty thousand dollars, after paying ten per cent. to the Congo government. The Belgians place no limit upon the number of elephants one may shoot, just so they get their rake-off. In British territory, however, sportsmen are limited to only two elephants a year to those holding licenses to shoot. Our elephant hunter friend was now on his way back to shoot some more.

The Elephant Hunter and His Bag

There was another interesting character on board who caused many of us to stop and think. He was a young British army officer who was mauled by a lioness several months ago in Somaliland. He now walked with a decided limp and was likely to lose his commission in the army because of physical infirmities. He was cheerful, pleasant, and looked hopefully forward to a time when he could have another go at a lion. This is the way the thing happened: Last March he was shooting in Somaliland and ran across a lioness. He shot her, but failed to disable her. She immediately charged, chewed up his leg, arm and shoulder, and was then killed by his Somali gunbearer. He was days from any help. He dressed his own wounds and the natives tried to carry him to the nearest settlement. Finally his bandages were exhausted, the natives deserted, and it was only after frightful suffering that he reached help. In three weeks blood poisoning set in, as is usual after the foul teeth of a lion have entered the flesh, and for several months he was close to death. Now he was up and about, cheerful and sunny, but a serious object lesson to the lion hunters bound for the lair of the lion.

Having Fun with Mr. Woermann

In the smoking-room of the *Adolph Woermann* was a bronze bust of Mr. Woermann presented by himself. Whether he meant to perpetuate his own memory is not vital to the story. The amusing feature lies in the fact that some irreverent passenger, whose soul was dead to the sacredness of art, put a rough slouch hat on Mr. Woermann one night, with side-splitting results. Mr. W. is a man with a strong, intelligent German face, something like that of Prince Henry, and in the statue appears with bare neck and shoulders. The addition of a rakish slouch hat produced a startling effect, greatly detracting from the strictly artistic, but adding much to the interest of the bust. It looked very much as though he had been ashore at Aden and had come back on board feeling the way a man does when he wants his hat on the side of his head. Still, what can a shipowner expect who puts a nude bust of himself in his own ship?

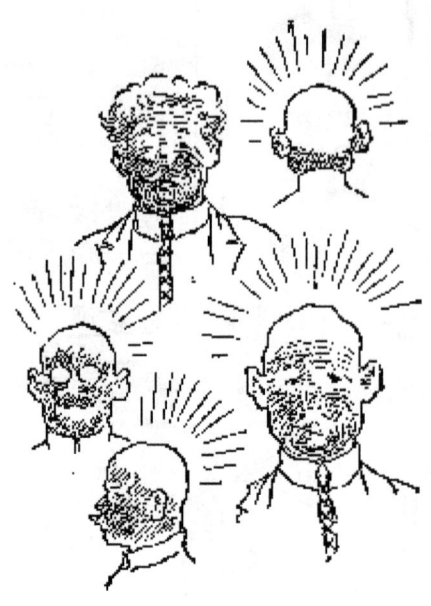

An African Hair-Cut

The ship's barber was the Associated Press of the ship's company, and his shop was the Park Row of the vessel. He had plenty of things to talk about and more than enough words to express them. Every vague rumor that floated about was sure to find lodgment in the barber shop, just as a piece of driftwood finally reaches the beach. He knew all the secrets of the voyage and told them freely.

One day I went down to have my hair trimmed. He asked if I'd have it done African style. "How's that?" I inquired. "Shaved," said he, and "No," said I. A number of the Germans on board were adopting the African style of hair-cut, and the effect was something depressing. Every bump that had lain dormant under a mat of hair at once assumed startling proportions, and red ears that were retiring suddenly stuck out from the pale white scalp like immense flappers. A devotee of this school of tonsorial art had a peeled look that did not commend him to favorable mention in artistic circles. But the flies, they loved it, so it was an ill wind that blew no good.

The Red Sea has a well-earned reputation of being hot. We expected a certain amount of sultriness, but not in such lavish prodigality as it was delivered. The first day out from Suez found the passengers peeling off unnecessary clothes, and the next day found the men sleeping out on deck. There wasn't much sleeping. The band concert lasted until ten-thirty, then the three Germans who were trying to drink all the beer on board gave a nightly saengerfest that lasted until one o'clock, and then the men who wash down the decks appeared at four. Between one and four it was too hot to sleep, so that there wasn't much restful repose on the ship until we got out of the Red Sea.

We Slept on Deck in the Red Sea

Down at the end of the Red Sea are the straits of Bab-el-Mandeb. In the middle of the straits is the island of Perim, a sun-baked, bare and uninviting chunk of land that has great strategic value and little else. It absolutely commands the entrance to the Red Sea, and, naturally, is British. Nearly all strategic points in the East are British, from Gibraltar to Singapore. A lighthouse, a signal station, and a small detachment of troops are the sole points of interest in Perim, and as one rides past one breathes a fervent prayer of thanksgiving that he is not one of the summer colony on Perim.

They tell a funny story about an English officer who was sent to Perim to command the detachment. At the end of six months an official order was sent for his transfer, because no one is expected to last longer than six months without going crazy or committing suicide. To the great surprise of the war office a letter came back stating that the officer was quite contented at Perim, that he liked the peace and quiet of the place, and begged that he be given leave to remain another six months. The war office was amazed, and it gladly gave him the extension. At the end of a year the same exchange of letters occurred and again he was given the extension.

I don't know how long this continued, but in the end the war office discovered that the officer had been in London having a good time while a sergeant-major attended to the sending of the biannual letter. I suppose the officer divided his pay with the sergeant-major. If he did not he was a most ungrateful man.

The *Adolph Woermann* is a German ship and is one of the best ones that go down the east coast. Its passengers go to the British ports in British East Africa, to the German ports in German East Africa, and to several other ports in South Africa. Consequently the passengers are about equally divided between the English and the Germans, with an occasional Portuguese bound for Delagoa Bay or Mozambique.

When we first went aboard our party of four desired to secure a table by ourselves. We were unsuccessful, however, and found it shared by a peaceful old gentleman with whiskers. By crossing with gold the palm of the chief steward, the old gentleman was shifted to a seat on the first officer's right. Later we discovered that he was Sir Thomas Scanlon, the first premier of South Africa, the man who gave Cecil Rhodes his start.

Mauled by a Lion

There were many interesting elements which made the cruise of the *Woermann* unusual. Mr. Boyce and his party of six were on board and were on their way to photograph East Africa. They took moving pictures of the various deck sports, also a bird's-eye picture of the ship, taken from a camera suspended by a number of box kites, and also gave two evenings of cinematograph entertainment.

There were also poker games, bridge games, and other forms of seaside sports, all of which contributed to the gaiety of life in the Indian Ocean. In the evening one might have imagined oneself at a London music-hall, in the daytime at the Olympian games, and in the early morning out on the farm. There were a number of chickens on board and each rooster seemed obliged to salute the dawn with a fanfare of crowing. They belonged to the governor and were going out to East Africa to found a colony of chickens. Some day, years hence, the proud descendents of these chickens will boast that their ancestors came over on the *Woermann*, just as some people boast about their ancestors on the *Mayflower*.

When we crossed the equator, a committee of strong-arm men baptized those of the passengers who had never before crossed the line. Those who had crossed the line entered into the fun of the occasion with much spirit and enthusiasm.

On the hottest day of the trip, just as we left Suez, when the mercury was sputtering from the heat, we heard that the north pole had been discovered. It cooled us off considerably for a while.

CHAPTER III
THE ISLAND OF MOMBASA, WITH THE JUNGLES OF EQUATORIAL AFRICA "ONLY A FEW BLOCKS AWAY." A STORY OF THE WORLD'S CHAMPION MAN-EATING LIONS

IN this voyage of the *Woermann* there were about twenty Englishmen and thirty Germans in the first class, not including women, and children. There was practically no communication between the two nationalities, which seemed deeply significant in these days when there is so much talk of war between England and Germany. Each went his way without so much as a "good morning" or a *guten abend*. And it was not a case of unfamiliarity with the languages, either, that caused this mutual restraint, for most of the Germans speak English. It was simply an evidence that at the present time there is decidedly bad feeling between the two races, and if it is a correct barometer of conditions in Europe, there is certain to be war one of these days. On the *Woermann*, we only hoped that it would not break out while the weather was as hot as it was at that time.

The Germans are not addicted to deck sports while voyaging about, and it is quite unusual to find on German ships anything in the way of deck competition. The German, while resting, prefers to play cards, or sing, or sit in his long easy chair with the children playing about. The Englishman likes to compete in feats of strength and takes to deck sports as a duck takes to water. I don't know who started it, but some one organized deck sports on the *Woermann*, and after we left Aden the sound of battle raged without cessation. Some of the competitions were amusing. For instance, there was the cockfight. Two men, with hands and knees hobbled with a stick and stout rope, seat themselves inside a circle, and the game is for each one to try to put the other outside the circle. Neither can use his hands.

The Cock Fight

It is like wrestling in a sitting position with both hands tied, the mode of attack being to topple over one's opponent and then bunt him out of the circle. There is considerable skill in the game and a fearful lot of hard work. By the time the victor has won, the seat of the trousers of each of the two contending heroes has cleaned the deck until it shines—the deck, not the trousers.

"Are You There?"

In a similar way the deck is benefited by the "are you there" game. Two men are blindfolded, armed with long paper clubs, and then lie at full length on the deck, with left hands clasped. One then says, "Are you there?" and when the other answers, "I am," he makes a wild swat at where he thinks the other's head to be. Of course, when the man says "I am," he immediately gets his head as far away from where it was when he spoke as is possible while clasping his opponent's hand. The "Are you there" man makes a wild swing and lands some place with a prodigious thump. He usually strikes the deck and seldom hits the head of the other man. If one of them hits the other's head three times he wins. In the meantime the deck has been thoroughly massaged by the two recumbent heroes as they have moved back and forth in their various offensive and defensive manœuvers.

A Study in Mombasa Shadows

Mombasa Is a Pretty Place

Transportation in Mombasa

The Spar and Pillow Fight

The pillow fight on the spar is the most fun. Two gladiators armed with pillows sit astride a spar and try to knock each other off. It requires a good deal of knack to keep your balance while some one is pounding you with a large pillow. You are not allowed to touch the spar with your hands, hence the difficulty of holding a difficult position. When a man begins to waver the other redoubles his attack, and slowly at first, but surely, the defeated gladiator tumbles off the spar into a canvas stretched several feet below. It is lots of fun, especially for the spectator and the winner.

Then, of course, there were other feats of intellectual and physical prowess in the *Woermann* competition, such as threading the needle, where you run across the deck, thread a needle held by a woman, and then drag her back to the starting point. The woman usually, in the excitement of the last spirited rush, falls over and is bodily dragged several yards, squealing wildly and waving a couple of much agitated deck shoes, and so forth.

Similar to this contest is the one where the gentleman dashes across the deck with several other equally dashing gentlemen, kneels at the feet of a woman who ties his necktie and then lights his cigarette. The game is to see who can do this the quickest and get back to the starting place first. If you have ever tried to light a cigarette in a terrible hurry and on a windy deck, you will appreciate the elements of uncertainty in the game.

These deck sports served to amuse and divert during the six days on the Indian Ocean, and then the ship's chart said that we were almost at Mombasa. The theoretical stage of the lion hunt was nearly over and it was now a matter of only a few days until we should be up against the "real thing." I sometimes wondered how I should act with a hostile lion in front of me—whether I would become panic-stricken or whether my nerve would hold true. There is lots of food for reverie when one is going against big game for the first time.

Chalking the Pig's Eye

We landed at Mombasa September sixteenth, seventeen days out from Naples.

Mombasa is a little island about two by three miles in extent. It is riotous with brilliant vegetation, and, as seen after a long sea voyage through the Red Sea and the Indian Ocean, it looks heavenly except for the heat. Hundreds of great baobab trees with huge, bottle-like trunks and hundreds of broad spreading mango trees give an effect of tropical luxuriance that is hardly to be excelled in beauty anywhere in the East. Large ships that stop at the island usually wind their course through a narrow channel and land their passengers and freight at the dock at Kilindini, a mile and a half from the old Portuguese town of Mombasa, where all the life of the island is centered. There are many relics of the old days around the town of Mombasa and the port of Kilindini, but since the British have been in possession a brisk air of progress and enterprise is evident everywhere. Young men and young women in tennis flannels, and other typical symptoms of British occupation are constantly seen, and one entirely forgets that one is several thousand miles from home and only a few blocks from the jungles of equatorial Africa. We dreaded Mombasa before we arrived, but were soon agreeably disappointed to find it not only beautiful and interesting, but also pleasantly cool and full of most hospitable social life.

When our ship anchored off Kilindini there was a great crowd assembled on the pier. There were many smart looking boats, manned with uniformed natives, that at once came out to the ship, and we knew that the town was *en fête* to welcome the newly appointed governor, Sir Percy Girouard.

He and his staff landed in full uniform. There were addresses of welcome at the pier, a great deal of cheering and considerable photographing. Then the rest of the passengers went ashore and spent several hours at the custom house. All personal luggage was passed through, and we embarked on a little train for Mombasa. The next day we registered our firearms and had Smith, Mackenzie and Company do the rest. This firm is ubiquitous in Mombasa and Zanzibar. They attend to everything for you, and relieve you from much worry, vexation and rupees. They pay your customs duties, get your mountains of stuff on the train for Nairobi, and all you have to do is to pay them a commission and look pleasant. The customs duty is ten per cent. on everything you have, and the commission is five per cent. But in a hot climate, where one is apt to feel lazy, the price is cheap.

Thanks to the governor, our party of four was invited to go to Nairobi on his special train. It left Mombasa on the morning of the nineteenth of September, and at once began to climb toward the plateau on which Nairobi is situated, three hundred and twenty-seven miles away. We had dreaded the railway ride through the lowlands along the coast, for that district has a bad reputation for fever and all such ills. But again we were pleasantly disappointed. The country was beautiful and interesting, and at four o'clock in the afternoon we arrived at Voi, a spot that is synonymous with human ailments. It is one of the famous ill health resorts of Africa, but on this occasion it was on its good behavior. We stopped four hours, inspected everything in sight, and at eight o'clock the special began to climb toward the plateau of East Africa. At nine o'clock we stopped at Tsavo, a place made famous by the two man-eating lions whose terrible depredations have been so vividly described by Colonel Patterson in his book, *The Man Eaters of Tsavo.* These two lions absolutely stopped all work on the railroad for a period of several weeks. They were daring beyond belief, and seemed to have no fear of human beings. For a time all efforts to kill them were in vain. Twenty-eight native workmen were eaten by them, and doubtless many more were unrecorded victims of their activity. The whole country was terrorized until finally, after many futile attempts, they were at last killed.

No book on Africa seems complete unless this incident is mentioned somewhere within its pages.

We looked out at Tsavo with devouring interest. All was still, with the dead silence of a tropical night. Then the train steamed on and we had several hours in a berth to think the matter over. In the early hours of morning, we stopped at Simba, the "Place of Lions," where the station-master has many lion scares even now. In the cold darkness of the night we bundled up in thick clothes and went forward to sit on the observation seat of the engine. Slowly the eastern skies became gray, then pink, and finally day broke through heavy masses of clouds. It was intensely cold. In the faint light we could see shadowy figures of animals creeping home after their night's hunting. A huge cheetah bounded along the track in front of us. A troop of giraffes slowly ambled away from the track. A gaunt hyena loped off into the scrub near the side of the railroad and then, as daylight became brighter, we found ourselves in the midst of thousands of wild animals. Zebras, hartebeests, Grant's gazelles, Thompson's gazelles, impalla, giraffes, wildebeests, and many other antelope species cantered off and stood to watch the train as it swept past them. It was a wonderful ride, perhaps the most novel railway ride to be found any place in the world. On each side of the Uganda Railroad there is a strip of land, narrow on the north and wide on the south, in which game is protected from the sportsman, and consequently the animals have learned to regard these strips as sanctuary. There were many tales of lions as we rode along, and the imagination pictured a slinking lion in every patch of reeds along the way. I heard one lion story that makes the man-eaters of Tsavo seem like vegetarians. It was told to me by a gentleman high in the government service—a man of unimpeachable veracity. He says the story is absolutely true, but refused to swear to it.

Once upon a time, so the story goes, there was a caravan of slaves moving through the jungles of Africa. The slave-drivers were cruel and they chained the poor savages together in bunches of ten. Each slave wore an iron ring around his neck and the chain passed through this ring and on to the rest of the ten. For days and weeks and months they marched along, their chains clanking and their shoulders bending beneath the heavy weight. From time to time the slave-drivers would jog them along with a few lashes from a four-cornered "hippo" hide *kiboko*, or whip. Quite naturally the life was far from pleasant to the chain-gang and they watched eagerly for a chance to escape. Finally one dark night, when the sentinels were asleep, a bunch of ten succeeded in creeping away into the darkness. They were unarmed and chained from neck to neck, one to another. For several days they made their way steadily toward the coast. All seemed well. They ate fruit and nuts and herbs and began to see visions of a pleasant arrival at the coast.

They Made Their Way Steadily Toward the Coast

But, alas! Their hopes were soon to be dispelled. One night a deep rumbling roar was heard in the jungle through which they were picking their unanimous way. A shudder ran through the slaves. "*Simba*," they whispered in terror. A little while later there was another rumble, this time much closer. They speedily became more frightened. Here they were, ten days' march from the coast, unarmed, and quite defenseless against a lion.

Presently the lion appeared, his cruel, hungry eyes gleaming through the night. They were frozen with horror, as slowly, slowly, slowly the great animal crept toward them with his tail sibilantly lashing above his back. They were now thoroughly alarmed and realized to the utmost that the lion's intentions were open to grave suspicion. Breathlessly they waited, or perhaps they tried to climb trees, but being chained together they could not climb more than one tree. And there was not a single tree big enough to hold more than nine of them. The record of the story is now obscure, but the horrid tale goes on to relate that the lion gave a frightful roar and leaped upon the tenth man, biting him to death in a single snap. The dilemma of the others is obvious. They knew better than to disturb a lion while it is eating. To do so would be to court sudden death. So they sat still and watched the beast slowly and greedily devour their comrade. Having finished his meal the great beast, surfeited with food, slowly moved off into the jungle.

The Lion's Intentions Were Open to Grave Suspicions

Immediately the nine remaining slaves took to their heels, dragging the empty ring and chain of the late number ten. All night long they ran until finally they became exhausted and fell asleep. In the afternoon they again resumed their march, hopeful once more. But alas! again.

Along about supper-time they heard the distant roar of a lion. Presently it sounded nearer and soon the gleaming eyes of the lion appeared once more among the jungle grass. Once again they were frozen with horror as the hungry beast devoured the last man in the row—number nine. Again they sat helpless while the man-eater slowly finished his supper, and again they were overjoyed to see him depart from their midst. As soon as the last vestige of his tail had disappeared from view they scrambled up and hiked briskly toward the coast, nine days away.

While the Man-Eater Finished His Supper

They were now thoroughly alarmed, and almost dreaded the supper hour. The next night the lion caught up with them again and proceeded to devour number eight. He then peacefully ambled away, leaving another empty ring.

The next night there was a spirited contest to see which end of the chain should be last, but a vote was taken and it was decided six to one in favor of continuing in their original formation. The one who voted against was eaten that night and the remaining six, with the four empty rings clanking behind them, resumed their mournful march to the coast, six days away.

Two to One

For five nights after this, the lion caught up with them and diminished their number by five. Finally there was only one left and the coast was a full day's march away. Could he make it? It looked like a desperate chance, but he still had hopes. He noticed with pleasure that the lion was becoming fat and probably could not travel fast. But he also noticed with displeasure that he had forty feet of chain and nine heavy iron neck rings to lug along and that extra weight naturally greatly handicapped him. It was a thrilling race—the coast only one day away and life or death the prize! Who can imagine the feelings of the poor slave? But with a stout heart he struggled on through poisonous morasses, and pushed his way through snaky creepers. The afternoon sun slowly sank toward the western horizon and—

The locomotive at this point of the story screeched loudly. The wheels grated on the track and my official friend leaped off the cow-catcher.

"Here!" I shouted, "what's the finish of that story?"

"I'll tell you the rest the next time I see you," he sang out, and so I don't know just how the story ended.

CHAPTER IV
ON THE EDGE OF THE ATHI PLAINS, FACE TO FACE WITH GREAT HERDS OF WILD GAME. UP IN A BALLOON AT NAIROBI

BEFORE Colonel Roosevelt drew the eyes of the world on British East Africa Nairobi was practically unheard of. The British colonial office knew where it was and a fair number of English sportsmen had visited it in the last six or eight years. Perhaps twenty-five or thirty Americans had been in Nairobi on their way to the rich game fields that lie in all directions from the town, but beyond these few outsiders the place was unknown. Now it is decidedly on the map, thanks to our gallant and picturesque Theodore. It has been mentioned in book and magazine to a degree that nearly everybody can tell in a general way where and what it is, even if he can not pronounce it.

Before coming to Nairobi I had read a lot about it, and yet when I reached the place it seemed as though the descriptions had failed to prepare me for what I saw. We arrived under unusual conditions. Files of native soldiers were lined up on the platform of the station to welcome the new governor, and the whole white population of the town, several hundred in number, were massed in front of the building. The roofs and trees were filled with natives and the broad open space beyond the station was fringed with pony carts, bullock carts, rickshaws, cameras, and some hotel 'buses. Several thousand people, mostly East Indians and natives, were among those present. Lord Delamere, who has adopted East Africa as his home, and who owns a hundred thousand acres or so of game preserves, read an address of welcome, and Sir Percy, in white uniform and helmet, responded with a speech that struck a popular note. There were dozens of cameras snapping and the whole effect was distinctly festive in appearance.

In the Back Yard of Nairobi

The town lies on the edge of the Athi Plains, a broad sweep of sun-bleached grass veldt many miles in extent. From almost any part of the town one may look out on plains where great herds of wild game are constantly in sight. In an hour's leisurely walk from the station a man with a gun can get hartebeest, zebra, Grant's gazelle, Thompson's gazelle, impalla, and probably wildebeest. One can not possibly count the number of animals that feed contentedly within sight of the town of Nairobi, and it is difficult to think that one is not looking out upon a collection of domesticated game. Sometimes, as happened two nights before we reached Nairobi, a lion will chase a herd of zebra and the latter in fright will tear through the town, destroying gardens and fences and flowers in a mad stampede. We met one man who goes out ten minutes from town every other day and kills a kongoni (hartebeest) as food for his dogs. If you were disposed to do so you could kill dozens every day with little effort and almost no diminution of the visible supply.

Dressed to Kill

The Balloon Ascension

The Norfolk Hotel, Nairobi

Nairobi is new and unattractive. There is one long main thoroughfare, quite wide and fringed with trees, along which at wide intervals are the substantial looking stone building of the Bank of India, the business houses, the hotels, and numbers of cheap corrugated iron, one-story shacks used for government purposes. A native barracks with low iron houses and some more little iron houses used for medical experiments and still some more for use as native hospitals are encountered as one takes the half-mile ride from the station to the hotel. A big square filled with large trees marks the park, and a number of rather pretentious one-story buildings display signs that tell you where you may buy almost anything, from a suit of clothes to a magazine rifle.

The Main Street Is a Busy Place

Goanese, East Indian, and European shops are scattered at intervals along this one long, wide street. Rickshaws, pedestrians, bullock carts, horsemen, and heavily burdened porters are passing constantly back and forth, almost always in the middle of the street. Bicycles, one or two motorcycles, and a couple of automobiles are occasionally to be seen. The aspect of the town suggests the activity of a new frontier place where everybody is busy. At one end the long street loses itself in the broad Athi Plains, at the other it climbs up over some low hills and enters the residence district on higher ground. Here the hills are generously covered with a straggly growth of tall, ungraceful trees, among which, almost hidden from view, are the widely scattered bungalows of the white population.

An Embo Apollo

The Askari Patrols the Camp

Branching off from the main street are side streets, some of them thronged with East Indian bazaars, about which may be found all the phases of life of an Indian city. Still beyond and parallel with the one main street are sparsely settled streets which look ragged with their tin shacks and scattered gardens.

Nairobi is not a beautiful place, but it is new and busy, and the people who live there are working wonders in changing a bad location into what some day will be a pretty place. It is over five thousand feet high, healthy, and cold at night. Away off in the hills a mile or more from town is Government House, where the governor lives, and near by is the club and a new European hospital, looking out over a sweep of country that on clear days includes Kilima-Njaro, over a hundred miles to the southeast, and Mount Kenia, a hundred miles northeast.

You are still in civilization in Nairobi. Anything you want you may buy at some of the shops, and almost anything you may want to eat or drink may easily be had. There are weekly newspapers, churches, clubs, hotels, and nearly all the by-products of civilization. One could live in Nairobi, only a few miles from the equator, wear summer clothes at noon and winter clothes at night, keep well, and not miss many of the luxuries of life. The telegraph puts you in immediate touch with the whole wide world, and on the thirtieth of September you can read the Chicago *Tribune* of August thirty-first.

At present the chief revenue of the government is derived from shooting parties, and the officials are doing all they can to encourage the coming of sportsmen. Each man who comes to shoot must pay two hundred and fifty dollars for his license as well as employ at least thirty natives for his transport. He must buy supplies, pay ten per cent. import and export tax, and in many other ways spend money which goes toward paying the expenses of government. The government also is encouraging various agricultural and stock raising experiments, but these have not yet passed the experimental stage. Almost anything may be grown in British East Africa, but before agriculture can be made to pay the vast herds of wild game must either be exterminated or driven away. No fence will keep out a herd of zebra, and in one rush a field of grain is ruined by these giant herds. Experiments have failed satisfactorily to domesticate the zebra, and so he remains a menace to agriculture and a nuisance in all respects except as adding a picturesque note to the landscape.

Colonel Roosevelt, in a recent speech in Nairobi, spoke of British East Africa as a land of enormous possibilities and promise, but in talks with many men here I found that little money has been made by those who have gone into agriculture in a large way. Drought and predatory herds of game have introduced an element of uncertainty which has made agriculture, as at present developed, unsatisfactory.

Colonel Roosevelt has become a popular idol in East Africa. Everywhere one meets Englishmen who express the greatest admiration for him. He has shrewdly analyzed conditions as they now exist and has picked out the weak spots in the government. For many years prior to the arrival of Sir Percy Girouard the country has been administered by weak executives, and its progress has been greatly retarded thereby. The last governor was kind, but inefficient, and some months ago was sent to the West Indies, where he is officially buried. Roosevelt came, sized up the situation, and made a speech at a big banquet in Nairobi. Nearly two hundred white men in evening clothes were there. They came from all parts of East Africa, and listened with admiration to the plain truths that Theodore Roosevelt told them in the manner of a Dutch uncle. Since then he has owned the country and could be elected to any office within the gift of the people. He talked for over an hour, and it must have been a great speech, if one may judge by the enthusiastic comments I have heard about it. When an Englishman gets enthusiastic about a speech by an American it must be a pretty good speech.

Newland and Tarlton is the firm that outfits most shooting parties that start out from Nairobi. They do all the preliminary work and relieve you of most of the worry. If you wish them to do so, they will get your complete outfit, so you need not bring anything with you but a suitcase. They will get your guns, your tents, your food supplies, your mules, your head-man, your cook, your gunbearers, your askaris (native soldiers), your interpreter, your ammunition, and your porters. They will have the whole outfit ready for you by the time you arrive in

Nairobi. When you arrive in British East Africa, a-shooting bent, you will hear of Newland and Tarlton so often that you will think they own the country.

Mr. Newland met us in Mombasa, and through his agents sent all of our London equipment of tents and guns and ammunition and food up to Nairobi. When we arrived in Nairobi he had our porters ready, together with tent boys, gunbearers, and all the other members of our *safari*, and in three days we were ready to march. The firm has systematized methods so much that it is simple for them to do what would be matters of endless worry to the stranger. In course of time you pay the price, and in our case it seemed reasonable, when one considers the work and worry involved. Most English sportsmen come out in October and November, after which time the shooting is at its height. Two years ago there were sixty *safaris*, or shooting expeditions, sent out from Nairobi. When we left, late in September, there were about thirty.

The Great White Way in Nairobi

The Busiest Place in Nairobi

Umbrella Acacias

The New Governor Looks Something Like Roosevelt

Each party must have from thirty to a couple of hundred camp attendants, depending upon the number of white men in the party. Each white man, requires, roughly, thirty natives to take care of him. In our party of four white people we had one hundred and eighteen. One would presume that the game would speedily be exterminated, yet it is said that the game is constantly increasing. After one day's ride on the railway it would be hard to conceive of game being more plentiful than it was while we were there. Mr. Roosevelt carried nearly three hundred men with him, collected a great quantity of game, and necessarily spent a great deal of money. It is said that the expenses of his expedition approached ten thousand dollars a month, but the chances are that this figure is much more than the actual figure.

At the time of our arrival there was a shortage in the porter supply, and we were obliged to take out men from a number of different tribes. Swahili porters are considered the best, but there are not enough to go round, so we had to take Swahilis, Bagandas, Kikuyus, Kavirondos,

Lumbwas, Minyamwezis, and a lot more of assorted races. Each porter carries sixty pounds on his head, and when the whole outfit is on the trail it looks like a procession of much importance.

The Norfolk Hotel is the chief rendezvous of Nairobi. In the course of the afternoon nearly all the white men on hunting bent show up at the hotel and patronize the bar. They come in wonderful hunting regalia and in all the wonderful splendor of the Britisher when he is afield. There is nearly always a great coming and going of men riding up, and of rickshaws arriving and departing. Usually several tired sportsmen are stretched out on the veranda of the long one-storied building, reading the ancient London papers that are lying about. Professional guides, arrayed in picturesque Buffalo Bill outfits, with spurs and hunting-knives and slouch hats, are among those present, and amateur sportsmen in crisp khaki and sun helmets and new puttees swagger back and forth to the bar. There is no denying the fact that there is considerable drinking in Nairobi. There was as much before we got there as there was after we got there, however. After the arrival of the European steamer at Mombasa business is brisk for several days as the different parties sally forth for the wilds.

At the Norfolk Hotel Bar

On our ship there were four different parties. A young American from Boston, who has been spending several years doing archæological work in Crete, accompanied by a young English cavalry officer, were starting out for a six-weeks' shoot south of the railway and near Victoria Nyanza.

Two professional ivory hunters were starting for German East Africa by way of the lake. Mr. Boyce and his African balloonograph party of seven white men were preparing for the photographing expedition in the Sotik, and our party of four was making final preparations for our march. Consequently there was much hurrying about, and Newland and Tarlton's warehouse was the center of throngs of waiting porters and the scene of intense activity as each party sorted and assembled its mountains of supplies.

Seager and Wormald got off first, going by train to Kijabe, where they were to begin their ten days' march in the Sotik. Here they were to try their luck for two or three weeks and then march back, preparatory to starting home.

The professional ivory hunters were slow in starting. There was delay in getting mules. One of them had shot three hundred elephants in the Belgian Congo during the last four years, and it was suspected he had been poaching. The other had been caught by the Belgian authorities on his last trip, lost all his ivory and guns by confiscation, but was ready to make another try. The ivory game is a rich one and there are always venturesome men who are willing to take chances with the law in getting the prizes.

The Boyce party with its two balloons and its great number of box kites and its moving picture equipment and its twenty-nine cameras and its vast equipment was slow in starting, but it expected to get away on September twenty-fourth, the day after we left. They planned to fill their balloon in Nairobi and tow it at the end of a special train as far as Kijabe, where they were to strike inland from the railway. They were encamped on a hill overlooking the city, with their two hundred and thirty porters ready for the field and their balloon ready to make the first ascension ever attempted in East Africa.

Throngs of natives squatted about, watching the final preparations, and doubtless wondered what the strange, swaying object was. On the evening of the twenty-second the party gave a moving picture show at one of the clubs for the benefit of St. Andrew's church. A great crowd of fashionably dressed people turned out and saw the motion picture records of events which they had seen in life only a couple of days before. There were moving pictures of the arrival of the governor's special train, his march through the city, and many other events that were fresh in the minds of the audience. There were also motion pictures taken on the ship that brought us down from Naples to Mombasa, and it was most interesting to see our fellow passengers and friends reproduced before us in their various athletic activities while on shipboard. Mr. Boyce gave an afternoon show for children, an evening show for grown-ups, and was to give another for the natives the following night. The charities of Nairobi were much richer because of Mr. Boyce and his African Balloonograph Expedition.

While in Nairobi we visited the little station where experiments are being made in the "sleeping sickness." An intelligent young English doctor is conducting the investigations and great hopes are entertained of much new information about that most mysterious ailment that has swept whole colonies of blacks away in the last few years.

In many little bottles were specimens of the deadly tsetse fly that causes all the infection. And the most deadly of all was the small one whose distinguishing characteristic was its wings, which crossed over its back. These we were told to look out for and to avoid them, if possible. They occur only in certain districts and live in the deep shade, near water. They also are day-biting insects, who do their biting only between eleven o'clock in the morning and five o'clock in the afternoon.

In the station there were a number of monkeys, upon which the fly was being tried. They were in various stages of the disease, but it seemed impossible to tell whether their illness was due to the sleeping sickness germ or was due to tick fever, a common malady among monkeys. In one of the rooms of the laboratory there were natives holding little cages of tsetse flies against the monkeys, which were pinioned to the floor by the natives. The screened cages were held close to the stomach of the helpless monkey, and little apertures in the screen permitted the fly to settle upon and bite the animal.

There are certain wide belts of land in Africa called the "tsetse fly belts," where horses, mules and cattle can not live. These districts have been known for a number of years, long before the sleeping sickness became known. In the case of animals, the danger could be minimized by keeping the animals out of those belts, but in the case of humans the same can not be done. One infected native from a sleeping sickness district can carry the disease from one end of the country to the other, and when once it breaks out the newly infected district is doomed. Consequently the British authorities are greatly alarmed, for by means of this deadly fly the whole population of East Africa might be wiped out if no remedy is discovered. It has not yet been absolutely proven that East Africa is a "white man's country," and in the end it may be necessary for him to give up hope of making it more than a place of temporary residence and exploration.

We were also shown some ticks. They are the pests of Africa. They exist nearly every place and carry a particularly malicious germ that gives one "tick fever." It is not a deadly fever, but it is recurrent and weakening. There are all kinds of ticks, from little red ones no bigger than a grain of pepper to big fat ones the size of a finger-nail, that are exactly the color of the ground. They seem to have immortal life, for they can exist for a long time without food. Doctor Ward told us of some that he had put in a box, where they lived four years without food or water. He also told us of one that was sent to the British museum, put on a card with a pin through it, and lived over two years in this condition. It is assumed, however, that it sustained fatal injuries, because after a two years' fight against its wound it finally succumbed.

We were told to avoid old camping grounds while on *safari*, because these spots were usually much infested with ticks waiting for new camping parties. Wild game is always covered with ticks and carries them all over the land. As you walk through the grass in the game country the ticks cling to your clothes and immediately seek for an opening where they may establish closer relations with you. Some animals, like the rhino and the eland, have tick birds that sit upon their backs and eat the ticks. The egrets police the eland and capture all predatory ticks, while the rhino usually has half a dozen little tick birds sitting upon him.

However, we were starting out in a day or so, and in a few days expected to learn a lot more about ticks than we then knew.

It is supposed to require a certain amount of nerve to go lion shooting. It is also supposed to require an additional amount to face an angry rhino or to attempt to get African buffalo. The last-named creature is a vindictive, crafty beast that is feared by old African hunters more than they fear any other animal. In consequence of these dangers we decided that it might be well to give our nerves a thorough test before going out with them. If they were not in good condition it would be well to know of it before rather than after going up against a strange and hostile lion.

That is why we went up in the balloon in Nairobi. The balloon was one of the two Boyce balloons and had never been tried. It was small, of twelve thousand cubic feet capacity, as compared with the seventy thousand foot balloons that do the racing. It was also being tried at an altitude of over five thousand feet under uncertain wind and heat conditions, and so the element of uncertainty was aggravated. We felt that if we could go up in a new balloon of a small size it might demonstrate whether we should later go up a tree or stand pat against a charging menagerie.

There was a great crowd gathered on the hill where this balloon was being inflated. Since five o'clock in the morning the gas had been generating in the wooden tanks, and from these was being conducted by a cloth tube to the mouth of the balloon. The natives squatted wonderingly about in a circle, mystified and excited. At three o'clock the balloon was over half filled and was swaying savagely at its anchorage. A strong wind was blowing, and Mr. Lawrence, who had charge of the ascension, was apprehensive. He feared to fill the balloon to its capacity lest the expansion of the gas due to the hot sun should explode it.

At half past three the basket was attached and it looked small—about the size of a large bushel basket, three feet in diameter and three feet deep. The balloon, heavily laden with sand-bags, was lightened until it could almost rise, and in this condition was led across to an open spot sufficiently far from the nearest trees. The crowd thronged up pop-eyed and quivering with excitement. Then there was a long wait until the wind had died down a bit, which it did after a while. The eventful moment had arrived, and Mr. Stephenson, of our party, climbed into the basket. He is only six feet five inches in height and weighs only two hundred and thirty pounds. He had on a pair of heavy hunting boots, for we were leaving for the hunting grounds immediately after the ascension. One by one the restraining bags of sand were taken off, but still the balloon sat on the ground without any inclination to do otherwise.

A wave of disappointment spread over the crowd. Suddenly a brilliant inspiration struck the gallant aëronaut. He took off one of his heavy hunting boots and cast it overboard. The balloon arose a foot or two and then sagged back to earth. Then the other boot was cast over and the balloon rose several feet, swaying and whipping savagely over the heads of the crowd. The wind was now blowing pretty hard, and when the wire was run out the balloon started almost horizontally for the nearest tree, rising slightly.

Throwing Out Ballast

The wire was stopped at once and the balloon thus suddenly restrained, changed its horizontal course to an upward one. At about sixty feet up the wire was again paid out and the balloon made a dash for the trees again. Once more the balloon was stopped and rose to a height of one hundred and fifty feet, where it swayed about with the pleasant face of Stephenson looking over the edge of the basket. He had to sit down, as there was not room to stand. The ascension seemed a failure with the handicap of two hundred and thirty pounds, and so the balloon was reeled down to the earth again. It was not a great ascension, but the amateur aëronaut had gained the distinction of making the first balloon ascension ever made in East Africa. He would have gone higher if his shoes had been heavier.

To me fell the next chance, and I knew that my one hundred and forty pounds would not seriously handicap the balloon. Once more there was a long wait until the wind died down, and all of a sudden the cylinder of wire was released and the ground sank hundreds of feet below me. The horizon widened and the whole vast plain of the African highlands stretched out with an ever-widening horizon. New mountain peaks rose far away and native villages with ant-like people moving about appeared in unexpected quarters. Away below, the crowd of people looked like little insects as they gazed up at the balloon. Grasping the ropes that led from the basket to the balloon, I stood and waved at them and could hear the shouts come up from a thousand feet below.

I was not frightened. There was no sensation of motion as long as the balloon was ascending. Aside from looking at the wonderful scene that opened out before me, I believe I thought chiefly about where I should land in case the wire broke. The balloon would undoubtedly go many miles before descending, and five miles in any direction would lead me into a primitive jungle or veldt. A hundred miles would take me into almost unexplored districts in some directions, where the natives would greet me as some supernatural being. Perhaps I might be greeted as a god and—just in the midst of these reflections they began to reel in the balloon. The sudden stopping was not pleasant, for then the balloon began to sway. Slowly the earth came nearer and the wind howled through the rigging and the partly filled bag flapped and thundered. The wire, about as thick as a piano wire, looked frail, but at last after a slow and tedious descent a safe landing was made amid the wondering natives. Cameras clicked and the moving picture machine worked busily as the balloon was secured to earth again.

To Mrs. Akeley of our party fell the next chance to go up. As she was lifted into the basket the feminine population of Nairobi gazed in wonder that a woman should dare venture up in a balloon. The cameras clicked some more, somebody shook hands with her, and it began to look quite like a leave-taking. Just when all was ready the wind sprang up savagely and an ascension seemed inexpedient. There was a long wait and still the wind continued in gusts. At last it was determined that we might as well settle down for better conditions, so Mrs. Akeley was lifted out and we waited impatiently for the wind to die down.

At last it died down, all was hurriedly prepared for the ascension, and Mrs. Akeley took her place again in the basket. In an instant the balloon shot up a couple of hundred feet and was held there for a moment. The wind once more sprang up and the balloon was drawn down amid the cheers of the crowd. She had been the first woman to make an ascension in British East Africa, if not in all of Africa.

We then mounted our mules and rode out on the open plains. Several hours before, our entire camp had moved and we were to join them at a prearranged spot out on the Athi Plains. All our preliminary worries were over and at last we were actually started. At six o'clock, far across the country we saw the gleaming lights of our camp-fires and the green tents that were to be our homes for many weeks to come. Enormous herds of hartebeest and wildebeest were on each side, and countless zebras. That night two of us heard the first bark of the zebra, and we thought it must be the bark of distant dogs. It was one of our first surprises to learn that zebras bark instead of neigh.

CHAPTER V
INTO THE HEART OF THE BIG GAME COUNTRY WITH A RETINUE OF MORE THAN ONE HUNDRED NATIVES. A SAFARI AND WHAT IT IS

WHEN I first expressed my intention of going to East Africa to shoot big game some of my friends remarked, in surprise: "Why, I didn't know that you were so bloodthirsty!" They seemed to think that the primary object of such an expedition was to slay animals, none of which had done anything to me, and that to wish to embark in any such project was an evidence of bloodthirstiness. I tried to explain that I had no particular grudge against any of the African fauna, and that the thing I chiefly desired to do was to get out in the open, far from the picture post-card, and enjoy experiences which could not help being wonderful and strange and perhaps exciting.

The shooting of animals merely for the sake of killing them is, of course, not an elevating sport, but the by-products of big game hunting in Africa are among the most delightful and inspiring of all experiences. For weeks or months you live a nomadic tent life amid surroundings so different from what you are accustomed to that one is both mentally and physically rejuvenated. You are among strange and savage people, in strange and savage lands, and always threatened by strange and savage animals. The life is new and the scenery new. There is adventure and novelty in every day of such a life, and it is that phase of it that has the most insistent appeal. It is the call of the wild to which the pre-Adamite monkey in our nature responds.

Even if one never used his rifle one would still enjoy life on *safari*. *Safari* is an Arabic word meaning expedition as it is understood in that country. If you go on any sort of a trip you are on *safari*. It need not be a shooting trip.

Of course everybody who has read the magazines of the last year has been more or less familiarized with African hunting. He has read of the amount of game that the authors have killed and of the narrow escapes that they have had.

He also has read about expeditions into districts with strange names, but naturally these names have meant nothing to him. I know that I read reams of African stuff about big game shooting and about *safari*, yet in spite of all that, I remained in the dark as to many details of such a life. I wanted to know what kind of money or trade stuff the hunter carried; what sort of things he had to eat each day; what he wore, and how he got from place to place. Most writers have a way of saying: "We equipped our *safari* in Nairobi and made seven marches to such and such a place, where we ran into some excellent eland." All the important small details are thus left out, and the reader remains in ignorance of what the tent boy does, who skins the game that is killed, and what sort of a cook stove they use.

The purpose of this chapter is to tell something about the little things that happen on *safari*. First of all, at the risk of repeating what has been written so often before, I will say a few words about the personnel of a *safari*, such as the one I was with.

There were four white people in our expedition—Mr. and Mrs. Akeley, Mr. Stephenson, and myself. Mr. Akeley's chief object was to get a group of five elephants for the American Museum of Natural History and incidentally secure photographic and moving picture records of animal life. Both he and Mrs. Akeley had been in Africa before and knew the country as thoroughly perhaps as any who has ever been there. Mr. Akeley undoubtedly is the foremost taxidermist of the world, and his work is famous wherever African animal life has been studied. Mr. Stephenson went for the experience in African shooting, and I for that experience and any other sort that might turn up.

To supply an expedition of four white people, we had one head-man, whose duty it was to run the *safari*—that is, to get us where we wanted to go. The success and pleasure of the *safari* depends almost wholly upon the head-man. If he is weak, the discipline of the camp will disappear and all sorts of annoyances will steadily increase. If he is strong, everything will run smoothly.

The Cook—A Toto—The Head-Man

Our head-man was a young Somali, named Abdi. For several years he was with Mr. McMillan of Juja farm, and he spoke English well and knew the requirements of white men. He was strikingly handsome, efficient, and ruled the native porters firmly and kindly. Each day we patted ourselves on the back because of Abdi.

It Is Tropical Along the Athi River

Hippos in the Tana River

Our Camp Down on the Tana

Second in the list came our four gunbearers, all Somalis, they being considered the best gunbearers. The duty of the gunbearer is always to be with you when you are hunting, to carry your gun, and to have it in your hand the instant it is needed. Then there were four second gunbearers, who came along just behind the first gunbearers. The second men were, in our case, selected from the native porters, and were subject to the orders of the first gunbearer. The first gunbearer carries your field-glasses and your light, long-range rifle; the second gunbearer carries your camera, your water bottle, and your heavy cordite double-barreled rifle. In close quarters, as in a lion fight, the first gunbearer crouches at your elbow, hands the big rifle to you; you fire, and he immediately takes the rifle and places in your hands the other rifle, ready for firing. By the time you have fired this one the first is again ready, and in this way you always have a loaded rifle ready for use. There frequently is no time for turning around, and so the first gunbearer is at your elbow with the barrel of one rifle pressed against your right leg that you may know that he is there. Sometimes they run away, but the Somali gunbearers are the most fearless and trustworthy, and seldom desert in time of need. The gunbearer has instructions never to fire unless his master is disarmed and down before the charge of a beast. When an animal is killed the gunbearers skin it and care for the trophy. Usually when on a shooting jaunt of several hours from camp several porters go along to carry home the game.

Third in the social scale came the askaris—armed natives in uniforms who guard the camp at night. One or more patrol the camp all night long, keep up the fires and scare away any marauding lion or hyena that may approach the camp. We had four askaris, one of whom was the noisiest man I have ever heard. He reminded me of a congressman when congress is not in session.

Gunbearer—Askari—Tent Boy—Porter

Then came the cook, who is always quite an important member of the community, because much of the pleasure of the *safari* depends upon him. Our cook was one that the Akeleys had on their former trip. His name was Abdullah, he had a jovial face and a beaming smile, cooked well, and was funny to look at. He wore a slouch hat with a red band around it, a khaki suit and heavy shoes. When on the march he carried his shoes and when in camp he wore a blue jersey and a polka-dotted apron which took the place of trousers. He was good-natured, which atoned somewhat for his slowness. The suggestion may be made that he might not have been slow, but that our appetites might have been so fast that he seemed slow.

The cook usually picks out a likely porter to help him, or a *toto*, which means "little boy" in Swahili. There are always a lot of boys who go along, unofficially, just for the fun and the food of the trip. They are not hired, but go as stowaways, and for the first few days out remain much in the background. Gradually they appear more and more until all chance of their being sent back has disappeared, and then they become established members of the party. They carry small loads and help brighten up the camp. Then there are the tent boys, personal servants of the white people. Each white person has his tent boy, who takes care of his tent, his bedding, his bath, his clothes, and all his personal effects. A good tent boy is a great feature on *safari*, for he relieves his master of all the little worries of life. The tent boys always wait on the table and do the family washing. They also see that the drinking water is boiled and filtered and that the water bottles are filled each evening.

Last of all come the porters, of whom we had eighty. There were Swahilis, Wakambas, Kikuyus, Masai, Minyamwezis, Lumbwas, Bagandas, Kavirondos, and doubtless members of various other tribes. It was their duty to carry the camp from place to place, each porter carrying sixty pounds on his head. When they arrive at the spot selected for camp they put up the tents, get in firewood, and carry in what game may later be shot by the white men.

Then, lowest in the social scale, are the saises, or grooms. There is one for each mule or horse, of which we had four. The sais is always at hand to hold the mount and is supposed to take care of it after hours.

The foregoing members of our personally conducted party, therefore, included:

Head-man	1	Tent Boys	4
Gunbearers	4	Porters	80
Askaris	4	Saises	4
Cook	1	"Totos"	20

The head-man and the four gunbearers get seventy-five rupees a month, the askaris fifteen rupees, the cook forty rupees, the tent boys twenty and twenty-five rupees, depending upon experience, the porters ten rupees, and the saises twelve rupees. The *totos* get nothing except food and lodging, as well as experience, which may be valuable when they grow up to be porters at ten rupees a month. A rupee is about thirty-three cents American. We were also required by law to provide a water bottle, blanket, and sweater for each porter, as well as uniforms and water bottles, shoes and blankets for all the other members of the party. We also supplied twenty tents for them.

For the first day or two on *safari* there may be little hitches and delays, but after a short time the work is reduced to a beautiful system, and camp is broken or pitched in a remarkably short time. The porters get into the habit of carrying a certain load and so there is usually little confusion in distributing the packs.

At the Edge of the Athi River

The Totos Are Not Fastidious

Life and activity begin early in camp. You go to bed early and before dawn you are awakened by the singing of countless birds of many kinds. The air is fresh and cool, and you draw your woolen blankets a little closer around you. The tent is closed, but through the little cracks you can see that all is still dark. In a few moments a faint grayness steals into the air, and off in the half darkness you hear the Somali gunbearers chanting their morning prayers—soft, musical, and soothing. Then there are more voices murmuring in the air and the camp slowly awakens to life. Some one is heard chopping wood, and by that time day breaks with a crash. All is life, and the birds are singing as though mad with the joy of life and sunshine. A little later a shadowy figure appears by your cot and says, "*Chai, bwana*" which means, "Tea, master."

You turn over and slowly sip the hot tea, while outside in the clear morning air the sound of voices grows and grows until you know that eighty or a hundred men are busy getting their breakfasts. The crackling of many fires greets your ears and the pungent smell of wood fires salutes your nostrils. You look at your watch and it is perhaps five or half past. The air is still cold and you hasten to slip out of your cot. It is never considered wise to bathe in the morning here.

Your shoes or boots are by your bed, all oiled and cleaned, and your puttees are neatly rolled, ready to be wound around you from the tops of the shoes to the knee. Your clean flannels (one always wears heavy flannel underclothes and heavy woolen socks in this climate) are laid out and your clothes for the day's march are ready for you. You get into your clothes and boots, go out of your tent, and find there a basin of hot water and your toilet equipment. The basin is supported on a three-pronged stick thrust into the ground and makes a thoroughly satisfactory washstand. The fire in front of the cook's tent is burning merrily and he and his assistants are busily at work on the morning breakfast. Twenty other camp-fires are burning around the twenty small white tents that the porters and others occupy, and scores of half-clad natives are cooking their breakfasts. The ration that we were required to give them was a pound and a half of ground-corn a day for each man, but in good hunting country we got them a good deal of meat to eat. They are very fond of hartebeest, zebra, rhino, and especially hippo. In fact, they are eager to eat any kind of meat, so that anything we killed was certain to be of practical use as food for the porters. This fact greatly relieves the conscience of the man who shoots an animal for its fine horns. Six porters sleep in each of the little shelter tents which we were required to supply them, and this number sleeping so closely packed served to keep them warm through the cold African highland nights.

By six o'clock our folding table in the mess tent is laid with white linen and white enamel dishes for breakfast. So we take our places. If we are in a fruit country we have some oranges and bananas or papayas, a sort of pawpaw that is most delicious; it is a cross between a cantaloupe and a mango. Then we have oatmeal with evaporated cream and sugar; then we have choice cuts from some animal that was killed the day before—usually the liver or the tenderloin. Then we have eggs and finish up on jam or marmalade and honey. We have coffee for breakfast and tea for the other meals.

While we are eating the tent boys have packed our tin trunks, our folding tent table, our cots and our pillows, cork mattresses and blankets. The gunbearer gets our two favorite rifles and cameras, field-glasses and water bottles. Then down comes the double-roofed green tents, all is wrapped into closely-packed bags, and before we are through with breakfast all the tented village has disappeared and only the mess tent and the two little outlying canvas shelters remain. It is a scene of great activity. Porters are busily making up their packs and the head-man with the askaris are busy directing them. In a half-hour all that remains is a scattered assortment of bundles, all neatly bound up in stout cords.

One man may carry a tent-bag and poles, another a tin uniform case with a shot-gun strapped on top; another may have a bedding roll and a chair or table, and so on until the whole outfit is reduced to eighty compact bundles which include the food for the porters, the ant-proof food boxes with our own food, and the horns and skins of our trophies. The work of breaking camp is reduced to a science.

Our gunbearers are waiting and the saises with the mules are in readiness. So we start off, usually walking the first hour or two, with gunbearers and saises and mules trailing along behind. Soon afterward we look back to see the long procession of porters following along in single file. Our tent boys carry our third rifle, and behind them all comes the head-man, ready to spur on any lagging porters.

Our Safari on the March

The early morning hours are bright and cool, but along about nine o'clock the equatorial sun begins to beat down upon our heavy sun helmets and our red-lined and padded spine protectors. But it is seldom hot for long. A cloud passes across the sun and instantly everything is cooled. A wave of wind sweeps across the hill and cools the moist brow like a camphor compress. An instant later the sun is out again and the land lies swimming in the shimmer of heat waves. Distant hills swim on miragic lakes, and if we are in plains country the mirages appear upon all sides.

We rarely shot while on a march from camp to camp. We walked or rode along, watching the swarms of game that slowly moved away as we approached. The scenery was beautiful. Sometimes we wound along on game trails or native trails through vast park-like stretches of rolling hills; at other times we climbed across low hills studded with thorn scrub, while off in the distance rose the blue hills and mountains. To the northward, always with us, was the great Mount Kenia, eighteen thousand feet high and nearly always veiled with masses of clouds. On her slopes are great droves of elephants, and we could pick out the spot where three years before Mrs. Akeley had killed her elephant with the record pair of tusks.

Our marches were seldom long. At noon or even earlier we arrived at our new camping place, ten or twelve miles from our starting of the morning. Frequently we loitered along so that the porters might get there first and the camp be fully established when we arrived. At other times we arrived early and picked out a spot, where ticks and malaria were not likely to be bothersome.

We usually camped near a river. Our first camp was on the Athi Plains, near Nairobi; our second at Nairobi Falls, where the river plunges down a sixty-foot drop in a spot of great beauty. Our third camp was on the Induruga River, in a beautiful but malarious spot; our fifth was on the Thika Thika River, where it was so cold in the morning that the vapor of our breathing was visible; and our sixth on a windblown hill where a whirlwind blew down our mess tent and scattered the cook's fire until the whole grass veldt was in furious flames. It took a hundred men an hour to put out the flames.

Our next camp was at Fort Hall, where a poisonous snake came into my tent while I was working. It crawled under my chair and was by my feet when I saw it. It was chased out and killed in the grass near my tent, and a porter cut out the fangs to show me. For a day or two I looked before putting on my shoes, but after that I ceased to think of it.

After that time our camps were along the Tana River, in a beautiful country thronged with game, but, unhappily, a district into which comparatively few hunters come on account of the fever that is said to prevail there. We were obliged to leave our mules at Fort Hall because it was considered certain death to them if we took them into this fly belt.

When the porters arrive at a camping place a good spot is picked out for our four tents and mess tent, the cook tent is located, and in a short time the camp is ready. In my tent the cot is spread, with blankets airing; the mosquito net is up, the table is ready, with toilet articles, books and cigars laid out. The three tin uniform cases are in their places, my cameras are in their places, as are also the guns and lanterns. A floor cloth covers the ground and a long easy chair is ready for occupancy. Towels and water are ready, and pajamas and cholera belt are on the pillow of the cot. Everything is done that should be done, and I am immediately in a well established house with all my favorite articles in their accustomed places.

The Safari in Camp

A luncheon, with fruit, meat, curry and a pastry is ready by the time we are, and then we smoke or sleep through the broiling midday hours. Mr. Stephenson—or "Fred," as he is with us—and I go out on a scouting expedition and look for good specimens to add to our collection of horns or to get food for the porters. Sometimes the whole party went out, either photographing charging rhinos or shooting, but this part of the daily program was usually too varied to generalize as part of the daily doings. Several porters went with each of us to bring in the game, which there is rarely any uncertainty of securing.

In the evening we return and find our baths of hot water ready. We take off our heavy hunting boots and slip into the soft mosquito boots. After which dinner is ready and our menu is strangely varied. Sometimes we have kongoni steaks, at other times we have the heart of waterbuck or the liver of bushbuck or impalla. Twice we had rhino tongue and once rhino tail soup. We eat, and at six o'clock the darkness of night suddenly spreads over the land. We talk over our several adventures of the afternoon, some of which may be quite thrilling, and then, with camp chairs drawn around the great camp-fire, and with the sentinel askari pacing back and forth, we spend a drowsy hour in talking. Gradually the sounds of night come on. Off there a hyena is howling or a zebra is barking, and we know that through all those shadowy masses of trees the beasts of prey are creeping forth for their night's hunting. The porters' tents are ranged in a wide semicircle, and their camp-fires show little groups of men squatting about them. Somewhere one is playing a tin flute, another is playing a French harp, and some are singing. It is a picture never to be forgotten, and rich with a charm that will surely always send forth its call to the restless soul of the man who goes back to the city.

Sometimes the evening program is different. When one of us brings in some exceptional trophy there is a great celebration, with singing and native dances, and cheers for the Bwana who did the heroic deed. The first lion in a camp is a signal for great rejoicing and celebrating—however, that is another story—the story of my first lion.

At nine o'clock the tents are closed and all the camp is quiet in sleep. Outside in the darkness the askari paces to and fro, and the thick masses of foliage stand out in inky blackness against the brilliant tropic night. We are far from civilization, but one has as great a feeling of security as though he were surrounded by chimneys and electric lights. And no sleep is sweeter than that which has come after a day's marching over sun-swept hills or through the tangled reed beds where every sense must always be on the alert for hidden dangers.

CHAPTER VI
A LION DRIVE. WITH A RHINO IN RANGE SOME ONE SHOUTS "SIMBA" AND I GET MY FIRST GLIMPSE OF A WILD LION. THREE SHOTS AND OUT

LIKE every one who goes to Africa with a gun and a return ticket, I had two absorbing ambitions. One was to kill a lion and the other to live to tell about it. In my estimation all the other animals compared to a lion as latitude eighty-seven and a half compares to the north pole. I wanted to climb out of the Tartarin of Tarascon class of near lion hunters into the ranks of those who are entitled to remark, "Once, when I was in Africa shooting lions," etc. A dead lion is bogey in the big game sport—the score that every hunter dreams of achieving—and I was extremely eager to make the dream a reality.

When speaking with English sportsmen in London my first question was, "Did you get any lions?" If they had, they at once rose in my estimation; if not, no matter how many elephants or rhinos or buffaloes they may have shot, they still remained in the amateur class.

On the steamer going down to Mombasa the hunting talk was four-fifths lion and one-fifth about other game. The cripple who had been badly mauled by a lion was a person of much distinction, even more so than the ivory hunter who had killed three hundred elephants.

Mr. Stephenson's Lion

A Post Mortem Inquiry

On the railway to Nairobi every eye was on the lookout for lions and every one gazed with intense interest at the station of Tsavo and remembered the famous pair of man-eaters that had terrorized that place some years before.

In Nairobi the men who had killed lions, and those who had been mauled by them (and there are many of the latter), were objects of vast concern, and the little cemetery with its many headstones marked "Killed by lion" added still greater fire to my interest.

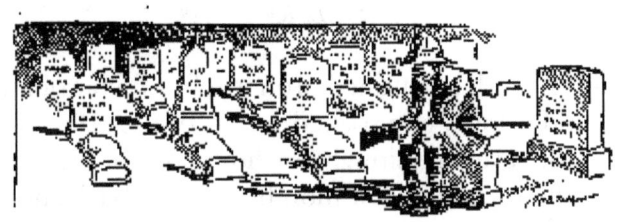

The Jolly Little Cemetery

Consequently, when we marched out of Nairobi on the evening of September twenty-third, with tents and guns and a hundred and twenty men, the dominating thought was of lions. If ever any one had greater hope and less expectation of killing a lion I was the one.

We had planned a short trip of from three to five weeks northeast of Nairobi in what is called the Tana River country. While there are some lions in that section, as there are in most parts of British East Africa, it is not considered a good lion country. Buffaloes, rhinos, hippos, giraffes, and many varieties of smaller game are abundant, largely because the Tana River is in a bad fever belt and hunting parties generally prefer to go elsewhere. This preliminary trip was intended to perfect our shooting, so that later, when in real lion country, we might be better equipped to take on the king of beasts with some promise of hitting him.

Peering for Lions

The tree-tops and corrugated iron roofs of Nairobi had hardly dropped behind a long, sun-soaked hump of the Athi Plains when I began to peel my eyes inquiringly for lions. All the lion stories that I had heard for the preceding few months paraded back and forth in my memory, and if ever a horizon was thoroughly scanned for lion, that horizon just out of Nairobi was the one. Hartebeests in droves loped awkwardly away from the trail and then turned and looked with wondering interest at us. Zebras, too fat to run, trotted off, and also turned to observe the invaders. Gazelles did the same, and away off in the distance a few wildebeests went galloping slowly to a safe distance. They were probably safe at any distance had they only known it, for up to the hour when I cantered forth from Nairobi in quest of lions and rhinos I had not shot at anything for three years, nor hit anything for ten.

Night came on—the black, sudden night of Africa—and we went into camp four miles from Nairobi without ever having heard the welcome roar of a lion. It was a distinct disappointment. I remembered the story about the lions that stampeded the zebras through the peaceful gardens of Nairobi only a few nights before—also the report that some man-eaters had been recently partaking of nourishment along the very road upon which we were now camping. I also remembered hearing that lions had been seen prowling around the edge of the town and that the Athi Plains are a time-honored habitat of the lion family. On the other hand, I thought of Mr. Roosevelt, who had recently been reducing the supply. I also remembered how many hunters had spent years in Africa without ever seeing a lion, and how Doctor Rainsford had made two different hunting trips to Africa, always looking for lions, but without success.

During our first three days of marching, we looked industriously for lions. On broad, grassy plain, in low scrub, on the slopes of low hills—everywhere we looked for them. If a flock of vultures circled above a distant spot we went over at once in the hope of surprising a lion at his kill. Every reed bed was promptly investigated, every dry nullah was explored. McMillan's farm, which is a farm only in name, was scoured without ever a sign or a hint that a lion lurked thereabouts. Mr. McMillan has four lions in a cage, but they snarled so savagely that we hastened away to look for lions elsewhere. The second day we crossed the Nairobi River, the third day we crossed the Induruga River, and the fourth day we camped down on the Athi River. Here we struck a clue. Two English settlers came over and told us that lions had been heard the night before near their ranch house, on the slopes of Donyo Sabuk, a high solitary round top mountain rising from the Athi Plains, and we determined to organize our first lion hunt. It was here that Mr. Lucas was killed by a lion a short time before.

A lion hunt, or a lion drive, is quite a ceremony. You take thirty or forty natives, go to the place where the lion was heard, and then beat every bit of cover in the hope of scaring out the beasts. Lions are fond of lying up during the day in dry reed beds, and when you go out looking for them, you are most likely to find them in such places.

Mr. Stephenson's Splendid Buffalo

"Lion Camp"

The Lion and Lioness in Camp

We started, three of us, with forty porters, at about daybreak. At seven o'clock we had climbed up the side of the mountain to the spot where the lions were supposed to be lurking—a long, reed-filled cleft in the side of the slope. The porters were sent up to one end of the reed bed, twenty on each side, while we went below to where the lion would probably be driven out by their shouting and noise. The porters bombarded the reeds with stones while we waited with rifles ready for the angry creature to dash out in our vicinity. It was an interesting wait, with plenty of food for thought. I wondered why the Englishmen had not come out to get the lions themselves, and then remembered that one of them had been mauled by a lion and had henceforth remained neutral in all lion fights. I wondered many other things which I have now forgotten. I was quite busy wondering for some time as I waited. In the meantime the lions failed to appear.

Bushbuck, waterbuck, and lots of other herbivora appeared, but no carnivora. We raked the reed bed fore and aft, and combed the long grass in every direction. A young rhino was startled in his morning nap, ran around excitedly for a while, and then trotted off. Birds of many varieties fluttered up and wondered what the racket was about. At ten o'clock we decided that the lions had failed to do their part of the program, and that no further developments were to be expected. So we marched back homeward, got mixed up with another rhino, and finally gained camp, seven miles away, just as our hunger had reached an advanced stage.

The next day we marched to the Thika Thika River, then to Punda Milia, and then to Fort Hall. Some one claimed to have heard a lion out from Fort Hall early in the morning, but I more than half suspect it was one of our porters who reverberates when he sleeps. From Fort Hall we crossed the Tana and made three marches down the river. Rhinos were everywhere jumping out from behind bushes when least expected and in many ways behaving in a most diverting way. For a time we forgot lions while dodging rhinos. There were dozens of them in the thick, low scrub, with now and then a bunch of eland, or a herd of waterbuck, or a few hundred of the ubiquitous kongoni.

We camped in a beautiful spot down on the Tana. The country looked like a park, with graceful trees scattered about on the rolling lawn-like hills. On all sides was game in great profusion. Hippos played about in the river, baboons scampered about on the edge of the water, monkeys chattered in the trees, and it seemed as though nearly all of the eight hundred varieties of East African birds gave us a morning serenade. A five-minutes' walk from camp would show you a rhino, while from the top of any knoll one could look across a vast sweep of hills upon which almost countless numbers of zebras, kongoni, and other animals might be seen.

But never a lion. It certainly looked discouraging.

As a form of pleasant excitement, we began to photograph rhinos, Mr. Akeley took out his moving-picture machine, advanced it cautiously to within a few yards of the unsuspecting rhino, and then we tried to provoke a charge. We took a dozen or more rhinos in this way, often approaching to within a few yards, and if there is any more exciting diversion I don't know what it is. I've looped the loop and there is no comparison. It is more like being ambushed by Filipino insurgents—that is, it's the same kind of excitement, with more danger.

One day it was necessary to shoot a big bull rhino. He staggered and fell, but at once got up and trotted over a hill. Having wounded him, it was then necessary for me to follow him, which I did for three blazing hours. From nine o'clock till twelve I followed, with the sun beating down on the dry, grass-covered hills as though it meant to burn up everything beneath it. If any one had asked me, "Is it hot enough for you?" I should have answered "Yes" without a moment's hesitation. The horizon shimmered in waves of heat. From the top of one hill I could see my rhino half a mile away on the slope of another. When I reached the slope he was a mile farther on. I began to think he was a mirage. For a wounded animal, with two five-hundred-grain shells in his shoulder, he was the most astonishing example of vitality I have ever seen. He would have been safe against a Gatling gun. There were more low trees a mile farther on, and I plodded doggedly on in the hope of getting a little relief from the sun. As I drew near I noticed a rhino standing under the trees, but he was not the wounded one. I decided that the shade was insufficient for both of us and moved swiftly on. Across the valley on the slope of another blistered hill stood the one I was looking for. He didn't seem to be in the chastened mood of one who is about to die. He seemed vexed about something, probably the two cordite shells he was carrying. I at last came up within a hundred yards of him. He had got my wind and was facing me with tail nervously erect. The tail of a rhino is an infallible barometer of his state of mind. With his short sight, I knew that he could not see me at that distance, but I knew that he had detected the direction in which the danger lay. By slowly moving ahead, the distance was cut to about seventy yards, which was not too far away in an open country with a wounded rhino in the foreground. I resolved to shoot before he charged or before he ran away, and so I prepared to end the long chase with an unerring shot.

Suddenly a sound struck my ear that acted upon me like an electric shock:

"*Simba!*"

It was the one word that I had been hoping to hear ever since leaving Nairobi, for the word means "lion." My Somali gunbearer was eagerly pointing toward a lone tree that stood a hundred yards off to the left. A huge, hulking animal was slowly moving away from it. It was my first glimpse of a wild lion. He was half concealed in the tall, dry grass and in a few seconds had entirely disappeared from view. We rushed after him. The rhino was completely forgotten and was left to charge or run away as he saw fit. When we reached the spot where the lion was last seen there was no trace of him. He apparently was not "as brave as a lion." We followed the course that he presumably took and presently reached the crest of a ridge. Then the second gunbearer, a keen-eyed Kikuyu, discovered the lion three hundred yards off to the right. After reaching the top of the hill the animal had swung directly off at right angles with the idea of reaching cover in a dry creek bed some distance away. I started to shoot at three hundred yards, but before I could take a careful aim the lion had disappeared in the grass. For an hour we thrashed the high reeds in the dry creek bed with never a sign of the king of beasts. He had apparently abdicated. He had vanished so completely that I thought he had escaped toward some low hills a mile farther on. The disappointment of seeing a lion and not getting it, or at least shooting at it, was keen to a degree that actually hurt.

Game Was Plenty for a Minute or Two

There was nothing left but to resume our chase after the wounded rhino. It was like going back to work after a pleasant two weeks' vacation. We presently found him on a far distant hill, and after an hour's tramp in the sun we came up to him in the middle of the rolling prairie. There was not a tree for a mile, nor a single avenue of escape in case he charged. Horticulture had never interested me especially, but just at this moment I think a tree, even a thorn tree, would have been a pleasant subject for intimate study. However, to make a long story longer, I shot him at a hundred yards and felt certain that both shells struck. Yet he wheeled around and, stumbling occasionally, was off like a railway train. Again we followed, two miles of desperate tramping in that merciless sun, up hills and down hills, until finally we entirely lost all trace of him. It was now two o'clock. I had eaten nothing since five o'clock in the morning, my water bottle was so nearly empty that I dared take only a swallow at a time, my knees were sore from climbing hills and wading through the tall, dry prairie grass, and I decided to give up this endless pursuit of a rhino who wouldn't die after being hit with four cordite shells.

The dry creek bed lay in the course of our homeward march, and we resolved to take a final look at it. There seemed no likelihood that the lion was there, and I walked into the place with the supreme courage of one who doesn't expect to find anything hostile. My head gunbearer and I had crossed and were walking down in the grass at one side. My second gunbearer was on the opposite side, and the stillness of death hung over the burning plain.

There was not a sign of life in any direction. The second gunbearer was instructed to set fire to the grass in the hope of awakening some protest from the lion in case he was still in the vicinity. There was a dry crackling of flames, and before we could count ten a deep growl came from somewhere in front of me, evidently on one of the edges of the creek bed. The second gunbearer was the first to locate him, and he signaled for me to come over on his side of the creek. In a moment I had dashed down and had climbed out on the other side and was eagerly gazing at a clump of bushes indicated by the Kikuyu. At first I could distinguish nothing, but soon I saw the tawny flanks and the lashing tail of the lion. His head was hidden by the bushes. At that time we were about a hundred yards from him and it was necessary to circle off to a point where the rest of his body could be seen. A little side ravine intervened, and I had to cross it and come directly down through the clump of bushes. The grass was high, and it was not until I had come within forty yards of the lion that I could get a clear view of him. He was glaring at me, with tail waving angrily, and his mouth was opened in a savage snarl. I could see that he didn't like me.

I raised the little .256 Mannlicher, aimed carefully at his open mouth and fired. The lion turned a back somersault and a great thrill of exultation suffused me. Already I saw the handsomely mounted lion-skin rug ornamenting my den at home. We approached cautiously, always remembering that the real danger of lion hunting comes after the lion has been shot. We threw stones in the grass where he had lain, but no answering growl was heard. I thought he was dead, but when we finally reached the spot where he had been there was no sign of him. He had vanished again. I searched the ravine and then crossed to the high grass on the other side. Then we saw him for an instant, half-concealed, just in front of us. His head was hanging, and he looked as though he had been hard hit. Again he disappeared and we searched high and low for him. For several hundred feet we beat the grass without result.

Then the grass was again fired and again the hoarse growl came in angry protest. Walking slowly, with guns ready for instant use, we advanced until we could see him under a tree seventy yards ahead on my side of the ravine. He was growling angrily. This time I used the double-barreled cordite rifle and the first shot struck him in the forehead without knocking him down. He sprang up and the second shot stretched him out. He was still alive when I came up to him, and a small bullet was fired into the base of his brain to reduce the danger of a final charge.

Old hunters always caution one about approaching a dying lion, for often the beast musters up unexpected vitality, makes a final charge, kills somebody, and then dies happy. So we waited a few feet away until the last quiver of his sides had passed. One of the boys pulled his tail and shook him, but there was no sign of life. He was extinct.

A new danger now threatened. The grass fire that the second gunbearer had started was sweeping the prairie, fanned by a strong wind, and there seemed to be not only the danger of abandoning the lion, but of being forced to flee before the flames. So we fell to work beating out the nearest fires, and trusted that a shifting of the wind would send the course of the flames in another direction.

It was now four o'clock. We were nine miles from camp and food, and we knew that at six o'clock darkness would suddenly descend, leaving us out in a rhino-infested country, far from camp. The water was nearly gone and the general outlook was far from pleasing.

The gunbearers skinned the lion. My first shot had struck one of his back teeth, breaking it squarely off, and then passed through the fleshy part of the neck. It was a wound that would startle, but not kill. The second shot had hit him between the eyes, but had glanced off the skull, merely ripping open the skin on the forehead for five inches. The third shell had killed him, except for the convulsive heaving that was finally stilled by the small bullet in the base of the brain.

As I Planned to Look in the Photograph of "My First Lion"

The skinning was interesting. All the fat in certain parts of the body was saved, for East Indians bid high for it and use it as a lubricant for rheumatic pains. The two shoulder blades are always saved and are considered a valuable trophy. They are little bones three inches long, unattached and floating, and have long since ceased to perform any function in the working of the body. The broken tooth was found and saved, and, of course, a photograph was taken. My gunbearer took the picture, and when it was developed there was only a part of the lion and part of the lion slayer visible. It was a good picture of the tree, however.

As I Looked—From Photograph by Gunbearer

At four-thirty the homeward march was begun. At five-thirty two rhinos blocked the path and one of them had to be shot. At six we were still several miles from camp, with the country wrapped in darkness. The water was gone and only one shell remained for the big gun. Somewhere ahead were miles of thorn scrub in which there might be rhinos or buffaloes. Two days before I had killed two large buffaloes in the district through which we must pass, and there was every likelihood of others still being there. At seven we were hopelessly lost in a wide stretch of hippo grass, and I had to fire a shot in the hope of getting an answering shot from camp. In a couple of moments we heard the distant shot, and then pressed on toward camp. The lion had been carried on ahead while we stopped with the rhino, and so the news reached the camp before us. A long line of porters came out to greet us and a great reception committee was waiting at the camp. It was the first lion of the expedition, and as such was the signal for great celebration. That night there were native dances and songs around the big central camp-fire and a wonderful display of pagan hilarity.

It had been a hard day. Fourteen hours without food, several hours without water, and miles of hard tramping through thorn scrub in the darkness and of long, broiling stretches in the blazing sunlight. It seemed a good price to pay even for a lion, but that night, as I finally stretched out on my cot, I was conscious from time to time of a glow of pleasure that swept over me. It seemed that of all human gratifications there was none equal to that experienced by the man who has killed his first lion.

My second lion experience came three days later. With a couple of tents and about forty porters our party of four had marched across to a point a couple of miles from where I had killed the lion. We hoped to put in a day or two looking for lions, some of which had been reported in that district. The porters went on ahead with the camp equipment, while we came along more slowly. Mr. Akeley had taken some close-range photographs of rhinos, and we were just on the point of starting direct for the new camp when we ran across two enormous rhinos standing in the open plain. One was extremely large, with an excellent pair of horns, and it was arranged that I should try to secure this one as a trophy, while Mr. Akeley secured a photograph of the event. At thirty-five yards I shot the larger one of the two, and it dropped in its tracks. The other started to charge, but was finally driven away by shouting and by shots fired in the air. The photograph was excellent and quite dramatic.

For an hour the gunbearers worked on the dead rhino and finally secured the head and feet and certain desirable parts of the skin. At noon we resumed our march for camp, two or three miles away. We had hardly gone half the distance when one of the tent boys was seen far ahead, riding the one mule that we had dared to bring down the Tana River. It was evident that something important had occurred and we hurried on to meet him.

"*Simba!*" he shouted, as soon as he could be heard. In a moment we had the details. One of the saises had seen two lions, a large male and female, quite near the camp. Porters were instructed to watch the beasts until we should arrive, and now were supposed to be in touch with them. We omitted luncheon and struck off at once in the direction indicated by the tent boy. We soon came up to the porters and an instant later saw the lions. It was a beautiful sight. The two animals were majestically walking up the rocky slope of a low, fire-scorched hill a few hundred yards away. The male was a splendid beast, with all the splendid dignity of one who fears nothing in the whole wide world. From time to time the two lions stopped and looked back at us, but with no sign of fear. Several times they lay down, but soon would resume their stately course up among the rocks.

I shall never forget the picture that lay before me. It was as though some famous lion painting of Gérôme or Landseer had come to life, sometimes the animals being outlined clearly against the blue sky and at other times standing, with splendid heads erect, upon the rocks of the low ridge that rose ahead of us.

We stalked them easily. Several porters were left where the lions could constantly see them, while we three, Akeley, Stephenson and I, with our six gunbearers, worked around the base of the hill until we were able to climb up on the crest of it, being thus constantly screened from view of the lions. At the crest was an abrupt outcropping of blackened rocks, where we stopped to locate the two animals. They were nowhere to be seen. Twenty-five yards farther along on the crest was another little ledge of rocks, and we worked our way silently along to it in the expectation that the lions might have advanced that far. But even then our search disclosed nothing. For some time we waited, scouring the neighborhood with our glasses, and had almost reached the conclusion that the lions had made off down the other side of the hill and had reached the cover of a shallow ravine some distance away. Then we saw them—exactly where we had last seen them before we had started our stalk. They were still together and showed no sign of alarm nor knowledge of our presence so near them. At this time they were one hundred and ten yards away. They lay down again behind the rocks and we waited twenty minutes for them to show themselves. Off to our right and in the valley another large male lion appeared and moved slowly away among the low scrub trees.

Finally we decided to rouse the two lions by shouting, but before this decision could be carried out the male rose above the rocks and stood plainly in view. It had previously been arranged that Mr. Stephenson should try for the male, while I should try for the female. In an instant he fired with his big rifle, the lion whirled around and then started running down the hill to the right.

Then the lioness appeared and I wounded her with my first shot. She ran out in the open toward us, but evidently without knowing from where the firing came. A second shot was better placed and I saw her collapse in her tracks. Leaving the lioness, I went down to where Stephenson had followed the lion. Several shots had been fired, but the lion was still running, although badly wounded. Just as it reached a small tree down on the slope a shot was put into a vital spot, and the lion went wildly over on his side. Even then he managed to drag himself under the small bushes surrounding the tree, where a moment later Mr. Stephenson killed him with a shot from his .318 Mauser.

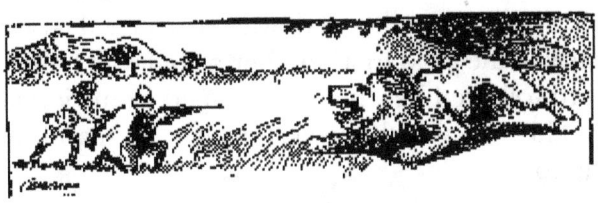

"A Very Interesting Experience," Said I Coolly, a Couple of Days Later

We measured and photographed the lion, and then I took my camera to get a picture of the dead lioness up on the ridge. She was sitting up snarling, and I was the most surprised person in the world. I shot at her and she ran fifty yards to a small tree, where she came to a stop. Two more shots from my big gun finished her, and the photograph was finally secured.

Leaving the porters to watch the two lions, we followed the third lion that had been seen in the valley. He had not gone far and we soon found him, but too far away to get a shot. For an hour we followed him, but he finally disappeared and could not be located again.

It was sundown when our porters reached camp with the two lions, and it was then that we ate our long-deferred luncheon.

A week later, while marching from the Tana River to the Zeka River, Mr. and Mrs. Akeley and I came across a large lion, accompanied by a lioness. They were first seen moving away across a low sloping ridge of the plains within a couple of miles of where we had killed the lion and lioness a week before. We followed them and came up with them after a brisk walk of ten minutes. Both were hiding in the grass near the crest of the slope, and we could see their ears and eyes above the long grass. We crouched down a hundred yards away and the lion rose to see where we had gone. Mrs. Akeley fired and missed, but her second shot pierced his brain and he fell like a log. We expected a charge from the lioness and waited until she should declare herself. But she did not appear and her whereabouts remained an anxious mystery until she was finally seen several hundred yards away making her way slowly up a distant hill. Half-way up she sat down and watched us as we made our way cautiously in the grass to where her mate lay as he fell, stone dead. We afterward followed her, but she escaped from view and could not be located. This lion was the largest we had seen and measured nine feet from tip to tip.

This was our last experience with lions in the Trans-Tana country. After that we went up in the elephant country on Mount Kenia, but that is a story all in itself.

Lion hunting is the best kind of African hunting in one respect. One feels no self-reproach in having killed a lion, for there is always the comforting thought that by killing one lion you have saved the lives of three hundred other animals. Every lion exacts an annual toll of at least that number of zebras, hartebeests, or other forms of antelopes, all of which are powerless to defend themselves against the great creature that creeps upon them in cover of darkness. So a lion hunter may consider himself something of a benefactor.

CHAPTER VII
ON THE TANA RIVER, THE HOME OF THE RHINO. THE TIMID ARE FRIGHTENED, THE DANGEROUS KILLED, AND OTHERS PHOTOGRAPHED. MOVING PICTURES OF A RHINO CHARGE

DOWN on the Tana River the rhinos are more common than in any other known section of Africa. In two weeks we saw over one hundred—perhaps two hundred—of them—so many, in fact, that one of the chief diversions of the day was to count rhinos. One day we counted twenty-six, another day nineteen, and by the time we left the district rhinos had become such fixtures in the landscape as to cause only casual comment. Perhaps there were some repeaters, ones that were counted twice, but even allowing for that there were still some left. We saw big ones and little ones, old ones and young ones, and middle-aged ones; ones with long ears, short horns, double horns, and single horns; black ones and red ones—in fact, all the kinds of rhinos that are resident in British East Africa. One had an ear gone and another had a crook in his tail. If we had stayed another week we might have got out a Tana River Rhino Directory, with addresses and tree numbers. We studied them fore and aft, from in front of trees and from behind them, from close range and long range, over our shoulders, and through our cameras, every way whereby a conscientious lover of life and nature can study a prominent member of the Mammalia. We called the place Rhino Park because the country looks like a beautiful park studded with splendid trees and dotted with rhinos.

A Morning Walk on the Tana River

When I went to Africa I was equipped with the following fund of knowledge concerning the rhinoceros: First, that he is familiarly called "rhino" by the daring hunters who have written about him; second, that he is a member of the Perissodactyl family, whose sole representatives are the horse, the rhino, and the tapir; third, that he savagely charges human beings who write books about their thrilling adventures in Africa, and, finally, that he looks like a hang-over from the pterodactyl age. The books and magazine stories that have come out since Mr. Roosevelt made African hunting the vogue invariably describe the rhino as being one of the most dangerous of African animals. A charging rhino, a wounded lion, a cape buffalo, and a frenzied elephant are the four terrors of the African hunters. All other forms of danger are slight compared with these, and I was full to the guards with a vast and fearful respect for the rhino. I fancied myself spinning around like a pinwheel with the horn of a rhino as a pivot, and the thought had little to commend itself to a lover of longevity—such as myself, for instance.

A Comfortable Hammock of Zebra Skin

Mrs. Akeley and Her Tana River Monkey

After going to Africa and meeting some of the best members of the rhino set I was able to form some conclusions of my own, chief of which is the belief that he is dangerous only if he hits you. As long as you can keep out of his reach you are in no great danger except from the thorns.

The prevailing estimate of the rhino is that he is an inoffensive creature who likes to bask under the shade of a tree and watch the years go parading by. His thick skin and fierce armament of horns seem to make of him a relic of some long-forgotten age—the last survivor of the time when mammoths and dinosauruses roamed the manless waste and time was counted in geological terms instead of days and minutes. His eyes are dimmed and he sees nothing beyond a few yards away, but his hearing and sense of smell are keen, and he sniffs danger from afar in case danger happens to be to windward of him. His sensitive nose is always alert for foreign and, therefore, suspicious odors, and when he smells the blood of an Englishman, or even an American, his tail goes up in anger, he sniffs and snorts and races around in a circle while he locates the direction where the danger lies—and then, look out. A blind, furious rush which only a well-sped bullet can prevent causing the untimely end of whatever happens to be in the way. That is the popular estimate of the rhino.

Popular Conception of Rhino

Here are some of the conclusions I have formed: If the hunter carefully approaches the rhino from the leeward he may often come within a few yards of the animal and might easily shoot him in a leisurely way. The rhino can see only at close range and can smell only when the wind blows the scent to him. Consequently he would be defenseless and at the mercy of the hunter if it were not for one thing. Nature, in her wisdom, has sent the little rhino bird to act as a sentinel for the great pachyderm. These little birds live on the back of the rhino and, as recompense for their vigilance, are permitted to partake of such ticks and insects as inhabit the hide of their host. Whenever danger, or, in other words, whenever a hunter tries to approach their own particular rhino from any direction, windward, leeward, or any other way, the ever alert and watchful rhino birds sound a tocsin of warning. The rhino pricks up his ears and begins to show signs of taking notice. He doesn't know where or what the danger may be, but he knows the C.Q.D. code of danger signals as delivered to him from the outposts on his back and hastens to get busy in an effort to locate the foe. As a general thing the little birds, on sight of danger, begin a wild chatter, rising from the back of the rhino and flying in an opposite direction from the danger. Then they return, light on the rhino's back, and repeat, often several times, the operation of flying away from the danger. If the rhino is a wise rhino he learns from the birds which is the safe way to go and soon trots swiftly off. In a measure the habits of the rhino bird are as interesting as those of the rhino itself, and as an example of the weak protecting the strong, the Damon and Pythias relationship between bird and beast is without parallel in the animal kingdom.

Before and After the Rhino Birds Give the Alarm

The rhino is a peaceful animal. He browses on herbs and shrubs and dwells in friendly relationship with the rest of the animal kingdom. Perhaps once or twice a day he ambles down to some favorite drinking place for a drink, but the rest of the time he grazes along a hillside or stands or lies sleepily under a tree. At such times as the latter he may be approached quite near without much danger. Each day he also goes to a favorite wallowing place, where he rolls in the red dirt and emerges from this dirt bath a dull red rhino. In the rhino country dozens of these red dirt rolling places may be found, each one trampled smooth for an area of fifteen or twenty feet in evidence of the great number of times it has been used by one or more rhinos. This dirt bath is a defensive measure against the hordes of ticks that infest the rhino. It is a subject for wonder that the six or eight tick birds do not keep the rhino free of ticks, and it has even been argued by some naturalists that the rhino bird does not eat ticks, but merely uses the rhino as a convenient resting-place. Also perhaps they enjoy the ride. We had planned to get a rhino bird and perform an autopsy on him in order to analyze his contents, but did not do so.

The Ford of Tana River

The Baby Rhino

After the rhino has taken his dirt wallow, and looks fine in his new red coat, he then slowly and painstakingly proceeds to kill time during the rest of the day. If danger threatens he becomes exceedingly nervous and excited. His anxiety is quite acute. In vain he tries to locate the danger, rushing one way for a few yards, then the other way, and finally all ways at once. His tail is up and he is snorting like a steam engine. When he rushes toward you in this attitude it looks very much as though he were charging you with the purpose of trampling you to flinders. As a matter of fact, or, rather, opinion, he is merely trying to locate where you are in order that he may run the other way. He looks terrifying, but in reality is probably badly terrified himself. He would give a good deal to know which way to run, and finally becomes so excited and nervous that he starts frantically in some direction, hoping for the best. If this rush happens to be in your direction you call it a charge from an infuriated rhino; if not, you say that he looked nasty and was about to charge, but finally ran away in another direction. In most rhino charges it is my opinion that the rhino is too rattled to know what he is doing, and, instead of charging maliciously, he is merely trying to get away as fast as possible. And in such cases the hunter blazes away at him, wounds him, and the rhino blindly charges the flash.

Trying to Provoke a Charge

It was our wish to get moving pictures of a rhino charge. Mr. Akeley had a machine and our plan of action was simple. We would first locate the rhino, usually somnolent under a thorn tree or browsing soberly out in the open. We would then get to the leeward of him and slowly advance the machine; Mr. Akeley in the middle and Stephenson and I on each side with our double-barreled cordite rifles. In case the charge became too serious to escape we hoped to be able to turn him or kill the rhino with our four bullets. If we were unsuccessful in doing so—well, we had to manage the situation by jumping.

Our first experience was most thrilling, chiefly because we expected a charge. We thought all rhinos charged, as per the magazine articles, and so prepared for busy doings. A rhino cow and half-grown calf were discovered on a distant hillside. We stopped in a ravine to adjust the picture machine and then crept cautiously up the hill until we were within about seventy yards of the unsuspecting pair. Then the rhino birds began to flutter and chatter and the two beasts began to sniff nervously. Finally they turned toward us, with tails erect and noses sniffing savagely. Now for the charge, we thought, for it was considered an absolute certainty that a rhino cow accompanied by its calf would always attack. We moved forward a few yards, clapped our hands to show where we were, and their attitude at once became more threatening. They rushed backward and forward a couple of times and faced us again.

By this time we knew that they saw us and our fingers were within the trigger guards. It was agreed that, if they charged, they should be allowed to come within forty feet before we fired, thus giving the picture machine time to get a good record. The situation was intense beyond description, and seconds seemed hours. When they started trotting toward us we thought the fatal moment had come, but instead of continuing the "charge," they swung around and trotted swiftly off in an opposite direction. As far as we could see them they trotted swiftly and with the lightness of deer, sometimes zigzagging their course, but always away from us. The charge had failed in spite of all our efforts to provoke it. The whistling and hand-clapping which we had hoped would give them our location without doubt had merely served to tell them the way not to go.

The moving picture record of a "charging rhino" would have been a brilliant success but for one thing—the rhino refused to charge.

During the following ten days we made many similar attempts to get a charge and always with nearly the same results. Once or twice we got within thirty yards before they finally turned tail after a number of feints that looked much like the beginning of a nasty charge. It was always intensely thrilling work because there was the likelihood that we might get a charge in spite of the fact that a dozen or so previous experiences had failed to precipitate one.

In several cases the first rush of the rhino was toward us, but instead of continuing, he would soon swing about and make off, four times as badly scared as we were. It seemed as though these preliminary rushes toward us were efforts to verify the location of danger in order to determine the right direction for escape. In all, we made between fifteen and twenty different attempts on different rhinos to get a charge, but with always practically the same result, yet with always the same thrill of excitement and uncertainty.

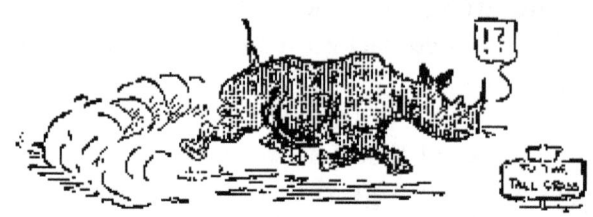

The End of the Charge

Comprehensive statistics on a rhino's charges are hard to obtain. The district commissioner at Embo told me that he had been ordered to reduce the number of rhinos in his district in the interest of public safety and that he had killed thirty-five in all. Out of this number five charged him. That would indicate that one rhino in seven will charge. Captain Dickinson, in his book, *Big Game Shooting on the Equator*, tells of a rhino that charged him so viciously that he threw down his bedding roll and the rhino tossed it and trampled it with great emphasis, after which it triumphantly trotted away, elated probably in the thought that it had wiped out its enemy. A number of fatalities are on record to prove that the rhino is a dangerous beast at times, and so I must conclude that the rhino experiences we had were exceedingly lucky ones, and perhaps exceptional ones in that respect.

In only one instance was it necessary for us to kill a rhino and even then it was done more in the interest of photography than of urgent necessity. On our game licenses we were each allowed to kill two rhinos, and as I wanted, one of the Tana River variety it was arranged that I should try to get the first big one with good horns. After a hunt of several hours we found two of them together out on the slope of a long hill. Our glasses showed that one of them was quite large and equipped with a splendid front horn nearly two feet long and a rear horn about a foot long. At the lower slope of the hill were two or three trees that screened our approach so that we were easily enabled to get within about one hundred and fifty yards of them without danger of discovery. From the trees onward the country was an open prairie for two or three miles.

Armed with a double-barreled cordite rifle and the comforting reflection that the chances were seven to one that the rhinos would not charge, I slowly advanced alone toward the two rhinos. Behind me about fifty yards was the long range camera and a second gun manned by Mr. Stephenson. When fifty yards from the rhinos I stopped, but as no offensive tactics were apparent in the camp of the enemy, I slowly walked forward to thirty-five yards. Then they saw me. They faced me with what seemed like an attitude of decided unfriendliness. Their tails were up and they were snorting like steam engines. When the big one started toward me I fired and it fell like a log. The other one, instead of thundering away, according to expectations, became more belligerent. It ran a few steps, then swung around, and I felt certain that it was going to avenge the death of its comrade. The camera brigade rushed forward, clapping their hands to scare it away, as there was no desire to kill both of the animals. But it refused to go. It would sometimes run a few steps, then it would turn and come toward us. It was evidently in a fighting mood, with no intention of deserting the field of action. Finally by firing shots in the air and yelling noisily it turned and dashed over the side of the hill. The photograph, taken at the instant the big rhino was struck, was remarkably dramatic and showed one rhino in an aggressive attitude and the other just plunging down from the shot of the big bullet.

The front horn of the dead rhino was twenty and three-quarters inches long and in many places the animal's hide was over an inch thick. Strips of this were cut off to make whips, and a large section was removed to be made into a table top. These table tops, polished and rendered translucent by the curing processes, are beautiful as well as extremely interesting. The rhino's tongue is even more delicious to eat than ox tongue and rhino tail soup is a great luxury on any white man's table; while the native porters consider rhino meat the finest of any meat to be had in Africa. The conscience of one who slays a rhino is somewhat appeased by the fact that a hundred native porters will have a good square meal of wholesome meat to help build up their systems.

A Real Rhino Charge

Our expedition sustained only one real rhino charge. One day Mr. Stephenson stumbled on a big cow rhino that was lying in the grass. The meeting was as unexpected to him as to her, and before he could count five she was rushing headlong toward him. He clapped his hands, whistled, and shouted to turn her course, but she came on, snorting loudly and with head ready to impale everything in its way. Stephenson did not want to kill her, neither did he desire to be killed, so when all other means had failed he fired a soft nose bullet into her shoulder in the hope that it would turn her away without seriously hurting her. The bullet seemed to have no effect and she did not change her course in the slightest degree. By this time she was within a short distance of Stephenson, who was obliged to run a few feet and take refuge behind a tree.

The Sultan Looked Like an American Indian

In the Thorn Brush on the Tana

The Dummy Rhino

The gunbearers and porters, who had fled in all directions, thought that Stephenson was caught, but the rhino, passing him with only a small margin of five feet, continued thunderously on her way. In a few yards she slowed down, and when last seen was walking. She had evidently been hit very hard by the soft nose bullet and was already showing signs of sickness. Suddenly a terrific squealing made the party aware that the cow rhino had been accompanied by a little rhino calf. The calf, only a couple of weeks old, charged savagely at every one in sight and every one in sight took refuge behind trees and bushes. Instead of trying to escape, the animal turned and continued to attack in all directions whenever a man showed himself. When a man leaped behind a tree the calf would charge the tree with such force that it would be hurled back several feet, only to spring up and charge again. His squealing could be heard for a mile. After a long time the porters succeeded in capturing it and they conveyed it back to camp strung on a pole. If that little rhino was any criterion of rhino pugnacity, then surely the rhino is born with the instinctive impulse to charge and to fight as savagely as any animal alive.

We fed our little pet rhino on milk and then swung it in a comfortable hammock made of zebra skin. In this more or less undignified fashion it was carried by eight strong porters to Fort Hall, two marches away, where it lived only a week or ten days and then, to our sorrow and regret, succumbed from lack of proper nourishment.

Retiring in Favor of Rhino

Sometimes, when the *safari* is marching through bush country, the rhino becomes an element of considerable anxiety; An armed party must precede the caravan and clear the route of rhinos, otherwise the porters are likely to be scattered by threatened charges. It is no uncommon sight to see a crowd of heavily laden porters drop their loads and shin up the nearest tree in record time. Consequently, strong protective measures are always demanded when a long train of unarmed natives is moving through bush or scrub country where there are many rhinos.

Favorite Way of Being Photographed

The lower Tana River country is admirably adapted to the life habits of the rhinos. Formerly the district was well settled by natives, but now, owing to the fever conditions prevailing there, the natives have all moved away to more wholesome places and only the forlorn remains of deserted villages mark where former prosperity reigned. The country has been abandoned to game, with the result that it has been enormously increasing during the last few years. In addition to the great numbers of rhinos there are big herds of buffalo, enormous numbers of hippo in the river, and many small droves of eland. Waterbuck, bushbuck, steinbuck, impalla, hartebeest and zebra dwell in comparative immunity from danger and may be seen in hundreds, grazing on the hills or in the woods that fringe the river. It is a sportsman's paradise, if he manages to escape the fever, and we enjoyed it tremendously, even though we shot only a hundredth part of what we might easily have shot. The charm of hunting in such a region lies in what one sees rather than in what one kills.

CHAPTER VIII
MEETING COLONEL ROOSEVELT IN THE UTTERMOST OUTPOST OF SEMI-CIVILIZATION. HE TALKS OF MANY THINGS, HEARS THAT HE HAS BEEN REPORTED DEAD, AND PROMPTLY PLANS AN ELEPHANT HUNT

AFTER one has been in British East Africa two months he begins to readjust his preconceived ideas to fit real conditions. He discovers that nothing is really as bad as he feared it would be, and that distance, as usual, has magnified the terrors of a far-away land. In spite of the fact that he is in the heart of a primitive country, surrounded by native tribes that still are mystified by a glass mirror, and perhaps many days' march from the nearest white person, he still may feel that he is in touch with the great world outside. His mail reaches him somehow or other, even if he is in the center of some vast unsettled district devoid of roads or trails.

How it is done is a mystery; but the fact remains that every once in a while a black man appears as by magic and hands one a package containing letters and telegrams. He is a native "runner," whose business it is to find you wherever you may be, and he does it, no matter how long it may take him. A telegram addressed to any sportsman in East Africa would reach him if only addressed with his name and the words "British East Africa." There are only four or five thousand white residents in the whole protectorate, and the names of these are duly catalogued and known to the post-office officials both in Mombasa and Nairobi.

In the Forest

If a strange name appears on a letter or despatch, inquiries are made and the identity of the stranger is quickly established. If he is a sportsman, the outfitters in Nairobi will know who he is. They will have equipped him with porters and the other essentials of a caravan, and they will know exactly in which section of the protectorate he is hunting. So the letter is readdressed in care of the *boma* or government station, nearest to that section. The letter duly arrives at the *boma*, and a native runner is told to go out and deliver the message. He starts off, and by inquiry of other natives and by relying on a natural instinct that is little short of marvelous he ultimately finds the object of his search and delivers his message.

If you look at a map of British East Africa you will be amazed at the number of names that are marked upon it. You would quite naturally think that the country was rather thickly settled, whereas in fact there are very few places of settlement away from the single line of railroad that runs from Mombasa to Victoria Nyanza. The protectorate is divided into subdistricts, each one of which has a capital, or *boma*, as it is called. This *boma* usually consists of a white man's residence, a little post-office, one or two Indian stores where all the necessities of a simple life may be procured, and a number of native grass huts. There is usually a small detachment of askaris, or native soldiers, who are necessary to enforce the law, repress any native uprising, and collect the hut tax of one dollar a year that is imposed upon each household in the district.

Other names on the map may look important, but will prove to be only streams, or hills, or some landmarks that have been used by the surveyors to signify certain places. In our five weeks' trip through Trans-Tanaland we found only two *bomas*, Fort Hall and Embo, and three or four ranches where one or more white men lived. In our expedition to Mount Elgon we encountered only two places where the mark of civilization showed—Eldoma Ravine and Sergoi. In the former place the only white man was the subcommissioner, and in the latter there was one policeman, and a general store kept by a South African. A number of Boer settlers are scattered over the plateau, trying to reclaim little sections of land from its primitive state.

Between Sergoi and Londiani, on the railroad, ninety miles south, there is one little store where caravans may buy food for porters and some of the simpler necessities that white men may require. All the rest of the country for thousands of square miles is given up to the lion and zebra and the vast herds of antelope that feed upon the rich grass of the plateau.

Yet in spite of the sparsity of settlement the native runner manages to find you, even after days of traveling, without compass or directions to aid him.

An Askari Who Looked Like a Tragedian

Mr. Akeley

Hunters who come to East Africa usually are sent to certain districts where game is known to be abundant. These districts are well defined and oftentimes there may be a number of *safaris* in them at the same time, but so large are the districts that one group of hunters very rarely encroaches upon the others.

Some parties are sent to Mount Kilima-Njaro, in the vicinity of which there is good hunting. Others are sent out from points along the railroad for certain classes of game that may be found only in those spots. Simba, on the railroad, is a favorite place for those who are after the yellow-maned or "plains" lion. Muhorini, also on the railroad, is a favorite place for those who want the roan antelope; Naivasha is a good place for hippo, and south of Kijabe, in what is called the Sotik, is a district where nearly all sorts of game abound. The Tana River is a favorite place for rhino, buffalo, nearly all sorts of antelope, and some lion; Mount Kenia is an elephant hunting ground, and the Aberdare Range, between Kenia and Naivasha, also is good for elephant. North of Kenia is the Guas Nyiro River, a rich district for game of many kinds. And so the country is divided up into sections that are sure to attract many sporting parties who desire certain kinds of game.

Our first expedition out from Nairobi was across the Athi Plains to the Tana River and Mount Kenia, a wonderful trip for those who are willing to take chances with the fever down the Tana River. In five weeks we saw lion, rhino, buffalo, and elephant—the four groups of animals that are called "royal game"; also hippo, giraffe, eland, wildebeest, and many varieties of smaller game. It is doubtful whether there is any other section of East Africa where one could have a chance for so many different species of game in such a short time as the Tana River country.

For our second expedition we selected the Guas Ngishu Plateau, the Nzoia River, and Mount Elgon. It is a long trip which involves elaborate preparation and some difficulty in keeping up supplies for the camp and the porters. It is the most promising place, however, for black-maned lion and elephant, and on account of these two capital prizes in the lottery of big game hunting occasional parties are willing to venture the time and expense necessary to reach this district.

We disembarked, or "detrained," as they say down there, at a little station on the railroad called Londiani, eight miles south of the equator and about eighty miles from Victoria Nyanza. Then with two transport wagons drawn by thirty oxen, our horses for "galloping" lions, and one hundred porters, we marched north, always at an altitude of from seventy-five hundred to ninety-two hundred feet, through vast forests that stretched for miles on all sides. The country was beautiful beyond words—clean, wholesome, and vast. In many places the scenery was as trim, and apparently as finished as sections of the wooded hills and meadows of Surrey. One might easily imagine oneself in a great private estate where landscape gardeners had worked for years.

One of the Transport Wagons

At night the cold was keen and four blankets were necessary the night we camped two miles from the equator. In the day the sun was hot in the midday hours, but never unpleasantly so. After two days of marching through forests and across great grassy folds in the earth we reached Eldoma Ravine, a subcommissioner's *boma* that looks for all the world like a mountain health resort. From the hill upon which the station is situated one may look across the Great Rift Valley, two thousand feet below, and stretching away for miles across, like a Grand Cañon of Arizona without any mountains in it. Strong stone walls protect the white residence, for this is a section of the country that has suffered much from native uprisings during the last few years. We called on the solitary white resident one evening, and, true to the creed of the Briton, he had dressed for dinner. The sight of a man in a dinner-coat miles from a white man and leagues from a white woman was something to remember and marvel at.

Northward from Eldoma Ravine for days we marched, sometimes in dense forests so thick that a man could scarcely force himself through the undergrowth that flanked the trail, and sometimes through upland meadows so deep in tall yellow grass as to suggest a field of waving grain, then through miles of country studded with the gnarled thorn tree that looks so much like our apple trees at home. It was as though we were traversing an endless orchard, clean, beautiful, and exhilarating in the cool winds of the African highlands. And then, all suddenly, we came to the end of the trees, and before us, like a great, heaving yellow sea, lay the Guas Ngishu Plateau that stretches northward one hundred miles and always above seven thousand feet in altitude.

Far ahead, like a little knob of blue, was Sergoi Hill, forty miles away, and beyond, in a fainter blue, were the hills that mark the limit of white man's passport. On the map that district is marked: "Natives probably treacherous." Off to the left, a hundred miles away, the dim outline of Mount Elgon rose in easy slopes from the horizon. Elgon, with its elephants, was our goal, and in between were the black-maned lions that we hoped to meet.

It would be hard to exaggerate the charm of this climate. And yet this, one thought, was equatorial Africa, which, in the popular imagination, is supposed to be synonymous with torrential rains, malignant fevers, and dense jungles of matted vegetation. It was more like the friendly stretches of Colorado scenery at the time of year when the grasses of the valley are dotted with flowers of many colors and the sun shines down upon you with genial warmth.

A Night on the Equator

Each morning we marched ten or twelve miles and then went into camp near some little stream. In the afternoon we hunted for lions, beating out swamps, scouting every bit of cover and combing the tall grass for hours at a time. Hartebeest, topi, zebra, eland, oribi, reedbuck, and small grass antelope were upon all sides and at all times.

The herds of zebra and hartebeest literally numbered thousands, but, except as the latter were occasionally required for food for the porters, we seldom tried to shoot them. Every Boer settler we saw was interviewed and every promising lion clue was followed to the bitter end, but without result. Sometimes we remained in one camp a day or more in order to search the lion retreats more thoroughly, but never a black-maned lion was routed from his lair. A few weeks later, when the dry grass had been burned to make way for new grass, as is done each year, the chances would be greatly improved, and we hoped for better luck when we retraced our steps from Elgon in December. Before that time it would be like trying to find a needle in a haystack to find a lion in the tall grass, and a good deal more dangerous if we did find one. There were lots of them there, but they were taking excellent care of themselves. In July, three months previous, Mr. McMillan, Mr. Selous, and Mr. Williams were in this same district after black-maned lions. They heard them every night, but saw only one in several weeks. This one, however, made a distinct impression. Williams saw it one day and wounded it at two hundred yards. The lion charged and could not be stopped by Williams' bullets. It was only after it had leaped on the hunter and frightfully mauled him that the lion succumbed to its wounds. And it was only after months of suffering that Williams finally recovered from the mauling.

We felt that if Frederick Selous, the world's greatest big game hunter, could not find the lion, then our chances were somewhat slim.

Lion Hunting in Tall Grass

There had been few parties in this district since McMillan's party left. Captain Ashton came in two months before us, and we met him on his way out. With him was Captain Black, a professional elephant hunter, who, three years before, on the Aberdare, had had a bad experience with an elephant. It was a cow that he had wounded but failed to kill. She charged him and knocked him down in a pile of very thick and matted brush. Three times she trampled him under her feet, but the bushes served as a kind of mattress and the captain escaped with only a few hones broken; although he was laid up for five weeks. Ashton and Black did not have much luck in the present trip and failed to get a single lion.

Two Spaniards passed our camp one day, inward bound. They were the Duke of Peñaranda and Sr. de la Huerta, and reported no lions during their few days in the district. Prince Lichtenstein was also somewhere on the plateau, but we didn't run across him. In addition to these three parties and ours, the only other expedition in the Guas Ngishu Plateau was Colonel Roosevelt's party, toward which, by previous agreement, we made our way.

A number of months before Mr. Akeley, who headed our party, was dining with President Roosevelt at the White House. In the course of their talk, which was about Africa and Mr. Akeley's former African hunting and collecting experiences, the latter had told the president about a group of elephants that he was going to collect and mount for the American Museum of History in New York. President Roosevelt was asked if he would coöperate in the work, and he expressed a keen willingness to do so. When our party arrived at Nairobi, in September, a letter awaited Mr. Akeley, renewing Colonel Roosevelt's desire to help in collecting the group.

It was in answer to this invitation that Mr. Akeley and our party had gone to the Mount Elgon country to meet Mr. Roosevelt and carry out the elephant-hunting compact made many months before at the White House.

Kermit, Leslie Tarlton and Colonel Roosevelt

Winding Through Unbroken Country

Our Safari on the March

Eleven days of marching and hunting from the railroad brought us to Sergoi, the very uttermost outpost of semi-civilization. Here we found another letter in which Mr. Akeley was asked to come to the Roosevelt camp, and which suggested that a native runner could pilot him to its whereabouts. The letter had been written some days before and had been for some time at Sergoi. Whether the Roosevelt camp had been moved in the meantime could not be determined at Sergoi, and we knew only in a general way that it was probably somewhere on the Nzoia River (pronounced Enzoya), two or three days' march west of Sergoi, toward Mount Elgon.

So we started across, meeting no natives who possibly could have given any information. On the afternoon of November thirteenth we went into camp on the edge of a great swamp, or *tinga-tinga*, as the natives call it, only a couple of hours' march from the river. Many fresh elephant trails had been discovered, and the swamp itself looked like a most promising place for lions. A great tree stood on one side of the swamp, and in its branches was a platform which an Englishman had occupied seven nights in a vain quest for lions some time before. A little grass shelter was below the tree, and as we approached a Wanderobo darted out and ran in terror from us. The Wanderobos are native hunters who live in the forests, and are as shy as wild animals. So we could not question him as to Colonel Roosevelt's camp. Later in the afternoon a native runner appeared from the direction of Sergoi with a message to the colonel, but he didn't know where the camp was and didn't seem to be in any great hurry to find out. He calmly made himself the guest of one of our porters and spent the night in our camp, doing much more sitting than running.

On the morning of the fourteenth we marched toward the river, two hours away, the native runner slowly ambling along with us. We had been on the trail about an hour and a half when a shot was heard off to our left; At first we thought it was our Spanish friends, but a few moments later we came to a point where we could see, about a mile away, a long string of porters winding along in the direction from which we came, it was plainly a much larger *safari* than the Spanish one, and we at once concluded that it was Colonel Roosevelt's.

Three or four men on horses were visible, but could not be recognized with our glasses. The number corresponded to the colonel's party, however, which we knew to consist of himself and Kermit, Edmund Heller and Leslie Tarlton. A messenger was sent across the hills to establish their identity and we marched on to the river, a half-hour farther, where we found the smoldering fires of their camp.

A transport wagon of supplies for the Duke of Peñaranda's *safari* was also there, and from the drivers it was definitely learned that the late occupants of the camp were Mr. Roosevelt and his party. In the meantime the messenger had reached Colonel Roosevelt, and when the latter learned that Mr. Akeley's *safari* was in the vicinity he at once ordered camp pitched forty-five minutes from our camp, and started across to see Akeley. The latter had also started across to see the colonel, and they met on the way. And during all this time the native runner with the message to Colonel Roosevelt was loafing the morning away in our camp. What the message might be, of course, we didn't know, but we hoped that it was nothing of importance. It was only when the colonel and his party reached our camp that the message was delivered. As we stood talking and congratulating everybody on how well he was looking the colonel casually opened the message.

He seemed amused, and somewhat surprised, and at once read it aloud to us. It was from America, and said: "Reported here you have been killed. Mrs. Roosevelt worried. Cable denial American Embassy, Rome." It was dated November sixth, eight days before.

"I think I might answer that by saying that the report is premature," he said, laughing, and then told the story of a Texas man who had commented on a similar report in the same words.

Colonel Roosevelt certainly didn't look dead. If ever a man looked rugged and healthy and in splendid physical condition he certainly did on the day that this despatch reached him. His cheeks were burned to a ruddy tan and his eyes were as clear as a plainsman's. He laughed and joked and commented on the news that we told him with all the enthusiasm of one who knows no physical cares or worries.

Reading the Report That He Had Been Killed

"If I could have seen you an hour and a half ago," he told Akeley, "I could have got you the elephants you want for your group. We passed within only a few yards of a herd of ten this morning, and Kermit got within thirty yards to make some photographs." They had not shot any, however, as they had received no answer to the letter sent several days before to Mr. Akeley and consequently did not know positively that his party had reached the plateau.

The colonel asked about George Ade, commented vigorously and with prophetic insight on the Cook-Peary controversy, and read aloud, in excellent dialect, a Dooley article on the subject, which I had saved from an old copy of the Chicago *Tribune*. He commented very frankly, with no semblance at hypocrisy, on Mr. Harriman's death, told many of his experiences in the hunting field, and for three hours, at lunch and afterward, he talked with the freedom of one who was glad to see some American friends in the wilderness and who had no objection to showing his pleasure at such a meeting.

He talked about the tariff and about many public men and public questions with a frankness that compels even a newspaper man to regard as being confidential. Our *safari* was the only one he had met in the field since he had been in Africa, and it was evident that the efforts of the protectorate officials to save him from interference and intrusion had been successful.

Arrangements were then made for an elephant hunt. Colonel Roosevelt was working on schedule time, and had planned to be in Sergoi on the seventeenth. He agreed to a hunt that should cover the fifteenth, sixteenth, and possibly the seventeenth, trusting that they might be successful in this period and that a hard forced march could get him to Sergoi on the night of the eighteenth.

It was arranged that he and Mr. Akeley, with Kermit and Tarlton and one tent should start early the next morning on the hunt, trusting to luck in overtaking the herd that he had seen in the morning. The hunt was enormously successful, and the adventures they had were so interesting that they deserve a separate chapter.

CHAPTER IX
THE COLONEL READS MACAULAY'S "ESSAYS," DISCOURSES ON MANY SUBJECTS WITH GREAT FRANKNESS, DECLINES A DRINK OF SCOTCH WHISKY, AND KILLS THREE ELEPHANTS

ON the afternoon of November fourteenth, a little cavalcade of horsemen might have been seen riding slowly away from our camp on the Nzoia River. One of them, evidently the leader, was a well-built man of about fifty-one years, tanned by many months of African hunting and wearing a pair of large spectacles. His teeth flashed in the warm sunlight. A rough hunting shirt encased his well-knit body and a pair of rougher trousers, reinforced with leather knee caps and jointly sustained by suspenders and a belt, fitted in loose folds around his stocky legs. On his head was a big sun helmet, and around his waist, less generous in amplitude than formerly, was a partly filled belt of Winchester cartridges. His horse was a stout little Abyssinian shooting pony, gray of color and lean in build, and in the blood-stained saddle-bag was a well-worn copy of Macaulay's *Essays*, bound in pigskin. Our hero—for it was he—was none other than Bwana Tumbo, the hunter-naturalist, exponent of the strenuous life, and ex-president of the United States.

Improving Each Shining Hour

If I were writing a thrilling story of adventure that is the way this story would begin. But as this is designed to be a simple chronicle of events, it is just as well at once to get down to basic facts and tell about the Roosevelt elephant hunt, the hyena episode, and the pigskin library, together with other more or less extraneous matter.

A Flag Flew Over the Colonel's Tent

Kermit and Mr. Stephenson Diagnosing the Case

Colonel Roosevelt, his son Kermit, Leslie Tarlton, who is managing the Roosevelt expedition, and Edmund Heller, the taxidermist of the expedition, came to our camp on the fourteenth of November to have luncheon and to talk over plans whereby Colonel Roosevelt was to kill one or more elephants for Mr. Akeley's American museum group of five or six elephants. The details were all arranged and later in the afternoon the colonel and his party left for their own camp, only a short distance from ours.

Mr. Akeley, with one of our tents and about forty porters, followed later in the evening and spent the night at the Roosevelt camp. The following morning Colonel Roosevelt, Mr. Akeley, Mr. Tarlton and Kermit, with two tents and forty porters and gunbearers, started early in the hope of again finding the trail of the small herd of elephants that had been seen the day before. The trail was picked up after a short time and the party of hunters expected that it would be a long and wearisome pursuit, for it was evident that the elephants had become nervous and were moving steadily along without stopping to feed. In such cases they frequently travel forty or fifty miles before settling down to quiet feeding again.

The country was hilly, deep with dry grass, and badly cut up with small gullies and jagged out-croppings of rock on the low ridges. At all times the ears of the hunting party were alert for any sound that would indicate the proximity of the herd, but for several hours no trumpeting, nor intestinal rumbling, nor crash of tusks against small trees were heard. Finally, at about eleven o'clock, Tarlton, who, strangely enough, is partly deaf, heard a sound that caused the hunting party to stop short. He heard elephants. They were undoubtedly only a short distance ahead, but as the wind was from their direction there was little likelihood that they had heard the approach of the hunters. So Tarlton, who has had much experience in elephant hunting, led the party off at a right angle from the elephant trail and then, turning, paralleled the trail a few hundred feet away. They had gone only a short distance when it became evident that they had passed the herd, which was hidden by the tall grass and the thickly-growing scrub trees that grew on all sides.

The wooded character of the country rendered it easy to stalk the elephant herd, and with careful attention to the wind, the four hunters and their gunbearers advanced under cover until the elephants could be seen and studied. Each of the four hunters carried a large double-barreled cordite rifle that fires a five-hundred-grain bullet, backed up by nearly a hundred grains of cordite.

As was expected, the herd consisted solely of cows and calves. There were eight cow elephants and two *totos*, or calves, a circumstance that was particularly fortunate, as Colonel Roosevelt was expected to secure one or two cows for the group, while some one else was to get the calf.

For some moments the hunting party studied the group of animals and finally decided which ones were the best for the group.

Two of the largest cows and the calf of one of them were selected. It is always the desire of collectors who kill groups of animals for museums to kill the calf and the mother at the same time whenever practicable, so that neither one is left to mourn the loss of the other. It is one of the unpleasant features of group collecting that calves must be killed, but the collector justifies himself in the thought that many thousands of people will be instructed and interested in the group when it is finished.

Elephant hunting is considered by many African hunters as being the most dangerous of all hunting. When a man is wounded by an elephant he is pretty likely to die, whereas the wounds inflicted by lions are often not necessarily mortal ones. Also, in fighting a wounded lion one may sometimes take refuge in the low branches of a tree, but with a wounded elephant there is rarely time to climb high enough and quick enough to escape the frenzied animal. In elephant shooting, also, the hunter endeavors to approach within twenty or thirty yards, so that the bullets may be placed exactly where their penetration will be the most instantaneously deadly. Consequently, a badly placed bullet may merely infuriate the elephant without giving the hunter time to gain a place of safety, and thus be much worse than if the hunter had entirely missed his mark.

Among elephant hunters it is considered more dangerous to attack a cow elephant than a bull, for the cow is always ready and eager to defend its calf, hence when Colonel Roosevelt prepared to open fire on a cow elephant, accompanied by a calf, at a range of thirty yards, in a district where the highest tree was within reach of an elephant's trunk, the situation was one fraught with tense uncertainty.

Colonel Roosevelt is undoubtedly a brave man. The men who have hunted with him in Africa say that he has never shown the slightest sign of fear in all the months of big game hunting that they have done together. He "holds straight," as they say in shooting parlance, and at short range, where his eyesight is most effective, he shoots accurately.

This, then, was the dramatic situation at about twelve o'clock noon on November fifteenth, eight miles east of the Nzoia River, near Mount Elgon: Eight cow elephants, two *totos*, one ex-president with a double-barreled cordite rifle thirty yards away, supported by three other hunters similarly armed, with native gunbearers held in the rear as a supporting column.

The colonel opened fire; the biggest cow dropped to her knees and in an instant the air was thunderous with the excited "milling" of the herd of elephants. For several anxious minutes the spot was the scene of much confusion, and when quiet was once more restored Colonel Roosevelt had killed three elephants and Kermit had killed one of the calves. It had not been intended or desired to kill more than two of the cows, but with a herd of angry elephants threatening to annihilate an attacking party, sometimes the prearranged plans do not work out according to specifications.

Kermit was hastily despatched to notify our camp and the work of preparing the skins of the elephants was at once begun.

In the meantime, we at our camp, eight miles away from the scene of battle, were waiting eagerly for news of the hunting party, although expecting nothing for a day of so. It seemed too much to expect that the hunt should have such a quick and successful termination. So when Kermit rode in with the news late in the afternoon it was a time for felicitation. We all solemnly took a drink, which in itself was an event, for our camp was a "dry" camp when in the field. Only the killing of a lion had been sufficient provocation for taking off the "lid," but on the strength of three elephants for the group the "lid" was momentarily raised with much ceremony and circumstance.

The burden of Kermit's message was "salt, salt, salt!" and porters and second gunbearers to help with the skinning. So James L. Clark, who has been connected with the American Museum of History for some time and who was with us on the Mount Elgon trip to help Mr. Akeley with the preparation of the group, started off with a lot of porters laden with salt for preserving the skins. It was his plan to go direct to the main Roosevelt camp, get a guide, and then push on to the elephant camp, where he hoped to arrive by ten o'clock at night. He would then be in time to help with the skinning, which we expected would be continued throughout the entire night. Kermit stopped at his own camp and gave Clark a guide for the rest of the journey, after which he went to bed.

At eleven o'clock the sound of firing was heard some place off in the darkness. The night guard of the Roosevelt camp, rightly construing it to be a signal, answered it with a shot, and, guided by the latter, Clark and his party of salt-laden porters once more appeared. They had traveled in a circle for three hours and were hopelessly lost. Kermit was routed out and again supplied more guides—also a compass and also the direction to follow. Unfortunately he made a mistake and said northwest instead of southeast—otherwise his directions were perfect.

For three hours more Clark and his porters went bumping through the night, stumbling through the long grass and falling into hidden holes. The porters began to be mutinous and the guides were thoroughly and hopelessly lost. It was then that they one and all laid down in the tall grass, made a fire to keep the lions and leopards away, and slept soundly until daylight. Even then the situation was little better, for the guides were still at sea. About the time that Clark decided, to return to the river, miles away, and take a fresh start, he fired a shot in the forlorn hope of getting a response from some section of the compass. A distant shot came in answer and he pushed on and soon came up with the colonel and Tarlton returning home after a night in the temporary elephant camp. The colonel gave him full directions and at nine o'clock the relief party arrived at their destination.

In the meantime we, Mrs. Akeley, Stephenson and myself, had left our camp on the river at six-fifteen, gone to the Roosevelt camp, and with Kermit guiding us proceeded on across country toward the elephant camp. On our way we also met the colonel and Tarlton, the former immensely pleased with the outcome of the hunt and full of enthusiasm about the adventure with the elephants. But the most remarkable thing of all, he said, was the hyena incident. He told us the story, and it is surely one that will make all nature fakers sit up in an incredulous and dissenting mood.

During the night, the story goes, many hyenas had come from far and near to gorge on the carcasses of the elephants. Their howls filled the night with weird sounds. Lions also journeyed to the feast, and between the two they mumbled the bones of the slain with many a howl and snarl. Early in the morning the colonel went out in the hope of surprising a lion at the spread. Instead, to his great amazement, he saw the head of a hyena protruding from the distended side of the largest elephant. It was inside the elephant and was looking out, as through a window. A single shot finished the hyena, after which a more careful examination was made.

There are two theories as to what really happened. One is that the hyena ate its way into the inside of the elephant, then gorged itself so that its stomach was distended to such proportions that it couldn't get through the hole by which it had entered the carcass.

The Hyena Episode

The other theory is that, after eating its way into the elephant, it started to eat its way out by a different route. When its head emerged the heavy muscles of the elephant's side inclosed about its neck like a vise, entrapping the hyena as effectively as though it had its head in a steel trap. In the animal's despairing efforts to escape it had kicked one leg out through the thick walls of the elephant's side.

Kermit Roosevelt

"Peeling" an elephant

The colonel, in parting, asked us to stop with him for lunch on our way back and he would tell us all about the elephant hunt and show us his pigskin library. In return we promised to photograph the hyena and thus be prepared to render expert testimony in case, some time in the future, he might get into a controversy with the nature fakers as to the truth of the incident.

We then resumed our journey and arrived at the elephant camp at nine-thirty. It was a scene of industry. The skins of the two largest elephants and that of the calf had been removed the afternoon before and were spread out under a cluster of trees. Twenty or thirty porters were squatted around the various ears and strips of hide and massive feet, paring off all the little particles of flesh or tissue that remained. As fast as a section of hide was stripped it was thickly covered with salt and rolled up. This is the preliminary step. Afterwards the skin, in many places an inch in thickness, is pared down to a condition of pliable thinness. This work requires hours or even days of hard labor by many skilful wielders of the paring knife. The skulls and many of the bones are saved when an animal is being preserved for a museum, but when we arrived they had not yet been removed from the carcasses.

Our first object was to visit the hyena, which we found still protruding from the side of his tomb. We photographed him from all angles, after which he was disinterred and exposed to full view. He had certainly died happy. He had literally eaten himself to death, and his body was so distended from gorging that it was as round as a ball. Colonel Roosevelt also photographed it, so that there will be no lack of evidence if the incident ever reaches the controversial stage.

The third cow killed by Colonel Roosevelt was too small for the group, so the skin was divided up as souvenirs of the day. We each got a foot, fifteen square feet of skin, and one of the ears was saved for the colonel.

We then started on the long two hours' ride back to the Roosevelt camp, arriving there at a few minutes before one o'clock. We had not been in camp ten minutes before a whirlwind came along, blew down a tent, and in another minute was gone.

A big American flag was flying from the colonel's tent, and he came out and greeted us with the utmost cordiality and warmth. In honor of the occasion he had put on his coat and a green knit tie. He was beaming with pleasure at the result of the elephant hunt and seemed proud that he was to have elephants in the American Museum group to be done by Mr. Akeley. Heller was stuffing some birds and mice and was as slouchy, deliberate and as full of dry humor as any one I've ever seen. He is a character of a most likable type. Tarlton, small, with short cropped red hair—a sort of Scotchman in appearance—is also a remarkable type. He has a quiet voice, never raised in tone, and talks like the university man that he is. He is a famous lion hunter and has killed numbers of lions and elephants, but now he says he is through with dangerous game.

"I've had enough of it," he says.

The colonel, Tarlton, Heller, and Kermit were the only members of the expedition present, Mearns and Loring having been engaged in a separate mission up in the Kenia country for several weeks, while Cuninghame had gone to Uganda to make preparations for the future operations of the party in that country.

Mrs. Akeley washed up in the colonel's tent, while Stephenson and I used Kermit's tent, and as we washed and scrubbed away the memories of the elephant carcasses the colonel stood in the door and talked to us.

We told him that each of us had taken a drink of Scotch whisky the evening before in honor of the elephants—the first drinks we had taken for weeks.

"I'd do the same," said the colonel, "but I don't like Scotch whisky. As a matter of fact, I have taken only three drinks of brandy since I've been in Africa, twice when I was exhausted and once when I was feeling a little feverish. Before I left Washington there were lots of people saying that I was a drunkard, and that I could never do any work until I had emptied a bottle or two of liquor."

We told him that we had heard these rumors frequently during the closing months of his administration, and he laughed.

"I never drank whisky," he said; "not from principle, but because I don't like it. I seldom drink wine, because I'm rather particular about the kind of wine I drink. We have some champagne with us, but the thought of drinking hot champagne in this country is unpleasant. Sometimes, when I can get wines that just suit my taste, I drink a little, but never much. The three drinks of brandy are all I've had in Africa, and I'm sure that I've not taken one in the last four months. They had all sorts of stories out about me before I left Washington—that I was drinking hard and that I was crazy. I may be crazy," he said, laughing, "but I most certainly haven't been drinking hard."

The luncheon was a merry affair. Heller had been out in the swamp in front of the camp and had shot some ducks for luncheon.

"On my way in," said the colonel, "I shot an oribi, but when I heard that Heller had shot some ducks I knew that my oribi would not be served."

It was evident that the most thorough good fellowship existed among the members of the colonel's party. His fondness for all of them was in constant evidence—in the way he joked with them and in the complete absence of restraint in their attitude toward him.

"They were told that I would be a hard man to get along with in the field," Colonel Roosevelt said, "but we've had a perfectly splendid time together."

I asked him whether he had been receiving newspapers, and, if not, whether he would like to see some that I had received from home. He answered that he had not seen any and really didn't want to see any.

"I don't believe in clinging to the tattered shreds of former greatness," he said, laughing.

He had not heard that Governor Johnson, of Minnesota, had died, and when we told him he said that Johnson would undoubtedly have been the strongest presidential candidate the Democrats could have nominated the next time. He wanted to know where he could address a note of sympathy to Mrs. Johnson.

Later, in speaking of a prominent public man who loudly disclaimed responsibility for an act committed by a subordinate, he said:

"It would have been far better to have said nothing about it, but let people think he himself had given the order. Very often subordinates say and do things that are credited to their superiors, and it is never good policy to try to shift the blame. Do you remember the time Root was in South America? Well, some president down there sent me a congratulatory telegram which reached Washington when I was away. Mr. —— of the state department answered it in my name and said that I and 'my people' were pleased with the reception they were giving Mr. Root. Well, the New York *Sun* took the matter up and when the fleet went around the world they referred to it as 'my fleet,' and that 'my fleet' had crossed 'my equator' four times and 'my ocean' a couple of times. It was very cleverly done and some people began to call for a Brutus to curb my imperialistic tendencies."

Writing His Adventures While They're Hot

He told a funny story about John L. Sullivan, who came to the White House to intercede for a nephew who had got into trouble in the navy. John L. told what a nice woman the boy's mother was and what a terrible disgrace it would be for himself and his family if the boy was dropped from the navy. "Why, if he hadn't gone into the navy he might have turned out very bad," said John L.; "taken up music or something like that."

We also told him that some of the American papers were keeping score on the game he had killed, and that whenever the cable reported a new victim the score up to date would be published like a base-ball percentage table. In the last report he was quoted as having killed seven lions, while Kermit had killed ten. This seemed to amuse him very much, although the figures were not strictly accurate. His score was nine and Kermit's eight up to date. He was also amused by the habit the American papers have of calling him "Bwana Tumbo," which means "The Master with the Stomach," a title that did not fit him nearly so appropriately then as it might have done before he began his active days in the hunting field. He said, so far as he knew, the porters called him "Bwana Mkubwa," which means "Great Master," and is applied to the chief man of a *safari*, regardless of who or what he is. It is merely a title that is always used to designate the boss. We told him that many natives we had met would invariably refer to him as the Sultana Mkubwa, or Great Sultan, because they had heard that he was a big chief from America.

He also laughingly quoted the attitude of Wall Street as expressed in the statement that they "hoped every lion would do his duty."

Later, in speaking generally of the odd experiences he had had in Africa, he spoke of one that will surely be regarded as a nature fake when he tells it. It was an experience that he and Cuninghame had with a big bull giraffe which they approached as it slept. When they were within ten feet of it it opened its eyes and stared at them. A slight movement on their part caused it to strike out with its front foot, but without rising. Then, as they made no offensive moves, it continued to regard them sleepily and without fear. Even when they threw sticks at it it refused to budge, and it was only after some time that it was chased away, where it came to a stop only fifty yards off.

"I suppose W.J. Long will call that a nature fake," he said, "and I wish that I had had a camera with me so that I could have photographed it. I'm afraid they won't believe Cuninghame, because they don't know him."

In the course of the luncheon the conversation ranged from politics, public men, his magazine work, some phases of Illinois politics, as involved in the recent senatorial election, his future plans of the present African trip and many of the little experiences he had had since arriving in the country. Much that was said was of such frankness, particularly as to public men, as to be obviously confidential.

Kermit Led the Way to the Elephant Camp

The Elephants' Skulls Were Saved

Removing an Elephant's Skin

He was asked whether he had secured, among his trophies, any new species of animal that might be named after him. In Africa there is a custom of giving the discoverer's name to any new kind or class of animal that is killed. For instance, the name "granti" is applied to the gazelle first discovered by the explorer Grant. "Thompsoni" is applied to the gazelle discovered by Thompson. "Cokei" is the name given the hartebeest discovered by Coke, and so on. If Colonel Roosevelt had discovered a new variation of any of the species it would be called the "Roosevelti ——."

The colonel said that he had not discovered any new animals, but that Heller, he thought, had found some new variety of mouse or mole on Mount Kenia. He supposed that it would be called the Mole Helleri.

He then told about an exciting adventure they had with a hippo two nights before. Away in the night the camp was aroused by screams coming from the big swamp in front. Kongoni, his gunbearer, rushed in and shouted: "Lion eat porter!" The colonel grabbed his gun and dashed out in the darkness. Kermit and one or two others, hastily armed, also appeared, and they charged down the swamp, where a hippo had made its appearance in the neighborhood of a terrified porter. Kermit dimly made out the hippo and shot at it, but it disappeared and could not be found again.

After luncheon the colonel said, "Now, I want to inflict my pigskin library on you," and together we went into his tent and he opened an oilcloth-covered, aluminum-lined case that was closely packed with books, nearly all of which were bound in pigskin. It was a present from his sister, Mrs. Douglas Robinson. The tent was lined with red, evidently Kermit's darkroom when he was developing pictures. A little table stood at the open flaps of the entrance and upon it were writing materials, with which Mr. Roosevelt already had started to write up the elephant hunt of the day before. His motto seems to be, "Do it now, if not sooner."

The Pigskin Library

I sat on his cot, Mrs. Akeley on a small tin trunk, and Stephenson on another. The colonel squatted down on the floor cloth of the tent and began to show us one by one the various literary treasures from his pigskin library. The whole box of books was so designed that it weighed only sixty pounds, and was thus within the limit of a porter's load. Some of the books were well stained from frequent use and from contact with the contents of his saddle-bags. Whenever he went on a hunt he carried one or more of these little volumes, which he would take out and read from time to time when there was nothing else to do. He never seemed to waste a moment.

His pride in the library was evident, and the fondness with which he brought forth the books was the fondness of an honest enthusiast.

"Some people don't consider Longfellow a great poet, but I do," he said, as he showed a little volume of the poet's works. "Lowell is represented here, but I think, toward the end of his life, he became too much Bostonian. The best American," he said later, "is a Bostonian who has lived ten years west of the Mississippi."

He then showed us his work-box, a compact leather case containing pads of paper, pens, lead pencils, and other requirements of the writer. I did not see a type-writing machine such as we cartoonists have so often represented in our cartoons of Mr. Roosevelt in Africa. But, then, cartoonists are not always strictly accurate.

Later on he spoke of the lectures he was to deliver in Berlin, at the Sorbonne in Paris, and in Oxford the following spring. I told him how surprised I had been to hear that he had prepared these lectures during the rush of the last few weeks of his administration. He said that he probably would be regarded as a representative American in those lectures and that he wanted to do them just as well as he possibly could. He knew that there would be no time nor library references in Africa, and so he had prepared them in Washington before leaving America.

In regard to his future movements he seemed sorry that he was obliged to take the Nile trip, and that he was only doing it as a matter of business—that he had to get a white rhino, which is found only along certain parts of the Nile.

"Going back by the Nile is a long and hard trip. For the first twelve days we will not fire a shot, probably. It will mean getting started every morning at three o'clock, marching until ten, then sweating under mosquito bars during the heat of the day, with spirillum ticks, sleeping-sickness flies, and all sorts of pests to bother one; then long days on the Nile, with nothing to see but papyrus reeds on each side."

And speaking of "rhinos" suggests a little incident that the colonel told and which he considers amusing.

"One day one of the party was stalking a buffalo, when a rhino suddenly appeared some distance away and threatened to charge or do something that would alarm the buffalo and scare it away. So they told me to hurry down and shoo the rhino off while they finished their stalk and got the buffalo. So, you see, there's an occupation. That settles the question as to what shall we do with our ex-presidents. They can be used to scare rhinos away."

On hearing this story I remembered that the thick-skinned rhino is sometimes used by cartoonists as a symbol for "the trusts," and the story seemed doubly appropriate as applied to this particular ex-president.

Some member of our party then modestly advanced the suggestion that the colonel might some day be back in the White House again. He laughed and said that the kaleidoscope never repeats.

"They needn't worry about what to do with this ex-president," he said. "I have work laid out for a long time ahead."

Another member of our party then told about the Roosevelt act in *The Follies of 1909*, in one part of which some one asks Kermit (in the play) where the "ex-president" is. "You mean the 'next president,' don't you?" says Kermit. When Colonel Roosevelt heard this he was immensely interested, not so much in the words of the play, but in the fact that Kermit had been represented on the stage—dramatized, as it were.

And as we left for our own camp the colonel called out: "Now, don't forget. Just as soon as we all get back to America we'll have a lion dinner together at my house."

CHAPTER X
ELEPHANT HUNTING NOT AN OCCASION FOR LIGHTSOME MERRYMAKING. FIVE HUNDRED THOUSAND ACRES OF FOREST IN WHICH THE KENIA ELEPHANT LIVES, WANDERS AND BRINGS UP HIS CHILDREN

THE peril and excitement of elephant hunting can not be realized by any one who has known only the big, placid elephants of the circus, or fed peanuts to a gentle-eyed pachyderm in the park. To the person thus circumscribed in his outlook, the idea of killing an elephant and calling it sport is little short of criminal. It would seem like going out in the barnyard and slaying a friendly old family horse.

That was my point of view before I went to Africa, but later experiences caused the point of view to shift considerably. If any one thinks that elephant hunting is an occasion for lightsome merrymaking he had better not meet the African elephant in the rough. Most people are acquainted with only the Indian elephant, the kind commonly seen in captivity, and judge from him that the elephant is a sort of semi-domesticated beast of burden, like the camel and the ox. Yet the Indian elephant is about as much like his African brother as a tomcat is like a tiger.

The Hyenas Had Feasted Well

Great Stretches of Dense Forest

Many African hunters consider elephant hunting more dangerous than lion, rhino, or buffalo hunting, any one of which can hardly be called an indoor sport. These are the four animals that are classed as "royal game" in game law parlance, and each one when aroused is sufficiently diverting to dispel any lassitude produced by the climate. It is wakeful sport—hunting these four kinds of game—and in my experience elephant hunting is the "most wakefullest" of them all.

Being Killed by an Elephant Is a Very Mussy Death

In my several months of African hunting I had four different encounters with elephants. The first two were on Mount Kenia and the last two were on the Guas Ngishu Plateau, near where it merges into the lower slopes of Mount Elgon. The first and the fourth experiences were terrifying ones, never to be forgotten. An Englishman, if he were to describe them, would say "they were rather nasty, you know," which indicates how really serious they were. The second and the third experiences were interesting, but not particularly dangerous.

Mount Kenia is a great motherly mountain that spreads over an immense area and raises its snow-capped peaks over eighteen thousand feet above the equator. The lower slopes are as beautiful as a park and are covered with the fields and the herds of the prosperous Kikuyus and other tribes. Scores of native villages of varying sizes are picturesquely planted among the banana groves and wooded valleys on this lower slope, each with its local chief, or sultan, and each tribe with its head sultan.

In a day's "trek" one meets many sultans with their more or less naked retinues, and every one of them spits on his hand, presses it to his forehead, and shakes hands with you. It is the form of greeting among the Kikuyus, and, in my opinion, might be improved. These people lead a happy pastoral life amid surroundings of exceptional beauty. Above the cultivated *shambas*, or fields of sweet potatoes and tobacco and sugar and groves of bananas, comes a strip of low bush country. It is a mile or two wide, scarcely ten feet high, and so dense that nothing but an elephant could force its way through the walls of vegetation. Most of the bushes are blackberry and are thorny.

Following the Trail

The elephants in their centuries of travel about the slopes have made trails through this dense bush, and it is only by following these trails that one can reach the upper heights of the mountain. Above the bush belt comes the great forest belt, sublimely grand in its hugeness and beauty, and above this belt comes the encircling band of bamboo forest that reaches up to the timber line. There are probably five hundred thousand acres of forest country in which the Kenia elephant may live and wander and bring up his children. He has made trails that weave and wind through the twilight shades of the forest, and the only ways in which a man may penetrate to his haunts are by these ancient trails. Mount Kenia, as seen from afar, looks soft and green and easy to stroll up, but no man unguided could ever find his way out if once lost in the labyrinth of trails that criss-cross in the forest.

For many years the elephants of Kenia have been practically secure from the white hunter with his high-powered rifles. Warfare between the native tribes on the slopes has been so constant that it was not until three or four years ago that it was considered reasonably safe for the government to allow hunting parties to invade the south side of the mountain. Prior to that time the elephant's most formidable enemies were the native hunter, who fought with poisoned spears and built deep pits in the trails, pits cleverly concealed with thin strips of bamboo and dried leaves, and the ivory hunting poachers. In 1906 the government granted permission to Mr. Akeley to enter this hitherto closed district to secure specimens for the Field Museum, and even then there was only a narrow strip that was free from tribal warfare. It was at that time that his party secured seven splendid tuskers, one of which, a one-hundred-fifteen-pound tusker shot by Mrs. Akeley, was the largest ever killed on Mount Kenia. And it was to this district that Mr. Akeley led our *safari* late in October to try again for elephants on the old familiar stamping ground. We pitched our camp in a lovely spot where one of his camps had stood three years before, just at the edge of the thick bush and on the upper edge of the *shambas*. News travels quickly in this country, and in a short time many of his old Kikuyu friends were at our camping place. One or two of the old guides were on hand to lead the way into elephant haunts and the natives near our camp reported that the elephants had been coming down into their fields during the last few days. Some had been heard only the day before. So the prospects looked most promising, and we started on a little hunt the first afternoon after arriving in camp.

The Old Wanderobo Guide

We took one tent and about twenty porters, for when one starts on an elephant trail there is no telling how long he will be gone or where he may be led. We expected that we would have to climb up through the strip of underbrush, and perhaps even as far up as the bamboos, in which event we might be gone two or three days. In addition to the porters we had our gunbearers and a couple of native guides. One of these was an old Wanderobo, or man of the forest, who had spent his life in the solitudes of the mountain and was probably more familiar with the trails than any other man. He wore a single piece of skin thrown over his shoulders and carried a big poisoned elephant spear with a barb of iron that remains in the elephant when driven in by the weight of the heavy wooden shaft. The barb was now covered with a protective binding of leaves. He led the way, silent and mild-eyed and very naked, and the curious little skin-tight cap that he wore made him look like an old woman. As we proceeded, other natives attached themselves to us as guides, so that by the time we were out half an hour there were four or five savages in the van.

He Was a Very Important Sultan

Saying Good-bye to Colonel Roosevelt

A Visiting Delegation of Kikuyus

No words can convey to the imagination the density of that first strip of bush. It was like walking between solid walls of vegetation, matted and tangled and bright with half-ripened blackberries. The walls were too high to see over except as occasionally we could catch glimpses of tree-tops somewhere ahead. We wound in and out along the tortuous path, and it was also torture-ous, for the thorn bushes scratched our hands and faces and even sent their stickers through the cloth into our knees. The effect on the barelegged porters was doubtless much worse.

After a couple of hours of marching in those cañons of vegetation we entered the lower edge of the forest and left the underbrush behind. We soon struck a fairly fresh elephant trail and for an hour wound in and out among the trees, stumbling over "monkey ropes" and gingerly avoiding old elephant pits. There were dozens of these, and if it had not been for the fact that our old guide carefully piloted us past them I'm certain more than one of us would have plunged down on to the sharpened stakes at the bottom. Some of the traps were so cleverly concealed that only a Wanderobo could detect them. In places the forest was like the stately aisles of a great shadowy cathedral, with giant cedars and camphor-wood trees rising in towering columns high above where the graceful festoons of liana and moss imparted an imposing scene of vastness and tropical beauty. In such places the ground was clean and springy to the footfall and the impression of a splendid solitude was such as one feels in a great deserted cathedral. At times we crossed matted and snaky-looking little streams that trickled through the decaying vegetation, where the feet of countless elephants had worn deep holes far down in the mud. Then, after long and circuitous marching, we would find ourselves traversing spots where we had been an hour before.

Elephant Pits

The elephant apparently moves about without much definition of purpose, at least when he is idling away his time, and the trail we were following led in all directions like a mystic maze. At this time I was hopelessly lost, and if left alone could probably never have found my way out again. So we quickened our steps lest the guides should get too far ahead of us. In those cool depths of the forest, into which only occasional shafts of sunlight filtered, the air was cold and damp, so much so that even the old Wanderobo got cold. It made me cold to look at his thin, old bare legs, but then I suppose his legs were as much accustomed to exposure as my hands were, and it's all a matter of getting used to it.

Our porters, especially those that were most heavily loaded, were falling behind and there was grave danger of losing them. In fact, a little later we did lose them. The trail became fresher and, to my dismay, led downward again and into that hopeless mass of underbrush which at this point extended some distance into the lower levels of the forest. We could not see in any direction more than twenty-five feet—except above. If our lives had depended on it we could not have penetrated the dense matted barriers of vegetation on each side of the narrow trail. The bare thought of meeting an elephant in such a place sent a cold chill down the back. If he happened to be coming toward us our only hope was in killing him before he could charge twenty-five feet, and, if we did kill him, to avoid being crushed by his body as it plunged forward. Without question it was the worst place in the world to encounter an elephant. And I prayed that we might get into more open forest before we came up with the ones we were trailing. You can't imagine how earnestly we all joined in that prayer.

It was at this unpropitious moment that we heard—startlingly near—the sharp crash of a tusk against a tree somewhere just ahead. It was a most unwelcome sound. There was no way of determining where the elephant was, for we were hemmed in by solid walls of bush and could not have seen an elephant ten feet on either side of the narrow trail. We also didn't know whether he was coming or going or whether he was on our trail or some other one of the maze of trails.

We quickly prepared for the worst. With our three heavy guns we crouched in the trail, waiting for the huge bulk of an elephant to loom up before us. Then came another thunderous crash to our right—and it seemed scarcely fifty yards away. Then a shrill squeal of a startled elephant off to our left and still another to the rear. Some elephants had evidently just caught our scent, and if the rest of the elephants became alarmed and started a stampede through the bush the situation would become extremely irksome for a man of quiet-loving tendencies. The thought of elephants charging down those narrow trails, perhaps from two directions at once, was one that started a copious flow of cold perspiration. We waited for several years of intense apprehension. There was absolute silence. The elephants also were evidently awaiting further developments.

A Clearing in the Forest

A Kikuyu "Cotillion"

Kikuyu Women Flailing Grain

Then we edged slowly onward along the trail, approaching each turning with extreme caution and then edging on to the next. Somewhere ahead and on two sides of us there were real, live, wild elephants that probably were not in a mood to welcome visitors from Chicago. How near they were we didn't know—except that the sounds had come from very near, certainly not more than a hundred yards—and we hoped that we might go safely forward to where the bush would be thin enough to allow us to see our surroundings. But there was no clearing. Several times a crash of underbrush either ahead or to one side brought us to anxious attention with fingers at the trigger guards. At last, after what seemed to be hours of nervous tension, we came to a crossing of trails, down which we could see in four directions thirty or forty feet. A large tree grew near the intersection of the trails, and here we waited within reach of its friendly protection. It was much more reassuring than to stand poised in a narrow trail with no possibility of sidestepping a charge. We waited at the crossing for further sounds of the elephants—waited for some time with rifles ready and then gradually relaxed our taut nerves. A line of porters with their burdens were huddled in one of the trails awaiting developments. I took a picture of the situation and had stood my rifle against the tree, and sat down to whisper the situation over. All immediate danger seemed to have passed. It seemed to, but it hadn't.

The Porters Came Down the Trail

Like a sudden unexpected explosion of a thirteen-inch gun there was a thundering crash in the bushes behind the porters, then a perfect avalanche of terrified porters, a dropping of bundles, a wild dash for the protection of the tree, and a bunch of the most startled white men ever seen on Mount Kenia. I reached the tree in two jumps, and three would have been a good record. The crashing of bushes and small trees at our elbows marked the course of a frenzied or frightened elephant, and to our intense relief the sounds diminished as the animal receded. I don't think I was ever so frightened in my life. But I had company. I didn't monopolize all the fright that was used in those few seconds of terror.

We then decided that there was no sane excuse for hunting elephants under such conditions. We at least demanded that we ought to see what we were hunting rather than blindly stumble through dense bush with elephants all around us. So we beat a masterly retreat, not without two more serious threats from the hidden elephants. A boy was sent up a tree to try to locate the elephants, but even up there it was impossible to distinguish anything in the mass of vegetation around. We fired guns to frighten away the animals, but at each report there was only a restless rustle in the brush that said that they were still there and waiting, perhaps as badly scared as we were.

My second elephant experience came the next day.

We started forth again, with a single tent, our guides and gunbearers, a cook and a couple of tent boys and twenty porters. This time we politely ignored all elephant trails in the dense bush and pushed on through the forest. Here it was infinitely better, for one could see some distance in all directions. We climbed steadily for a couple of thousand feet, always in forest so wild and grand and beautiful as to exceed all dreams of what an African forest could be. It more than fulfilled the preconceptions of a tropical forest such as you see described in stories of the Congo and the Amazon.

The air was cold in the shadows, but pleasant in the little open glades that occasionally spread out before us. Once or twice in the heart of that overwhelming forest we found little circular clearings so devoid of trees as to seem like artificial clearings. Once we found the skull of an elephant and scores of times we narrowly escaped the deep elephant traps that lay in our paths. Many times we saw evidences of the giant forest pig that lives on Mount Kenia and has only once or twice been killed by a white man. Sometimes we came to deep ravines with sides that led for a hundred feet almost perpendicularly through tangles of creepers and bogs of rotted vegetation.

We dragged ourselves up by clinging to vines and monkey ropes. On all sides was a solitude so vast as almost to overpower the senses. The sounds of bird life seemed only to intensify the effect of solitude. Once in a while we came upon evidences of human habitation, little huts of twigs and leaves, where the Wanderobo, or man of the forest, lived and hunted. Up in some of the trees were thin cylindrical wooden honey pots, some of them ages old and some comparatively new. And in the lower levels of the forest we saw where the Kikuyu women had come up for firewood. For some strange reason the elephants are not afraid of the native women and will not be disturbed by the sight of one of them. After seeing the women I am not surprised that they feel that way about it, but I don't see how they can tell the women from the men. Possibly because they know that only the women do such manual labor as to carry wood.

In the afternoon we reached the bamboos which lie above the forest belt. Here the ground is clean and heavily carpeted with dry bamboo leaves. The bamboos grow close together, all seemingly of the same size, and are pervaded with a cool, greenish shadow that is almost sunny in comparison with the deep, solemn shades of the great forest.

Then we struck a trail. The old Wanderobo guide said it was only an hour or so old and that we should soon overtake the elephant. It was evidently only one elephant and not a large one. It is fascinating to watch an experienced elephant hunter and to see how eloquent the trail is to him. A broken twig means something, the blades of grass turned a certain way will distinguish the fresh trail from the old one, the footprints in the soft earth, the droppings—all tell a definite story to him, and he knows when he is drawing down upon his quarry. As we proceeded his movements became slower and more cautious, and the plodding drudgery of following an elephant trail gave way to suppressed excitement.

It Looked Like the Rear Elevation of a Barn

Slower and slower he went, and finally he indicated that only the gunbearers and ourselves should continue. The porters were left behind, and in single file we moved on tiptoe along the trail. Then he stopped and by his attitude said that the quest was ended. The elephant was there. One by one we edged forward, and there, thirty yards away, partly hidden by slender bamboos, stood a motionless elephant. He seemed to be the biggest one I had ever seen. He was quartering, head away from us, and we could not see his tusks. If they were big, we were to shoot; if not, we were to let him alone. As we watched and waited for his head to turn we noticed that his ears began to wave slowly back and forth, like the gills of a fish as it breathes. The head slowly and almost imperceptibly turned, and Akeley signaled me to shoot. From where I stood I could not see the tusks at first, but as his head turned more I saw the great white shafts of ivory. The visible ivory was evidently about four feet long, and indicated that he carried forty or fifty pounds of ivory. Then, quicker than a wink, the great dark mass was galvanized into motion. He darted forward, crashing through the bamboo as though it had been a bed of reeds, and in five seconds had disappeared. For some moments we heard his great form crashing away, farther and farther, until it finally died out in the distance.

It was the first wild elephant I had ever seen, and it is photographed on my memory so vividly as never to be forgotten. I was more than half glad that I had not shot and that he had got away unharmed.

That night we camped in a little circular clearing which the Akeleys called "Tembo Circus," for it was near this same clearing that one of their large elephants had been killed three years before, and in the clearing the skin had been prepared for preservation. All about us stretched the vast forest, full of strange night sounds and spectral in the darkness. In the morning we awoke in a dense cloud and did not break camp until afternoon. Our Kikuyu and Wanderobo guides were sent out with promises of liberal backsheesh to find fresh trails, but they returned with unfavorable reports, so we marched back to the main camp again.

Thus ended our Kenia elephant experience, for a letter from Colonel Roosevelt, asking Mr. Akeley if he could come to Nairobi for a conference on their elephant group, led to our departure from the Mount Kenia country.

The other two elephant experiences were much more spectacular and perhaps are worthy of a separate story.

CHAPTER XI
NINE DAYS WITHOUT SEEING AN ELEPHANT. THE ROOSEVELT PARTY DEPARTS AND WE MARCH FOR THE MOUNTAINS ON OUR BIG ELEPHANT HUNT. THE POLICEMAN OF THE PLAINS

THE Mount Elgon elephants have a very bad reputation. The district is remote from government protection and for years the herds have been the prey of Swahili and Arab ivory hunters, as well as poachers of all sorts who have come over the Uganda border or down from the savage Turkana and Suk countries on the north. As a natural consequence of this unrestricted poaching the herds have been hunted and harassed so much that most of the large bull elephants with big ivory have been killed, leaving for the greater part big herds of cows and young elephants made savage and vicious by their persecution. Elephant hunters who have conscientiously hunted the district bring in reports of having seen herds of several hundred elephants, most of which were cows and calves, and of having seen no bulls of large size.

The government game license permits the holder to kill two elephants, the ivory of each to be at least sixty pounds. This means a fairly large elephant and may be either a bull or a cow. The cow ivory, however, rarely reaches that weight and consequently the bulls are the ones the hunters are after and the ones that have gradually been so greatly reduced in numbers. The elephants of this district roam the slopes of the mountains and often make long swinging trips out in the broad stretches of the Guas Ngishu Plateau to the eastward, in all a district probably fifty miles wide by sixty or seventy miles long.

The hunters who invade this section usually march north from the railroad at a point near Victoria Nyanza, turn westward at a little settlement called Sergoi, and continue in that direction until they reach the Nzoia River. Naturally, these names will mean nothing to one not familiar with the country, but perhaps by saying that the trip means at least ten days of steady marching in a remote and unsettled country, far from sources of supplies, I will be able to convey a faint idea of how hard it is to reach the elephant country.

Our purpose in making this long trip of ten weeks or more was to try for black-maned lion on the high plateau and to collect elephants for the group that Mr. Akeley is preparing for the American Museum of Natural History. The government gave him a special permit to collect such elephants as he would require, two cows, a calf, a young bull, and, if possible, two large bulls. One or more of these were to be killed by Colonel Roosevelt and one by myself. It seemed promising that the cows, calf, and young bull could be got on Mount Elgon, but the likelihood of getting the big bulls was far from encouraging. Lieutenant-Governor Jackson thought we might be successful if we directed our efforts to the southeastern slopes of the mountain and avoided the northeastern slopes along the River Turkwel, which had been hunted a good deal by sportsmen and poachers. If we were unable to get the big bulls on Elgon it might be necessary to make a special trip into Uganda for them. However, we determined to try, and try we did, through eight weeks of hard work and wonderful experiences in that remote district.

A Kikuyu Spearman

The Porters Like Elephant Meat

My Masai Sais and Gunbearers

At Sergoi, the very outpost of crude civilization, we were warned not to go up the southern side of the mountain on account of the natives that live there. We were told that they were inclined to be troublesome. We met Captain Ashton and Captain Black coming out after six weeks on the northern slopes. They reported seeing big herds, but mostly cows and calves. At Sergoi we also received word from Colonel Roosevelt and at once marched to the Nzoia River, where we met him.

During our march we saw no elephants, but as we neared the river there were fresh signs of elephant along the trail. It is strikingly indicative of the "Roosevelt luck" that he saw, on the morning we met him, the only elephants that he had seen in the district, and that within twenty-four hours from that time he had killed three elephants and Kermit one. Of this number two cows killed by Colonel Roosevelt were satisfactory for the group, and also the calf killed by his son, Kermit. This left one young bull and two large bulls still to be secured, and to that end we addressed our efforts during the succeeding weeks.

For nine days we hunted the Nzoia River region, but without seeing an elephant. There were kongoni, zebra, topi, waterbuck, wart-hogs, reedbuck, oribi, eland, and Uganda cob, but scour the country as we would, we saw no sign of elephant except the broad trails in the grass and the countless evidences that they had been in the region some time before. The country was beautiful and wholesome. There was lots of game for our table, from the most delicious grouse to the oribi, whose meat is the tenderest I have ever eaten. There were ducks and geese and Kavirondo crane; and sometimes eland, as fine in flavor as that of the prize steer of the fat-stock show. Then there were reedbuck and cob, both of which are very good to eat. So our tins of camp pie and kippered herring and ox tongue remained unopened and we lived as we never had before.

When the day's hunt was over the sun in a splendid effort painted such sublime sunsets above Mount Elgon as I had never dreamed of. And the music of hundreds of African birds along the river's edge greeted us with the cool, delightful dawn. Purely from an æsthetic standpoint, our days on the Nzoia were ones never to be forgotten, while from the standpoint of the man who loves to see wild game and doesn't care much about killing it, the bright, clear days on the Nzoia were memorable ones. The Roosevelt party went its way back to civilization; the Spaniards, De la Huerta and the Duke of Peñaranda, came and made a flying trip up the mountain for elephant, then returned and went their way. The young Baron Rothschild came on to the plateau for a couple of weeks and then disappeared. And still we lingered on, happy, healthy, generally hungry, and intoxicated with the languorous murmur of Africa.

With Sharp Stakes in Them

Then we marched for the mountain on our big elephant hunt. The details of those twelve days of adventuring in districts, some of which were probably never traversed before by white men, our experiences with the natives, our climb up the side of the mountain and our camp in the crater; our icy mornings, our ascent of the highest peak, and our explorations of the ancient homes of the cave-dwellers—all are part of a remarkable series of events that have nothing to do with an elephant story. In the forests we saw numberless old elephant pits, and on the grassy slopes there were mazes of elephants' trails, some so big that hundreds of elephants must have moved along them. But we saw no elephants. We scanned the hills for miles and tramped for days in ideal elephant country, but our quest was all in vain. Then our food supplies ran low, our last bullock was killed, and we hurried back to the base camp on the river, a hungry, tired band of a hundred and twenty men.

The matter of provisioning a large number of porters far from the railroad is a serious one. In addition to carrying the *safari* outfit, the porters must carry their *posho*, or cornmeal ration, and it is impossible for them to carry more than a limited number of days' rations. So the farther one gets from the base of supplies the more difficult it is to move, and a relay system must be employed. Porters must be sent back for food, often six or eight days; or else a bullock wagon must be used for that purpose. In our *safari* we used two wagons, drawn by thirty oxen, to supplement the porters in keeping up food supplies, and even by so doing there were times when rations ran low. In such times we would shoot game for them, either kongoni or zebra, both of which are considered great delicacies by the black man.

However, this is not telling about my memorable elephant experiences in the Guas Ngishu Plateau.

We got back to the Nzoia River on December third. On the fifteenth, after many more unsuccessful attempts to get in touch with a herd, Mr. Akeley and I resolved to try the mountain again. We thought that perhaps the elephants might have moved northward along the eastern slope, and so we thought we'd push clear up to the Turkwel River and find out beyond question. We outfitted for an eight days' march, carried only one tent and a small number of good porters. Only the absolute necessaries were taken, for we expected to move fast and hard. The first day we marched eight hours, crossed the Nzoia River, and by a curious chance at once struck a fresh trail which was diagnosed as being only a few hours old. The bark torn from trees was fresh and still moist; the leaves of the branches that had been broken off as the elephants fed along the way were still unwithered, and the flowers that had been crushed down by the great feet of the herd had lost little of their freshness and fragrance.

The trail led us first in one direction, then in another; sometimes it was a big trail that plowed through the long grass like a river, with little tributaries branching in and out where the individual members of the herd had swerved out of the main channel to feed by the way. And sometimes when all the herd were feeding, the main trail disappeared, to be replaced by a maze of lesser trails leading in all directions. But by the skilful tracking of our gunbearers the main trail would be found again some distance onward. We followed the trail for hours, and then, night coming on, we went into camp near a small stream, choked with luxuriant vegetation. Akeley thought he heard a faint squeal of an elephant far off, and while the porters made camp we went on for a mile or so to investigate. But no further sounds indicated the proximity of the herd.

Early the next morning we took up the trail again, and in less than an hour my Masai sais pointed off to a distant slope a couple of miles away, where a black line appeared. It looked like an outcropping of rock. Akeley looked at it and exclaimed, "By George, I believe he's got them!" and a moment later, after he had directed his glasses on the distant spot, he said briskly, "That's right, they're over there." And so, for the first time, after having scanned suspicious-looking spots in the landscape for weeks and always with disappointment, I saw a herd of real live elephants. To the naked eye they looked more like little shifting black beetles than anything else, but in the glasses they were plainly revealed with swaying bodies and flapping ears and swinging trunks.

In elephant hunting the first important thing to consider is the wind, for the elephant is very keen-scented and is quick to detect a breath of danger in the breeze. Fortunately we had seen them in time. If we had gone ahead a few hundred yards they would have got our wind and gone away in alarm, but this had not occurred. We could see that they were feeding quietly and without the slightest evidence of uneasiness.

Some Kikuyu Belles

Wanderobo Guides

We left our horses and the porters under a big tree and told the latter to come on if they heard any firing; otherwise, they were to await our return. Then, with only our gunbearers and a man carrying Akeley's large camera, we circled in a wide detour until we were safely behind the elephants. The wind continued favorable, and we cautiously approached the brow of a hill near where we had last seen them. They had disappeared, but their trail was as easy to follow as an open road. Before reaching the brow of the next hill one of the gunbearers was sent up a tree to reconnoiter the country beyond.

"*Hapa*," he whispered, as he carefully climbed down and indicated with his hand that they were near. Again we swung in a wide circle and came over the brow of the next hill. There, four or five hundred yards away, was the herd of elephants, standing idly under the low trees that studded the opposite slope. There were between forty and fifty of them, and from the number of *totos*, or calves, we assumed that many of the big ones were cows. We studied the herd for some minutes, estimating the ivory and trying in vain to pick out the bulls. There is very little difference between the appearance of a cow and a bull elephant when the latter has only moderate-sized tusks. Usually the tusks of the male are heavier and thicker, but except for this distinction there is very little noticeable difference between the two. Of course, an elephant with gigantic tusks is at once known to be a bull, but if he has small tusks it is a matter of considerable guesswork.

Two Kongoni on Guard

We could not tell which ones of this herd were bulls, but assumed that there must surely be several small-sized or young bulls among them. We decided to go nearer, knowing that the elephant's eyesight is very poor, and with such a favoring wind his sense of smell was useless. It seemed amazing that they did not see us as we walked up the slope toward them. When a couple of hundred yards away we climbed a tree to study them some more. They were in three separate groups, each of which was clustered sleepy and motionless under the trees. They had ceased feeding and had evidently laid up for their midday rest, although the hour was hardly ten in the morning.

From our "observation tower" in the tree we studied the three groups as well as we could. So far as we could judge there were at least three bulls of medium size, but as we looked those three lazily moved off toward the group on the extreme left. At that time we were within about a hundred yards of the nearest group with the wind still favorable, and except for one thing we might easily have crept up through the grass to within thirty or forty yards. Directly between us and the elephants were two kongoni, one lying down and the other alert and erect.

The Policemen of the Plains

The kongoni is the policeman of the plains. He is the self-appointed guardian of all the other animals, and for some strange, unselfish reason, he always does sentinel duty for the others. His eyes are so keen that he sees your hat when you appear over the horizon two miles away, and from that moment he never loses sight of you. If you approach too near he whistles shrilly, and every other animal within several hundred yards is on the alert and apprehensive. The kongoni often risks his own life to warn other herds of animals of the approach of danger, and if I were going to write an animal story I'd use the kongoni as my hero. The hunters hate him for the trouble he gives them, but a fair-minded man can not help but recognize the heroic, self-sacrificing qualities of the big, awkward, vigilant antelope. Why these two sentinels had not seen us is still and always will be a mystery, but it is certain that they had not.

At the same time we knew that any attempt to approach nearer would alarm them and they in turn would sound the shrill tocsin of warning to the unsuspecting elephant herd, in which event we might have to track the elephants for miles until they settled down again. So we cautiously climbed down, retreated below the edge of the hill, and worked our way up in the lee of the group farthest to our left in the expectation of finding the three bulls. From tree to tree, and in the protection of large ant-hills, we moved forward until we were less than fifty yards from the elephants. Then we studied them again, but could not locate the bulls.

Probably at this time something may have occurred to make the elephants nervous. Perhaps the warning cry of a bird or the suspicious rustling of our footsteps in the tall grass, but at any rate the herd began to move slowly away. Two of the larger groups marched solemnly down the slope away from us and the other disappeared among the low scrub trees to our right. We followed the two larger groups and soon were again within a few yards of them. An ant-hill four or five feet high gave us some protection, and over the top of this we watched the enormous animals as they stood under the trees ahead of us. While watching these two large groups we forgot about the one that had disappeared to the right.

Suddenly one of the gunbearers whispered a warning and we turned to see this group only a few yards from us and bearing directly down toward the ant-hill where we crouched in the grass. They had not yet seen us, but it seemed a miracle that they did not. If one of us had moved in the slightest degree they would have charged into us with irresistible force. We held our guns and our breath while these big animals, by a most fortunate chance, passed by us to the windward of the ant-hill, not more than thirty feet away. If they had passed to the leeward side they would have got our wind and trouble would have been unavoidable. I took a surreptitious snap-shot of them after they had passed by, and for the first time in some minutes took a long breath.

Then we circled the herd again and came up to them. They were now thoroughly uneasy. They knew that some invisible hostile influence was abroad in the land, but they could not locate in which direction it lay. We saw the sensitive trunks feeling for the scent and saw the big ears moving uneasily back and forth. One large cow with a broken tusk was facing us, vaguely conscious that danger lay in that direction. And then, by some code of signals known only to the elephant world, the greater number of elephants moved off down the slope and up the opposite slope. Only the big, aggressive cow and four or five smaller animals remained behind as a rear-guard. She stood as she had stood for some moments, gazing directly at us and nervously waving her ears and trunk.

The Rear-guard

Akeley climbed to the top of an ant-hill and made some photographs showing the big cow and her companions in the foreground, while off on the neighboring hillside three distinct groups of elephants were in view. The latter were thoroughly alarmed and moved away very swiftly for some distance and then came to a pause. The big cow and her attendants then moved off, feeling that the retreat had been successfully effected. Once more we followed them and came up to them, and then once more we were flanked by a number of elephants that had previously disappeared over the hill. They had swung around and were returning directly toward where we stood, unsuspecting.

We barely had time to fall back to some small bushes, where we waited while the flanking party approached. They came almost toward us, and when only about fifty feet away I ventured a photograph, feeling that, if successful, it would be the closest picture ever made of a herd of wild elephants. I used a Verascope, a small stereoscopic French machine whose "click" is almost noiseless. The elephants advanced and we huddled together with rifles ready in the patch of bushes. It seemed a certainty that they would charge, and that if our bullets could not turn them we would be completely annihilated. But as yet there was no sign that they saw us, or, if they did, they could not distinguish our motionless forms from the foliage of the scrub.

At last, the foremost elephant, barely thirty feet from us, came to the trail in the grass by which we had retreated when we first saw them. The trunk, sweeping ahead of it as if feeling for the scent of danger, paused an instant as it reached the trail and then the animal drew back sharply as though stung. Then it whirled about and the herd went crashing away through the sparse undergrowth. It was a time of the utmost nervous tension, and I don't believe the human system could undergo a prolonged strain of that severity.

It Started Back as Though Stung

During all this time we had not succeeded in positively locating a bull elephant. Of all the forty-four elephants that were visible at any one time, there was not one that we could feel safe in identifying as the elephant needed for the group. Three more times we stalked the herd to very close range, but they were now so restless that nothing could be ascertained. So finally we decided to get ahead of them and watch them as they passed us, but just as we had reached a point where they were approaching, the two kongoni gave a shrill alarm and the entire herd made off in tremendous haste. Later, on our way back to camp, we came up with one group of six or seven, but they seemed too angry and aggressive to take needless chances with, so we watched them a while and then left them behind.

During all that day we were with the herd nearly five hours, five hours of intense nervous strain, during which time there was never a moment when we were not in some danger of discovery. But in spite of the aggressive bearing of some of them at one time or another, I had the feeling that the elephants would run away from us the instant they definitely determined where we were. And it was while laboring under this impression that I met my second Mount Elgon herd of elephants and learned by bitter experience that the impression was wholly false. But that is still another story, the story of being charged five times in one day by angry elephants, and how I killed a bull elephant for the Akeley group.

CHAPTER XII
"'TWAS THE DAY BEFORE CHRISTMAS." PHOTOGRAPHING A CHARGING ELEPHANT. CORNERING A WOUNDED ELEPHANT IN A RIVER JUNGLE GROWTH. A THRILLING CHARGE. HASSAN'S COURAGE.

ON the night of December the twenty-third I sat out in a boma watching for lions. None came and at the first crack of dawn my two gunbearers and I crawled out of the tangled mass of thorn branches, and prepared to return to camp two miles away. We were expecting my sais to arrive with my horse soon after daybreak, and while waiting for him to come, and for my gunbearers to get the blankets tied up, I went across to a neighboring swamp in the hope of getting a bushbuck. I was about three hundred yards from the boma when my attention was drawn to a movement in the trees about a quarter of a mile away. I looked and saw what I first thought was a herd of zebras coming toward me. They looked dark against the faint light of early dawn and seemed surprisingly big. Then I realized! They were elephants! I had only my little gun and my big double-barreled cordite was at the boma, three hundred yards away. Breathlessly I ran for it, fearing that the elephants might cut me off before I could reach it. There seemed to be from seven to ten of them, but they soon disappeared in the trees, going at a fast swinging walk. Hassan, my first gunbearer, stopped to slip a couple of solid shells in the gun while I ran to the top of a hill in the hope of catching sight of the herd. But they had disappeared entirely. We soon found the trail strongly marked in the dew-covered grass. My sais then appeared with my horse. He had seen two elephants and they had taken alarm at his scent and were rapidly fleeing. So I galloped back to camp to tell the rest of the party and to prepare for a systematic pursuit.

After breakfast, with Akeley, Stephenson, Clark and our gunbearers, the trail was again picked up where I had left it. It was then a little past nine and the elephants had two hours' start of us. Their trail indicated that they were moving fast and so we prepared for a long chase. For nearly two hours we followed, Akeley tracking with remarkable precision. Sometimes the trail was faint and merged with older trails, but by looking carefully the fresh trail was kept. Soon we began to see newly broken branches from the trees which indicated that the elephants were getting quieted down and were beginning to feed. It must have been about eleven o'clock when Stephenson saw the herd far across on another slope. There were two of the animals distinctly visible and another partly visible. They were resting under some of the many acacia trees that dappled the slope of the hill. We stopped to examine them with our glasses. One seemed to have no tusks, but we finally saw that it had very small ones. The other and larger one had one good tusk and one that was broken off. After about twenty minutes we left our horses and with only our gunbearers moved across toward them, thinking that there must be others that we had not yet seen. The wind was bad, sometimes sweeping up in our direction through the depression between the two slopes and a moment later coming from another direction. At one time the wind blew from us directly toward the elephants and we expected to see them take alarm and run away. But they did not. We circled around and approached them from a better direction and advanced to within a couple of hundred yards without being detected. We then stopped for a conference. If there was a young bull I was to kill it for the Akeley group; if there was a large bull Stephenson was to kill it for himself; if there were only cows we were not to shoot unless absolutely necessary. In this event, Akeley was to take his camera, and with "Fred," "Jimmy" Clark, and I as escorts with our double-barreled cordite rifles, was to advance until he could get a photograph that would show an elephant the full size of the plate. If the elephants charged we were to yell and try to turn them without shooting; if they came on we were to shoot to hurt, but not to kill.

Fred was on one side of "Ake," Jimmy on another, and I on Fred's left. Thus we slowly moved toward the elephants. A reedbuck was startled out of the grass and noisily ran away, giving the alarm. The elephants began feeling in the air with their trunks and their ears began to wave uneasily. Finally they turned and seemed about to go away. Then Fred saw, a short distance to the right, some more elephants that had previously been hidden by the trees. We both whispered to Ake to stop, but he either did not hear us on account of his heavy sun hat or else was too intent upon the elephants in front to heed.

A Nandi Spearman

In the Deep Jungle Growth

As the Elephant Fell

"Ake," whispered Fred, "there's a good bull over there with good tusks. Wait a minute." But Ake, camera in position, continued to advance and so we followed. The elephants, a big cow and a half-grown one, were now facing us with ears wide spread. They looked very nasty. I thought they would turn and run away and was not uneasy about the outcome. But to my great surprise they started toward us, first slowly and then at a rapid trot, steadily gaining in swiftness. It was a real charge and we yelled to scare them off. The big cow was in the lead and she had not the slightest intention of being scared. Her one idea was to annihilate us. We raised our rifles and continued to yell, but on she rushed. She was only thirty yards away when Jimmy fired, Fred fired, and then I. The huge animal sank on her four knees and the half-grown one turned off and stopped, confused and angry. Akeley had got a splendid photograph of the charging cow and now he took one of the smaller beast before we approached the cow. Upon our advance the smaller one ran away but the big cow never moved again. She was stone dead. The three bullets had struck her, Jimmy's high as she was head on, Fred's between the eye and ear as she swung, and mine just behind the orifice of the ear as the head was still further swung by the shock of Fred's bullet. The elephant rested on her four knees in an upright position, quite lifelike in appearance. The small elephant ran off toward those that we had seen on our right. I suggested that we immediately follow the herd in the hope that a young bull might be found among them. So off we went and in a few moments we saw them to our right, apparently returning to where the cow had been killed. It is entirely likely that the big broken-tusked cow was going back to make trouble for us. Colonel Roosevelt had a similar experience with a bull elephant that returned and charged the hunters as they were standing about one that they had just killed.

They Whirled Around

As the elephants moved along slowly we paralleled them and studied them as well as we could. One was the big cow with the one broken and one good tusk. She was leading the group, and was doubtless a vicious animal. She was an enormous beast, probably over eleven feet in height. Another was the half-grown elephant, then a smaller one, and lastly a good-sized elephant with two fairly good tusks. We tried to determine the sex of this last one, I hoping that it was a bull, but fearing otherwise. Ake thought it was a cow with tusks about twelve or fourteen inches long, but the fact that its breasts showed no signs of milk fullness led me to hope that it was a young bull, and I determined to act on that supposition. I at once advanced with my big gun in readiness. The two largest elephants at the same moment whirled around and started swiftly toward us. I rested my gun against the side of a small tree and after their onward rush had brought them within fifty yards I fired as Ake suggested, "just between the eye and ear." The animal swerved but did not fall. Akeley and Stephenson fired at the big cow and under the shock of their heavy shells she dropped to her knees, then sprang up and came on again. Once more they shot and she again went down on her knees, but got up, shaking her head and turned a little to one side.

Stephenson started to shoot her again, but Ake shouted, "Don't shoot her again. She's got enough." Mr. Stephenson followed her for some distance and decided that she was going to recover, and so came back. In the meantime my elephant, with the two smaller ones, was moving off to the left, and with my small rifle I fired at its backbone, the only vulnerable spot visible. A spurt of dust rose, but the elephant did not stop. So, accompanied by Hassan and Sulimani, my two gunbearers, I started after the wounded elephant and the two younger ones. The big one was moving slowly, as though badly wounded. The wind was bad, so we circled around to head them off and in doing so completely lost them. Presently we struck their trail and followed them by the blood-stains on the grass.

After some minutes we saw them moving along in the tall grass near the Nzoia River. Again we swiftly circled to head them off before they could cross the river, but when we reached a point where they had last been seen they had disappeared in the dense tangle of trees and high reeds that grew at the river's edge. We thought they would cross the river, so we rushed after them. Suddenly Hassan yelled "Here they come!" and, ahead of us, came the large elephant, its head rising from above the sea of grass like the bow of a battleship bearing rapidly down upon us. The two smaller ones were almost invisible, only the back of one appearing above the reeds. We were out in the open and the situation looked decidedly dangerous. I hastily drew a bead on the big one's forehead, fired, but it didn't stop. There was barely time for us to get out of the way. I ran sideways toward a little mound that furnished some protection, while Hassan, with a coolness and courage that I both admired and envied, stood still until the big elephant was within ten feet of him and then leaped to one side as the three beasts swept by him, carried onward by the impetus of their mad rush. As the big one passed it made a vicious swing at him with its trunk.

Bow On

The Bull Elephant

Cooking Elephant Meat

Fortunately the elephants continued in their course and we followed them with my big rifle again reloaded and ready. Once more they turned in toward the river and were completely swallowed up in the tall reeds. We again waded in after them and had gone only a few yards when we once more saw the angry head of the big one looming up as it came toward us. I fired point-blank at the base of the trunk and the beast stopped suddenly. Then it slowly turned and as it was about to disappear in the tall elephant grass again I fired at its backbone. The huge bulk collapsed and disappeared, buried in the reeds. Hassan yelled that it was dead, but we couldn't see for the grass. The situation now was perilous in the extreme. The river made a sharp bend at this point like an incomplete letter O, with a narrow neck of land through which the elephants had passed when I had shot. At the narrow neck it was about a hundred feet across while the depth of the "O" was about three hundred feet and the width about two hundred and fifty feet. This small peninsula was matted with a jungle growth of high grass and reeds six or eight feet tall, while the edges of the river were thickly wooded with small trees tangled together and interlacing their branches over the narrow but deep waters of the Nzoia.

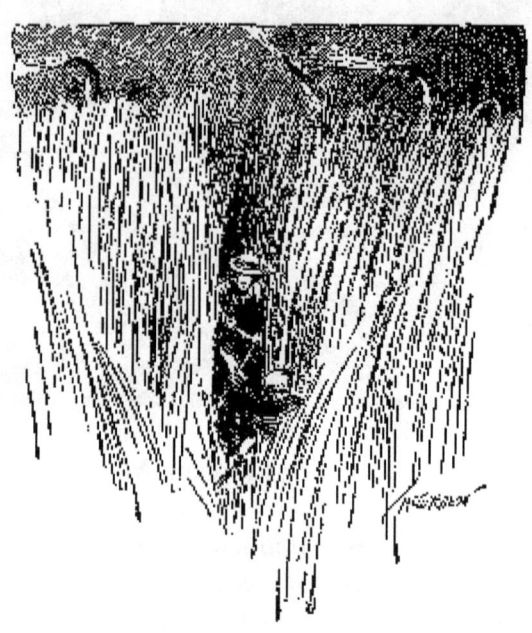

Awaiting the Charge

Down in the jungle depths of this peninsula there was a violent commotion among the low branches of these trees, an indication that the animal was not dead, but was thrashing madly about as if desperately wounded. Hassan said it was the young elephant and that the older one was dead, but this could not be determined without pushing on through the reeds until we would be almost upon them. This course seemed too dangerous to try.

The river at this point was absolutely impassable for animals. The banks were ten feet high and perpendicular. The water was perhaps five or six feet deep and the width of the swift stream not over twenty or thirty feet. The trees had interlaced their roots and branches across the river and in the water. No animal, not a tree climber, could possibly cross the stream on account of the straight up and down banks.

So after a time we crept along through the grass at the edge of the stream until we reached a point probably forty yards from where the elephants doubtless were, although quite hidden from our view. There was still a tremendous threshing in the low branches of the trees and in order to see the animals we had to creep cautiously across the peninsula to a point about half-way, where a large, rotten, dead tree stood. This gave us cover and from its screen we could see the three elephants, only fifteen yards away. The head of the big one was still up and it was turned directly at us. It was so close and so big that the effect was terrifying.

"*Mkubwa*," whispered Sulimani, and that means "big." So the big elephant, instead of being dead, was still alive, with an impassable river at its feet on one side, a dense tangle of trees on two other sides, and with a narrow open aisle between it and ourselves. The two smaller elephants were at its side. To see to fire I had to step out from the tree and expose myself, and as I stepped out the wounded beast saw me and reared its head as if to make a final rush. I fired point-blank; it swung around and a second shot sent it down. Hassan grabbed my arm and told me to hurry back before the two smaller elephants charged. If they did so it might be necessary to shoot them, which we didn't want to do. So we ran swiftly back to the edge of the river and waited. But all was quiet, and after a time we climbed across the river on the interlacing branches, circled around to where the elephants were visible just across the stream and scared the two smaller ones away. Once more we swung across from branch to branch over the swift waters of the river and reached the other bank where lay the mountainous bulk of the dead elephant. It was a young bull about eight feet high and with two well-shaped tusks twenty-two inches long in the open, or approximately thirty-eight inches in all.

Sulimani was sent to notify Mr. Akeley and Mr. Clark, and after a long search found them, and together they arrived a couple of hours later, followed by gunbearers and saises. Mr. Stephenson had gone back to camp to see that salt and supplies, with one tent, were sent out.

Then began the work of measuring the elephant, a work that must be done most thoroughly when the trophy is to be mounted entire. There were dozens of measurements of every part of the body, enough to make a dress for a woman, and then came the skinning, a prodigious task that took all of the late afternoon and evening. We investigated the position of an elephant's heart which Kermit Roosevelt had said was up in the upper third or at the top of the second third of the body, a spot which must be reached by a shot directed through the point of the ear as it lay back. As a matter of fact, an elephant's heart lies against the brisket, about ten or eleven inches from the bottom of the breast. A broadside shot through the front leg at the elbow would penetrate the heart.

At nine o'clock, Christmas Eve, the tent arrived and was soon put up in the jungle of high grass at the middle of the little peninsula. A more African scene can not be imagined. The porter's fires, over each of which sticks spitted with elephant meat *en brochette* were cooking, imparted a weird look to the river jungle grass and spectral trees.

At ten o'clock we had our dinner and at eleven we put on our pajamas and with the camp-fire burning before the tent and the armed askaris pacing back and forth, gave ourselves up to lazy talk, then meditation and then sound sleep.

It was a wonderful day—one always to be remembered.

The next day, Christmas, came without the usual customs of Christmas morn. In the forenoon we stuck with the bull elephant, getting its skin and bones ready for transportation back to camp; and in the afternoon came the work of saving the skull and part of the skin of the cow elephant. The porters must have thought the day a wonderful one, for they ate and gorged on elephant meat until they could hardly move.

CHAPTER XIII
IN THE SWAMPS ON THE GUAS NGISHU. BEATING FOR LIONS WE CAME UPON A STRANGE AND FASCINATING WILD BEAST, WHICH BECAME ATTACHED TO OUR PARTY. THE LITTLE WANDEROBO DOG

ONE of the most exciting phases of African hunting is the beating of swamps for lion. A long skirmish line of native porters is sent in at one end of the swamp and, like a gigantic comb, sweeps every live thing ahead of it as it advances through the reeds. All kinds of swamp life are stirred into action, and a fairly large swamp will yield forth the contents of a pretty respectable menagerie. Sometimes a hyena or two will be flushed and once in a while a lion will be driven out.

It is the constant expectation of the last-named animal that gives such keen and long sustained interest to the work of beating a swamp. One never knows what to expect. A suspicious stir in the reeds may mean a lion or only a hyena; an enormous crashing may sound like a herd of elephants, but finally resolve itself into a badly frightened reedbuck. Most of the time you expect reedbuck, but all the time you have to be ready for lion. As a general thing a lion will slink along in the reeds ahead of the beaters and not reveal himself until he is driven to the end of the cover. Then he will grunt warningly or show an ear or a lashing tail above the reeds, and instantly every one is in a state of intense expectancy. What the next move will be no one knows, but it is more than likely to be something of a supremely dramatic sort.

One day we were beating swamps on the Guas Ngishu Plateau. Lions seemed to be numerous in that district. Two days before I had killed two lions near by, and during the morning Stephenson and I had each killed a lioness in the same line of marshy reed beds. We now intended advancing to the next large swamp of the chain and see whether a large, black-maned lion might not be routed out.

Conditions seemed propitious, for in this selfsame swamp Colonel Roosevelt had seen the best lion of his trip some weeks before. Perhaps the lion might still be there.

The campaign was planned with great thoroughness. Forty or fifty porters were formed into the customary skirmish line and on each side we paralleled the beaters with our rifles. At the word of command the column began to advance and the interest reached a fever heat. The swamp was five or six hundred yards long, and for the first three hundred yards nothing of a thrilling sort occurred. The shouts of the beaters blended into a rhythmic, melodious chant and the swish of their sticks as they thrashed the reeds was enough to make even the king of beasts apprehensive.

Abdi, the Somali Head-man

Along the Nzoia River

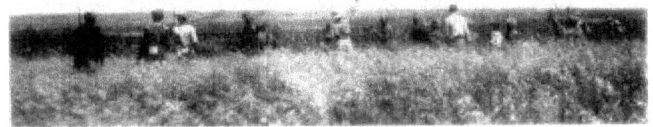

Beating a Swamp for Lions

Over on my side of the swamp there was a wide extension of dry reeds and bushes through which I was obliged to go in order to keep in touch with the skirmish line of porters. We had got three-quarters the full length of the swamp and any moment might reasonably expect to hear from a lion if there was one ahead of us. Every rifle was at readiness and the porters were advancing less impetuously. In fact, they were pretending to go forward without doing so.

Suddenly a wild shout from a porter near by, then a hurried retreat of other porters, and then a cautious advance gave sign that something desperate was about to happen. We caught a glimpse of reeds moving about and then saw something crouched in the grass beneath. Two ears were finally distinguished among the tangle of rushes, and there was no further doubt about it. It was not a lion. It wasn't even a hyena.

It was a little dog. His presence in the middle of that swamp was about as logical as if he had been a musk-ox or a walrus. However, there he was, gazing up at us from the bulrushes, with mild, friendly eyes and a little tail that was poised for wagging at the slightest provocation. He was instantly christened "Moses" for obvious reasons. Later the name was changed to Mosina, also for obvious reasons.

After the line of porters had regained their composure the lion beat continued, but no lion appeared. The sum total of the wild beasts yielded by that promising swamp was one (1) little black and tan dog with white feet.

It Was Not a Lion

Some of our genealogical experts addressed themselves to the task of figuring out the why and wherefore of little Mosina and what in the world she was doing out in a lion and leopard infested place. Leopards in particular are fond of dogs, not the way you and I are fond of them, but in quite a different way. A leopard, so it is said, prefers a dog to any other food and will take daring chances in an effort to secure one for breakfast, dinner, or supper. Therefore, how little Mosina escaped so long is a mystery yet unsolved.

The experts decided after a thorough consideration of the case, viewing it from all possible angles, that the little dog was a Wanderobo dog. The Wanderobo are natives who live solely by hunting and generally have the most primitive sort of a grass hut at the edge of a swamp or deep in the solitudes of the forest. They put rude honey boxes up in the trees to serve as beehives, and it is from this honey and from the game that they kill with their bows and arrows and traps and spears that they manage to eke out a meager living.

Like all true hunters, they keep dogs, and it is more than likely that little Mosina was the ex-property of some wild-eyed, naked Wanderobo who lived in the swamp. When our great crowd of noisy beaters appeared at the other end of the swamp the Wanderobo had doubtless crawled out of his hole and made off for the nearest tall grass. In going he had left behind Mosina as a rear-guard to cover his retreat or to stay the invaders' advance until he could reach the nearest spot available to a hasty man.

So we adopted this theory as to why Mosina was in the bulrushes, and in honor of her Wanderobo associations we again changed her name to "Little Wanderobo Dog." So far as I know, she is the only dog in history who has had three separate and distinct names within two hours. Of course, there are people who have called dogs more than three different names in much less time, but they were not Christian names. One of the bachelor members of the committee, who is known to be a woman-hater, conferred the honorary title of the pronoun "he" on Little Wanderobo Dog, and she has been "he" ever since. But not without a bitter fight by those of the committee who think the pronoun "she" is infinitely more to be admired.

Little Wanderobo Dog did not wait to be adopted. He adopted us, but not ostentatiously at first—just a friendly wag here and there to show that he had at last found what he was looking for. By degrees he became more friendly and genial, so that at the end of an hour he was thoroughly one of us.

I have never seen a milder-eyed dog than Little Wanderobo. Innocence and guilelessness struggled for supremacy, with "confidence in strangers" a close third. You couldn't help liking him, for with those meek and gentle eyes, together with manners above reproach, he simply walked into your heart and made himself at home.

I think that we were a good deal of a surprise to him. In all his short young life he had probably never known anything but kicks and cuffs. When he met a stranger he naturally expected to have something thrown at him, or to have a stubby toe or hard sandal projected into his side. Imagine his wonderment to find people who actually petted him and played with him. At first he didn't know how to play, but it was amazing to see how fast he learned. He was ready to play with any and all comers at any and all times. You could arouse him from a deep slumber and he would be ready to engage in any form of gaiety at a second's notice.

They talk about "charm." Some people have it to a wonderful degree. You like them the minute you meet them, and often don't really know why. Perhaps because you simply can't help it. Well, that was the chief characteristic of Little Wanderobo Dog. He had more charm than anything I've ever met, and so it is only natural that he should have walked into our affections in the most natural, unaffected sort of way.

I don't know what he thought of us, but I really believe that he thought he had gone to Heaven. We fed him and played with him, and finally he gained a little assurance, and actually barked. He barked at one of our roosters, and then we knew that he considered himself past the probation stage. He had confidence enough to assert himself in a series of lusty barks without fearing a hostile boot or an angry shout. The first time he barked we all rushed out of our tents in wonder and admiration. It was the most important event of the day, and it caused a great deal of talk of a friendly nature.

There was one umbrageous cloud on Little Wanderobo Dog's horizon, however—a cloud that he soon learned to evade. The Mohammedans didn't like him. It is a part of their creed to hate dogs almost as much as pork, and to be touched by a dog means many prayers to Allah to wipe away the stain of contact. But Little Wanderobo Dog was not conversant with the Mohammedan creed at first, and in his gladness and joy of life he embraced everybody in the waves of affection and friendliness that radiated from him like a golden aura.

The Somali gunbearers were disciples of Allah, and they began to kick at him before he was within eight feet of them. Two of the tent boys were also Mohammedans, but they had to be more circumspect in their hostility. Whenever Little Wanderobo Dog came around they would edge away, which gave the former a certain sense of importance because it was flattering to have a number of grown-up men fear him so much. Then there were a number of the porters who were Mohammedans of a sort, but these were wont to say, "O, what is a creed among friends?"

It was quite cold up on the plateau at night. Sometimes the wind swept down from the distant fringe of mountains and shook the tents until the tent pegs jumped out of the ground. The night guard would pile more wood on the big central camp-fire near our tents and the porters, in their eighteen or twenty little tents, would huddle closer together for warmth. They were nights for at least three blankets, and even four were not too many.

Consequently Little Wanderobo Dog was confronted by the necessity of adopting a place to sleep where he would be safe from those sharp arrows of the north wind that swept across the high stretches of the plateau. So he ingratiated himself into my tent with many friendly wags of his tail and a countenance of such benign faith in human nature that he was allowed to remain. At many times in the night I was awakened and I knew that Little Wanderobo Dog was dreaming about some wicked swamp ogre that was trying to kick him.

At first he was not a silent sleeper, but later on these awful nightmares came with less frequency and I presume his dreams took on a more beatific character. As a watch-dog I don't believe he had great value, because of his readiness to make friends with anything and anybody. If a leopard had come into the tent he would have said, "Excuse me, but I think you are in the wrong place," but he would never have barked or conducted himself in an ungentlemanly way.

One could never tell what was likely to come into one's tent at night, even with armed askaris patrolling the camp all night long. One cold night, before Little Wanderobo Dog had come to live with us, I was awakened by a curious rustle of the tent flaps. I listened and then watched the tent flap for some moments, thinking that the wind might have been responsible. But there was no wind and it seemed beyond doubt that some animal had entered.

For a long time I listened, but could hear nothing; and yet at the same time I had a positive conviction that I was not alone in the tent. I wondered if it could be a leopard, or some small member of the cat tribe. I knew that it wasn't a dog, for there were no dogs anywhere in the vicinity of the camp. As the minutes went by without any hostile move from the darkness, I decided to let whatever it was stay until it got ready to depart. So I went to sleep.

Once more in the night I was awakened by a noise in the tent and as nearly as I could diagnose the situation, the noise came from under my cot. But, I reasoned, if the animal is there, it's behaving itself and if it were on mischief bent it would have transacted its business long before. So I went to sleep again.

Just at dawn the clarion crow of a rooster came from under my bed. It was one of the roosters the cook had bought from a Boer settler and had come in to escape the coldness of the night air without. It was a most agreeable surprise, for there was a homelike sound in the crow of the rooster that was pleasantly reminiscent of the banks of the Wabash far away.

After Little Wanderobo Dog became "acclimated" to the warm and friendly atmosphere of hospitality of the camp, he began to show evidences of tact and diplomacy. He bestowed his attentions, with unerring impartiality to all of us. In the evening, and frequently during the day, he would pay ceremonial visits to each of the four tents of the *msungu*, as the white people are called. First he would approach the threshold of one tent, cock an inquiring ear at the occupant, and upon receiving the customary sign of welcome would wag himself in and pay his respects. After a short call he would wag his way out and call at the next tent, where the same performance was repeated.

A Ceremonial Call

He never burst into a place like a cyclone of happiness, but rather, he sort of oozed in and oozed out, his mild brown eyes brimming with gentleness and his tail, that eloquent insignia of canine gladness, wigwagging messages of good cheer.

In one of the tents of the *msungu* there was a pet monkey. It had been captured down on the Tana River months before and at first was wild and vicious. As time went by it lost much of its wildness and to those it liked was affectionate and friendly. To all others it presented variable moods, sometimes friendly and sometimes unexpectedly and unreasonably hostile. We feared that Little Wanderobo Dog would have some bad moments with the little Tana River monkey, and their first meeting was awaited with keen interest. We thought the monkey would scratch all the gentleness out of the Little Wanderobo Dog's eyes and that the two animals would become bitter enemies.

But nothing of the sort happened. Little Wanderobo Dog managed the matter with rare tact. He succeeded in slowly overcoming the monkey's prejudices, then in inspiring confidence, and finally in establishing play relations. It was worth a good deal to see the dog and monkey playing together, the latter scampering down from his tent-pole aery, leaping on the dog, and scampering hurriedly over the latter, with a quick retreat to the invulnerable heights of the tent-pole. Little Wanderobo Dog would allow the monkey to roam at will over his features and anatomy, thereby showing tolerance which I thought impossible for any animal to show. After Little Wanderobo Dog had paid his devoirs to his host, which he did each day with great punctiliousness, he would then retire to some sunny spot and enjoy his siesta. He was great on siestas and usually had several each day.

The Entente Cordiale

In time he learned to distinguish between Mohammedans and other dark-complexioned people and held himself aloof from the former, thereby escaping any humiliating races with the heavy boots of the gunbearers and other followers of Allah. He made friends with little Ali, the monkey's valet, a small Swahili boy who looked like a chocolate drop in color, and like a tooth-powder ad in disposition. It was Ali's duty to carry the monkey on our marches.

The little gray monkey, with its venerable looking black face fringed with a sunburst of white hair, would be tied to an old umbrella of the Sairey Gamp pattern, and would sit upon it as the small boy carried it along the trails on his shoulder, like a musket. Sometimes when the sun was strong the umbrella would be raised to shield the monkey's eyes, which could not stand the fierce glare incident to a long march upon sun-baked trails. At such times the monkey, who rejoiced in the brief name of J.T. Jr.—the same being emblazoned on the little silver collar around its neck—at such times the monkey would scamper from shoulder to shoulder of the small boy, with occasional excursions up in the woolly kinks of the heights above. It was a funny picture and one that never failed to amuse those who watched it.

Well, Little Wanderobo Dog, by some prescient instinct hardly to be expected in one brought up in a swamp, decided that little Ali and the monkey were to be his "companions of the march." So, when the tents were struck and Abdi, the head-man, shouted "*Funga nizigo yaka!*" and the tented city of yesterday became a scattered heap of sixty-pound porters' loads, Little Wanderobo would seek out Ali and prepare to bear him company during the long stretches of the march. And then when the long line of horsemen, native soldiers, porters, tent boys, gunbearers, ox gharries, and all began to wind their sinuous way over veldt or through forest, there was none in the line more picturesque than Ali and J.T. Jr. surrounded by the affable Little Wanderobo Dog.

Being Posed for a Post Mortem Picture

The Triumvirate

The Three Comrades

It is little wonder that friendship soon ripened into love, and that we all became speedily and irrevocably attached to the little swamp angel. His presence in any gathering was like a benediction of good cheer, and when his tail was in full swing he looked like a golden jubilee. As I say, it was no wonder we liked him, and I think I may also say, without flattering ourselves, that the sentiment was reciprocated. I don't believe the joy he showed at all times could have been assumed. It must have been pure joy, without alloy.

His table manners were above reproach. He would, never grab or show unseemly greed. He awaited our pleasure and each bone or chop that fell his way was received with every token of mute but eloquent gratitude. You were constantly made to feel that he loved you for yourself and not for what he hoped you would give him. If I were to be wrecked on a desert island, I believe there is hardly more than one person that I'd prefer to have as my sole companion than Little Wanderobo Dog.

Perhaps a few words about the architecture of the little dog might not come amiss. He was built somewhat on the lines of the German renaissance, being low and rakish like a dachshund, but with just a little more freeboard than the dachshund. His legs were straight instead of bowed, as are those of his distinguished German cousin. His ears were hardly as pendulous, being rather more trenchant than pendulous, and therefore more mobile in action. His tail was facile and retroussé, with a lateral swing of about a foot and an indicated speed of seventeen hundred to the minute. When you add to these many charms, those mild eyes, surcharged with love light, and a bark as sweet as the bark of the frangipanni tree and as cheerful as the song of the meadow-lark, you may realize some of the estimable qualities that distinguished Little Wanderobo Dog.

For some weeks he stayed with us, Tray-like in his faithfulness, and always in the vanguard when danger threatened the rear. One day our caravan passed through a group of migrating Wanderobos. There were a dozen or so of men, all armed with spears and bows and arrows; also fifteen or twenty women, thirty or forty *totos*, and about a score of dogs.

Here was the test. Would Little Wanderobo Dog, reclaimed from the swamp, harken to the call of the blood and join the band of his own kind? If he did, we could only bow our heads in grief and submission, for after all were not we only foster friends and not blood relations? But Little Wanderobo Dog never wavered in his allegiance to us. He had planted his lance by our colors and with these he would stick till death.

He passed those other Wanderobo dogs as if they were creatures from another world. If he felt tempted to join his fellow dogs, there was no indication of it, and at night when we reached our camp we found our faithful follower at his accustomed post, stanch, firm and true to his colors, which were black and tan.

But alas, there comes a time when the best of friends must part. And the dark day came when I saw Little Wanderobo Dog for the last time. It was at Escarpment. Our long months of hunting were over. Our horses and porters and all our equipment were on the train bound for Nairobi, where we were to settle our affairs and leave Africa and its happy hunting ground. Little Wanderobo Dog had been let out of his first-class compartment in the train and was running up and down the platform, wigwagging messages of gladness with his tail and sniffing friends and strangers with dog-like curiosity. Some friends of ours were at the train to say howdy-do and to shake our hands, and with these the little dog was soon on friendly terms.

When the train whistle blew and the bell was rung and some more whistles blew and more bells were rung, Little Wanderobo Dog was taken back into his car. The last good-bys were said and we were off for Nairobi. Suddenly there was a startled cry, a whisk of a tail, and the dog was gone—out of the car window. He lit on his nose, but as far back as we could see he sat in the middle of the next track and gazed at the receding train. Two days later Mrs. Tarlton came down from Escarpment and said that she had rescued the dog and that he was installed in the hospitable home of Mrs. Hampson, where he would remain until he rejoined those members of our party who were to remain in Africa some months longer. It is likely that Little Wanderobo Dog may be taken on a great elephant hunt in Uganda and, who knows, some time he may visit America. I hope so, for I'd like to give him a dinner.

Our Last View

CHAPTER XIV
WHO'S WHO IN JUNGLELAND. THE HARTEBEEST AND THE WILDEBEEST, THE AMUSING GIRAFFE AND THE UBIQUITOUS ZEBRA, THE LOVELY GAZELLE AND THE GENTLE IMPALLA

IN the course of the average shooting experience in British East Africa the sportsman is likely to see between twenty and thirty different species of animals. From the windows of the car as he journeys from Mombasa to Nairobi, three hundred and twenty-seven miles, he may definitely count upon seeing at least seven of these species: Wildebeest, hartebeest, Grant's gazelle, Thompson's gazelle, zebra, impalla, and giraffe, with the likelihood of seeing in addition some wart-hogs and a distant rhinoceros, and the remote possibility of seeing cheetah, lion, and hyena. Of the bird varieties the traveler will be sure of seeing many ostriches, some giant bustards, and perhaps a sedate secretary-bird or two.

Hassan and a Hartebeest

The Author's Home in Africa

Beautiful Upland Country

These animals are the common varieties, and after a short time in the country the stranger learns to tell them apart. He knows the zebra from his previous observation in circuses; he also does not have to be told what the giraffe is, but the other ones of the seven common varieties he must learn, for most of them are utterly strange to an American eye.

Gazelle, with Wildebeest in Background

He soon learns to pick out the wildebeest, or gnu, by its American buffalo appearance; he comes to know the little Thompson's gazelle by its big black stripe on its white sides and by its frisky tail that is always flirting back and forth. The Grant's gazelle is a little harder to pick out at first, and one is likely to get the Grant's and Tommy's confused. But after a short time the difference is apparent, the Grant's being much larger in stature and has much larger horns and is minus the Thompsonian perpetual motion tail. It certainly is a stirring tail! The impalla is about the same size as the Grant's gazelle, but has horns of a lyrate shape.

The hartebeest is speedily identified, because he is unlike any other antelope in appearance and exists in such large numbers in nearly every part of East Africa. Indeed, if a returned traveler were asked what animal is most typical of the country he would at once name the hartebeest. He sees it so much and so often that after a time it seems to be only a necessary fixture in the landscape. A horizon without a few hartebeests on it would seem to be lacking in completeness.

Furthermore, the stranger soon learns that the hartebeest is commonly called by its native name, kongoni, and by the time his shooting trip is over the sight of the ubiquitous kongoni has become as much of his daily experience as the sight of his tent or his breakfast table. To me the kongoni appealed most strongly because of his droll appearance and because of a many-sided character that stirs one's imagination.

He is big and awkward in appearance and action; his face is long and thin and always seems to wear a quizzical look of good humor, as if he were amused at something. Others besides myself have remarked upon this, so I am hoping that the kongoni wore this amused look even at times when he was not looking at me. His long, rakish horns are mounted on a pedicle that extends above his head, thus accentuating the droll length of his features. His withers are unusually high and add to the awkward appearance of the animal. Standing, the kongoni is a picture of alert, interested good humor; running, he is extremely funny, as he bounces along on legs that seem to be stiffened so that he appears to rise and fall in his stride like a huge rubber ball. We made quite a study of the kongoni, for he is a most interesting animal. He is unselfish and vigilant in protecting the other creatures of the plain. His eyes are as keen as those of a hawk, and when a herd is feeding there are always several kongoni sentinels posted on ant-hills in such a strategic way that not a thing moves anywhere on the plains that escapes their attention. Oftentimes I have cautiously crept to the top of a ridge to scan the plains, and there, a mile away, a kongoni would be looking at me with great interest.

If you try to approach he will remain where he is until his warning sneezes have alarmed all the other animals, and finally, when all have fled, he goes gallumphing along in the rear. He is the self-appointed protector of his fellow creatures, the sentinel of the plains. I have seen him run back into danger in order to alarm a herd of unsuspecting zebras.

He leads the wildebeests to water and he lends his eyes to the elephants as they feed. With nearly every herd of game, or near by, will be found the faithful kongoni, always alert, watchful, and vigilant, and it is nearly always his cry of warning that sends the beasts of the plains flying from dangers that they can not see.

The sportsman swears at the kongoni because it so often alarms the quarry he is stalking. How very often it happens! The hunter sees afar some trophy that he is eager to secure and straightway begins a careful stalk of many hundred yards. At last, after much patient work, he reaches a point where he feels that he can chance a shot. He takes a careful sight and at that moment a kongoni that has been silently watching him from some place or other gives the alarm, and away goes the trophy beyond reach of a bullet. And then how the hunter curses at the kongoni, who has stopped some little distance away and is regarding him with that quaint, lugubriously funny look. It almost seems to be laughing at him.

One day I tried to shoot a topi. It was a broiling hot day and the sun hung dead above and drove its burning javelins into me as I crept along. For seven hundred yards, on hands and knees, I slowly and painfully made my way. The grass wore through the knees of my trousers and the sharp stubbles cut my palms; once a snake darted out of a clump of grass just as my hand was descending upon it, and lizards frequently shot away within a yard of my nose. My neck was nearly broken from looking forward while on my hands and knees, and it was nearly an hour of creeping progress that I spent while stalking that topi.

When I got within two hundred and fifty yards, and was just ready to take a careful aim, with an ant-hill as a rest, a kongoni somewhere gave the alarm, and away went the topi, safe and sound but badly scared. The kongoni went a little way off and then turned and grinned broadly. I was momentarily tempted to shoot him, but on second thought I realized that he had acted nobly from the animal point of view, so I forgave him.

Outward Bound—Reading Your Thoughts—Concluding your Intentions Are Hostile

The kongoni seems to be gifted with a clairvoyant instinct. He knows when you don't want to shoot him and when you do. If you start out in the morning with no hostile intentions toward him he will allow you to approach to within a short distance. He will be alert and watchful, but he will show no anxiety. But just suppose for an instant that you change your mind. Suppose you say to yourself that the porters have had no meat for several days and that it might be well to shoot a kongoni. The latter knows what is passing in your mind long before you have made a single movement to betray your intentions. He begins to edge away, ready in an instant to go bounding rapidly beyond rifle shot.

I've seen a herd of kongoni standing quite near, watching me with curious interest, but without fear. Perhaps I was intent upon something else and hardly noticed them. Suddenly a villainous thought might enter my head, such as "That big kongoni has enormous horns," and instantly the herd would prick up their ears, run a few steps, and then turn to verify their suspicions. Then, if the villainous thought still lurked in my brain, they would sneeze shrilly and go galloping away in the distance. There is no way to explain this except to attribute it to thought transference, and this in spite of the fact that the kongoni doesn't understand English.

The kongoni is found nearly every place in East Africa. Along the railway between Makindu and Nairobi the species is called Coke's hartebeest. Farther up the railway the species is Neumann's hartebeest, while still beyond, on the Guas Ngishu Plateau and the Mau escarpment, the species is called Jackson's hartebeest. In the main the three varieties are almost the same; it is in the horns that the chief distinction lies, with lesser differences in color and stature. The hunter has been allowed to kill ten of each on his license, but under the new game ordinance in force since December, 1909, only four Jackson's are allowed and twenty Coke's instead of ten.

The Young Kongoni Is Very Funny

When we went across the Guas Ngishu Plateau in early November we saw thousands of Jackson's hartebeest, and never a calf. When we came back in late December and early January we saw hundreds and hundreds of calves, many of them less than a day old. The stork must have been busy, for they all arrived at once. These little calves come into the world fully equipped for running, and almost immediately after birth go bounding along after their mothers, so awkward and so funny that I'm not surprised that their own mothers look perpetually amused.

The hartebeest, or kongoni, is hard to kill. The Dutch gave him the name for that reason. It often seems as if bullets have no effect on him. He will absorb lead without losing a trace of his good-humored look, and after he has been shot several times he will go bounding earnestly away, as if nothing was the matter. If he succeeds in joining a herd there is little way of distinguishing which one has been shot, unless he suddenly exhibits signs or falls over. Otherwise he is quite likely to gallop away, far beyond pursuit, and then slowly succumb to his wounds.

Again I've seen them knocked over and lie as if dead, but before one could approach they would be up and off as good as ever. This is the great tragedy of the conscientious hunter's life—the escape of a wounded animal beyond pursuit—and the thought of it is one that keeps him awake at night with a remorseful heart and saddened thoughts. Whenever I shall think of Africa in the future, I shall think of my old friend, the kongoni, dotting the landscape and sticking his inquiring ears over various spots on the horizon. In four and a half months I think I must have seen at least a hundred thousand kongoni.

The giraffe is also a creature of most amusing actions. You are pretty certain to see a bunch of them as you come up the railway from the coast. They were the first wild animals I saw in British East Africa—a group of four or five quietly feeding within only a hundred yards of the thundering railway engine. They were in the protected area, however, and seemed to know that no harm would reach them there. Later on in the morning we saw other herds, but invariably at long range, sometimes teetering along the sky line or appearing and disappearing behind the flat-topped umbrella acacias.

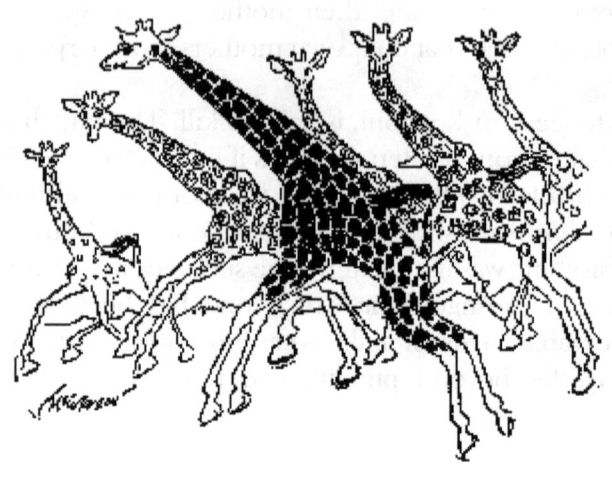

They Run Loosely but Earnestly

The giraffe is most laughable when in action. He first looks at you, then curls his tail over his back, and then lopes off with head and neck stuck out, and with body and legs slowly folding and unfolding in a most ungainly stride. It is hard to describe the gait of a giraffe to one who has never seen it, but any one would at once know without being told that a giraffe couldn't help being funny when running.

As a general thing it is difficult to approach a giraffe. With their keen eyes and great height they almost invariably see you before you see them, and that will be at seven or eight hundred yards' distance. From the moment they see you they never lose sight of you unless it is when they disappear behind a hill a mile or two away.

When seen on the sky-line a herd of giraffe will suggest a line of telegraph poles; when seen scattered along a hillside, partly sheltered under the trees, they blend into the mottled lights and shadows in such a way as to be almost invisible. I have been within two hundred yards of a motionless giraffe and, although looking directly at it, was not aware that it was a giraffe until it moved. It might easily have been mistaken for a bare fork of the tree, with the mottled shadows of the leaves cast upon it.

Along the Tana River I saw several herds of giraffe, perhaps fifty head in all, but it was on the great stretches of the scrub country that slopes down from Mount Elgon that I saw the great herds of them. One afternoon I saw twenty-nine together, big black males, beautifully marked tawny females, and lots of little ones that loomed up like lamp posts amidst a group of telegraph poles. Within two hours I saw two other herds of seven and nine each, and every day thereafter it was quite a common thing to run across groups of these strange-looking animals browsing among the trees.

One is not allowed to kill a giraffe except under a special license, which costs one hundred and fifty rupees, or fifty dollars. One of our party had a commission to secure a specimen for a collector and had been unsuccessful in getting it. That circumstance led to an amusing adventure that I had with a giant giraffe. One day, with my gunbearers, I had ridden out from camp in search of wild pigs. Ten minutes after leaving camp I drew rein hastily, for off to my left and in front a lone giraffe of great size and of splendid black color was slowly careening along toward me. If he continued in his course and did not see us he would pass within a hundred yards of me. So I hastily but quietly dismounted to try for a photograph as he passed.

A moment or two later he saw me for the first time and at once swung into a funny trot. I took the picture, and then the thought struck me, "Why not drive him into camp, where he could be secured by the one having a special license?" I jumped on my horse and galloped around him, but in a few moments struck a ravine so rocky that I had to walk my horse through the worst of it. By the time I had crossed the giraffe was some hundred yards ahead. Still farther ahead the prairie was burning and the long line of fire extended a mile or more across our front.

I thought this fire would swing the giraffe off, and so it became a race to reach the fire line first, in order to swing him in the right direction. The ground was deep with prairie grass, as dry as tinder, and scattered throughout were innumerable holes in the ground made by the ant-bears and wart-hogs. Any one of these holes was enough to throw a horse head over heels if he went into it. I had no gun, having left it with my gunbearer when I took the picture. So there was nothing to hinder me as we swept across the great plain.

We passed the camp half a mile away at a furious pace, the giraffe holding his own with the horse and keeping too far in front to be turned. By degrees we approached the prairie fire and the flames were leaping up three or four feet in a line many hundred yards long. The giraffe hesitated and then breasted the walls of fire; I didn't know whether my horse would take the salamander leap or not, and as we rushed down toward it I half-expected that he would stop suddenly and send me flying over his shoulders. But he never wavered. The excitement of the chase was upon him and he took the leap like an antelope. There was a moment of blinding smoke, a burning blast of air, and then we were galloping madly on across the blackened dust where the fire had already swept.

For two miles I galloped the giraffe, vainly endeavoring to swing him around, but once a swamp retarded me and another time a low hill shut the giraffe from view. When I passed the hill he had disappeared and could not be found again. There was no deep regret at having lost him, for I felt particularly grateful to him for having given me the most exhilarating and the most joyous ride I had in Africa.

The large male giraffes often appear solid black at a distance, for the yellow bands separating the splotches of black are so slender as to be invisible at even a short distance. The females are much lighter and usually look like the giraffes we see in the circuses at home.

Then there's the ubiquitous zebra, almost as numerous as the kongoni. You see vast herds of zebra at many places along the railway, and thereafter, as you roam about the level spots of East Africa, you are always running into herds of them. At first, the sight of a herd of zebras is a surprise, for you have been accustomed to seeing them in the small numbers found in captivity. It is a source of passing wonder that these rare animals should be roaming about the suburbs of towns in hundred lots. You decide that it would be a shame to shoot a zebra and determine not to join in this heartless slaughter.

Later on your sentiments will undergo a change. Everybody will tell you that the zebra is a fearful pest and must be exterminated if civilization and progress are to continue. The zebra is absolutely useless and efforts to domesticate him have been without good results. He tramps over the plains, breaks down fences, tears up the cultivated fields, and really fulfills no mission in life save that of supplying the lions with food. As long as the zebras stay the lions will be there, but the settlers say that the lions are even preferable to the zebras.

Under the old game ordinance expiring December fifteenth, 1909, a sportsman was allowed two zebras under his license; under the new one he is allowed twenty! That reveals the attitude of East Africa toward the jaunty little striped pony.

Zebra, Wildebeest and Gazelle (Wildebeest in Middle)

In action the zebra is dependent upon his friend, the kongoni. When the latter signals him to run, he trots off and then turns to look. If the kongoni sends out a 4-11 alarm, the zebra will hike off in a Shetland-pony-like gallop and run some distance before stopping. They have no endurance and may be easily rounded up with a horse.

On the Athi Plains may be found the bones of scores of zebras, each spot marking where a lion has fed; and in the barb-wire fences of the settlers other scores of withered hides and whitened skulls mark where they have fallen before the grim march of civilization.

With each sportsman granted an allowance of twenty zebras, it may not be so long before the zebra will be forced to seek the sanctuary of the game reserves, which, happily, are large enough to insure his escape from extinction.

The zebra's chief peculiarity, aside from his beautiful markings, is a dog-like bark which is much more canine than equine in its sound. The zebra's chief charm is its colt, for there is nothing alive that is prettier or more graceful than a young zebra a few weeks old.

The only Grant's gazelles that I saw were those along the railway at Kapiti Plains and Athi Plains. This animal is graceful and beautiful, with a splendid sweep of horns. With them, and in much greater numbers, is the little "Tommy," or Thompson's gazelle, a graceful, buoyant, happy, bounding little antelope with an ever active tail flirting gaily in the sunshine. The Tommy is small, about twice as big as a fox terrier, and is of a fawn color. Along the lower parts of his sides is a broad white belt, along the middle of which runs a bold black stripe. The effect is strikingly handsome.

The impalla is much bigger than the Tommy, and he usually travels in large herds of fifty or more. It is no uncommon sight to see one buck with twenty or thirty females, and it is probably due to the fact that hunters try to get the male specimens as trophies that accounts for the vast preponderance of females in the various antelope herds. The impalla is seen along the railroad and in enormous numbers out along the Thika Thika and Tana Rivers. There are also many up in the Rift Valley and doubtless in other sections. From my own experience and observation they were most abundant on the Tana River.

Impalla Buck and Lady Friends

The wildebeest, or gnu, is found on the Athi Plains and northward along the Athi River and the Thika Thika. One need never travel more than two hours' drive or walk from Nairobi to see wildebeest, but it's a different thing to get them. You would have to travel many hours, most likely, before you succeeded in bringing down a wildebeest.

My first shot in Africa was at a wildebeest at three hundred yards. The bullet struck, but so did the wildebeest. He struck out for northern Africa, and when last seen was still headed earnestly for the north pole. I am consoled in thinking that my shot must have inflicted more surprise than injury and so I hope he has now fully recovered, wilder and beastier than of yore.

My last shot in Africa, the day before leaving for the coast, was at a wildebeest an hour or so out of Nairobi. This time I missed entirely and repeatedly and the wildebeest remains unscathed to roam the broad plains of the Athi until some better or luckier shot passes his way. If I have anything on my conscience, it is certainly not the remorse of having reduced the supply of wildebeests.

Wildebeest With the White Man Only Eight Miles Away

In our last few days' shooting out on the Athi Plains we saw perhaps fifty or seventy-five of these great bison-like animals. Their bodies and legs and tails are slender and graceful, like those of a horse, but the heads are heavy-featured, heavy-horned and heavy-bearded. They are wild and when they see you a mile or so away will start and run for the nearest vanishing point, usually arriving there long before you do.

The foregoing seven species of animals are the ones most commonly seen in East Africa. Perhaps something about some of the less common ones will have some instructive value.

CHAPTER XV
SOME NATURAL HISTORY IN WHICH IT IS REVEALED THAT A SING-SING WATERBUCK IS NOT A SINGING TOPI, AND THAT A TOPI IS NOT A SPECIES OF HEAD-DRESS

WHILE reading an account of the trophies secured by Colonel Roosevelt on the Guas Ngishu Plateau, I was mystified by seeing the name of an animal I had never heard tell of—a singing topi. For a time I puzzled over this strange creature and finally evolved a satisfactory explanation of how the animal made its appearance in the despatches. Briefly, "there haint no sich animal," as the old farmer said when he saw his first dromedary in a circus; it was merely a mistake, due to the telegraphic abbreviations which foreign correspondents employ to save cable tolls.

What the correspondent meant to say was that the colonel had secured a sing-sing waterbuck *and* a topi. The word "waterbuck" was omitted because he assumed that everybody at home would know that a "sing-sing" was a species of waterbuck, wherein he was mistaken, for comparatively few people in America know what a sing-sing is, or, for that matter, what a topi is, or what a Uganda cob is. When his despatch had been transmitted through several operators on its way to the States the word "sing-sing" became "singing" and was supposed to be an adjective describing the topi. Hence the "singing topi."

The American paragraphers also had fun with the word "topi," for they thought a topi was a sun hat much worn in the hot countries. From this course of reasoning it was probably assumed that Colonel Roosevelt had shot some kind of a singing sun hat, which was certainly enough to cause comment.

There are two kinds of waterbuck that the East African hunter will find in the course of his travels, the common waterbuck which we saw in such numbers on the Tana River, and the Defassa, or "sing-sing" waterbuck, which is found in the higher altitudes up toward the Mau escarpment and Mount Elgon. Both of these varieties of waterbuck are beautiful animals, almost as large as a steer, and with great sweeping horns that often exceed twenty-five inches in length. In some instances the horns have been nearly three feet long, but the longest one that our party secured was only twenty-nine inches in length. As a trophy for a wall there are few heads in Africa more noble than that of the waterbuck.

In all our wanderings, during which we saw at least two thousand waterbuck, we found that the does outnumbered the males by ten to one and that usually in a herd of twenty there would be only one big male and one or two smaller ones. We also never saw them in water, but usually not a great distance from a marsh or stream. They were much shier than the hartebeest and zebra, and upon seeing our approach would be the first to run away. And by a curious chance the does seemed to know that it was the buck only that was in danger. They would often turn to watch us, while the buck himself would keep on running until he had put many hundreds of yards between himself and the threatened danger. Then, and then only, would he turn to watch, and it usually required careful stalking to get within gunshot of him again.

Waterbuck

The doe is not pretty, being thickly and clumsily built, with a heavy, ungraceful neck, but the buck is like a painting by Landseer, noble, graceful, and beautifully marked with white and black on his dark gray coat.

We didn't kill many waterbuck, because there is no excuse for doing so except to secure the heads as trophies. The meat is so coarse and tough that even the porters, who seldom draw the line at eating anything their teeth can penetrate, do not care for waterbuck meat except under the stress of great hunger. They do like the skin, however, for it is of the waterbuck skin that their best sandals are made. Consequently, when a waterbuck is killed there is a fierce scramble among the porters to secure portions of the hide for this purpose.

The male waterbucks are savage fighters among themselves, and it was not uncommon to see big bulls with one horn gone or with both horns badly broken or marred as a result of the jealous struggle for dominance of a herd of does.

The topi is something like the hartebeest, but much more beautiful and much more rare. It is over four feet high, with skin of a dark reddish brown, with a silklike bluish gray gloss. On the shoulders and thighs are bluish black patches and the forehead and nose are blackish brown. The under parts are bright cinnamon. We ran across this beautiful antelope only on the Guas Ngishu Plateau, although it is found in one or two other districts in East Africa. In all our weeks of rambling on the high plains near Mount Elgon I think I saw several hundred head of topi, always shy and quick to take alarm.

A Uganda Cob

The Lordly Eland

The meat is the most delicious of any of the large antelopes, and the skin, when properly cared for, is as soft as kid and as brilliant as watered silk. The head is a fine trophy on account of its rich coloring rather than because of its horns, which are not particularly graceful in curve or proportion, but which are wonderfully ridged.

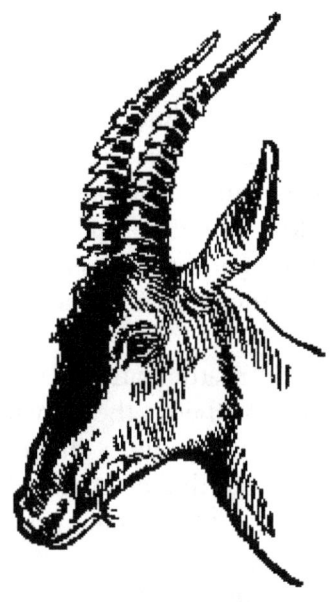

Topi

I am sure that if I were a beautiful topi with a skin like watered silk I should be deeply humiliated to be mistaken for a singing sun hat.

The topi's nearest relations are the sasseby, the tiang, and the korrigum. And now you know all about the topi. The game ordinance allows the sportsman to kill two topi, and the holder of a license will work hard to get his two, for they are splendid trophies.

The duiker is another little antelope that one meets frequently in the grassy places of East Africa. It is small, with dark complexion, and goes through the high grass in a way that strongly suggests the diving of a porpoise at sea. In fact, it gets its Dutch name for that reason, *duiker bok*, meaning "diving buck" in Dutch. There are a dozen or more different species of duikers, and they may be found scattered all over South and East Africa. They are difficult to shoot, for their diving habits make them a fleeting target; also their size, about twenty or thirty pounds in weight, makes them a small target.

Quite often the little duiker will hide in the grass until you have almost stepped on him, and then, if he considers discovery inevitable, he will spring away with his little huddled-up back rising and disappearing over the grass exactly as the porpoise does in the water. One day while we were beating some tall grass for lions, one of the porters stepped on a duiker, and its sharp horns, twisting suddenly, cut him on the ankle. The horns of the bucks are short and straight, from four to six inches long, but most often about four and a half inches.

It would take an expert mathematician to keep track of all the different kinds of duikers, for there's the crowned duiker, the yellow-backed duiker, the red duiker, Jentink's duiker, Abbott's duiker, the Ituri red duiker, the black-faced duiker, Alexander's duiker, the Ruddy duiker, Weyn's duiker, Johnston's duiker, Isaac's duiker, Harvey's duiker, Roberts' duiker, Leopold's duiker, the white-bellied duiker, the bay duiker, the chestnut duiker, the white-lipped duiker, Ogilby's duiker, Brooke's duiker, Peter's duiker, the red-flanked duiker, the banded duiker, Walker's duiker, the white-faced duiker, the black duiker, Maxwell's duiker, the black-rumped duiker, the Uganda duiker, the blue duiker, the Nyasa duiker, Heck's duiker, the Urori duiker, Erwin's duiker, and I suppose a lot more that the naturalists have not had time to catalogue.

Like a Popular Cemetery

One would assume that with all these duikers there would hardly be room left in Africa for any other animals. But there is. For instance, there's the oribi and the dik-dik, to say nothing of the steinbuck and the klipspringer. The last named is a rock-jumping antelope, the others little grass antelopes, and all of them are as pretty and cute as animals can be. They are all small, the dik-dik being scarcely larger than a rabbit, and they are divided into as many subspecies as the duiker. A list of the different kinds of oribi would take up several lines of valuable space without conveying any illuminating intelligence to the lay mind.

We found thousands of oribi on the Guas Ngishu Plateau. You couldn't go half a mile in any direction without stirring up large family parties of them, and a landscape looked lonely unless one could see a few oribi bounding over the ant-hills or rising and falling as they leaped through the grass. When we first went into the plateau the grass was long and the oribi were for the most part fleeting streaks of yellow over the tops of it, but later when we came out the grass had been burned and the young, tender grass had spread a green carpet over the plains. Then the oribi were visible everywhere, usually in groups of four or six. Also the mamma oribis had given birth to bouncing baby oribis, and the sight of the little ones was most pleasing to the eyes.

Mamma and the Little One

One day I was hot on the trail of a big waterbuck. The grass was deep at that part of the plateau and I was pushing rapidly through it. Suddenly one of my gunbearers, who was behind, called out and pointed to something in the grass. I hurried back, and there lay a little oribi only a few hours old and with big, wondering eyes that looked gravely up at me as I bent over it. It was plenty old enough to run and could easily have leaped away, but there it lay as tight as if nothing in the world could make it budge.

A Museum Specimen Must Be Preserved Entire

The Eland Is the Largest of the African Antelopes

The whole thing was as plain as could be. It was acting under instructions. I could almost hear the mother of the oribi tell the little one when it heard us coming to lay perfectly quiet and not to move the least bit until she came back. Then mamma hurried away to cover. The little oribi remembered his instructions and followed them out to the letter. Its mamma had told it not to move and it hadn't. We looked at it a little while and then said good-by and went our way. Some place near by an anxious mother oribi was watching us with her heart in her mouth, no doubt, and I'm sure that we had not gone many yards before she was back to see what had happened to the little one. It was quite an exciting adventure for the little oribi and quite incomprehensible to the mother that he had emerged from the peril so safely.

Another night I was going out to watch for lions. A bait had been placed near the tree where I was stationed and I had some hopes of seeing, if not killing, a lion. Night had already fallen, but there was still a trace of twilight in the air as I walked through the low scrub trees that lay between our camp and the tree, a mile and a half away. As I was walking along I heard a loud screaming to my left, and, looking across, I saw an oribi trying to beat off two jackals that had seized her young baby oribi. The jackals paid little attention to her and she was frantic in her efforts to save her little one.

It was too dark to see my sights plainly, but I shot at both of the jackals and sent them slinking away. I didn't go over to see if the little oribi was still alive, for I was certain that it had been killed. If it were dead I didn't want to see it and could not help either it or its mother; if it were alive its mother could get it safely away from the jackals. Since that moment I have hated jackals above all animals, not even excepting the odious hyena, and it is the chief regret of my hunting experience in East Africa that I did not kill those two cowardly vandals.

When the American reader picks up his paper and reads that Colonel Roosevelt has shot a Uganda cob, it is quite natural that he should not know what kind of a thing a cob is. If the colonel was out shooting "singing topis" or "singing sun hats," why, then, should he not also shoot corn cobs or cob pipes?

The cob, sometimes spelled kob, however, is only an antelope, although a graceful and handsome one. It is divided into several subspecies which live in different parts of the country. In one part will be found the large cob, almost the size of a waterbuck, which is called Mrs. Gray's cob, in honor of the wife of one of the former keepers in the London zoo; in another part is the species known as Vaughan's cob, and in still other parts are the dusky cob, the puku cob, the lechwi cob, the black lechwi, the Uganda cob and Buffon's cob.

It was Lady Constance Stewart-Richardson, the remarkable young English woman who is now dancing barefooted on the London music stage, who killed the record head of this last named species in Nigeria.

The Gregarious Cob

It is of the Uganda cob only that I am able to write about from my own observation and experience. We found them only in one place, on the banks of the Nzoia River near Mount Elgon and the Uganda border. They never were more than four or five hundred yards from the river and could not be driven away. If they were startled at one point they would circle around and quickly get back to the river at some other point. They seemed to become homesick unless they could see the river near by. We found them only in a short stretch of five or six miles, although they doubtless are found all the way down the Nzoia River to Victoria Nyanza.

The cob is a curiously reliable animal. He likes one certain place that he is accustomed to, and nothing can drive him away. If you see him there one afternoon, you are reasonably certain of coming back the next afternoon and seeing him there again. Usually they graze in some sheltered meadow along the river's edge, and for recreation, so far as I could see, amuse themselves by seeing how many can get on top of one ant-hill at one time. Some of those ant-hills were literally bristling with cobs, one male to each five females, and in herds of from thirty to fifty.

In architecture, the cob is nearly three feet high at the shoulder, has beautiful, sweeping horns of a lyrate shape, has a white patch around each eye, a white belly, and a coat of yellow with black on the forelegs. There is no handsomer antelope in Africa than the Uganda cob, and because it is found in such a restricted and remote district is accountable for the fact that one seldom sees a cob head in a collection of horns. Comparatively few sportsmen have killed them, although they are not hard to kill if one reaches a district where they are found. The extreme beauty of this antelope led us to secure a group of them for the Field Museum.

The reedbuck is another of the smaller antelopes that carries a beautiful head, and, like nearly all of the antelopes, comes in many varieties, or subspecies.

A Wounded Wart Hog

A Grass Fire

A Maribou Stork

Our own relations with the reedbuck were limited to the high altitudes near the Mau escarpment and the broad, rolling, grassy downs along the numerous streams of the Guas Ngishu Plateau. This subspecies is called the Uganda race of the bohor reedbuck—

sometimes abbreviated to "bohor." If you say you've shot a "bohor" you will be understood to mean a bohor reedbuck.

Reedbuck

You will find the reedbuck in the tall reeds and bulrushes of the swamps and low places, where he finds good cover and good feeding; and also you will find him along the low, undulating, grass-covered hills near his water supply. In the heat of the day they are up in the tall grass, where they remain until along in the afternoon. They lie close, and, if discovered, will dart off with neck outstretched in such a way as to make it difficult to tell which is male and which female.

I have also seen the females use every means for protecting their lords and masters, standing up before them as they lie secreted in the grass and seeking to divert the attention of the hunter from the bucks to themselves. This desire to protect the male is common to many of the antelope family, and numberless times I have seen a band of does attempt to screen the male and shield him from harm.

The reedbuck never travels in large numbers, seldom more than two or three, or at most, five or six, being bunched together.

They Watched While the Buck Ran Away

We had most of our reedbuck experiences while driving swamps for lions. On these occasions many reedbuck would be driven out of the cover of the reeds and rushes, and go crashing up the slopes leading away from the swamp. On one occasion a reedbuck lay so close that it did not stir until one of the beaters was almost upon it, when it sprang up, nearly knocking him over, and escaped behind the skirmish line of beaters. At other times, after the skirmish line apparently had traversed every foot of a swamp, reedbuck would spring up after the line had passed, thus illustrating how close they can lie and how effectually they can escape detection.

The reedbuck has short horns, usually between seven and ten inches in length, but one of our party secured one set of horns ten and a quarter inches long—an exceptionally fine head. The reedbuck's distinguishing characteristic is a sharp whistle, which he sounds shrilly when alarmed.

Another beautiful antelope that we met in small numbers on the Tana River and on the Guas Ngihsu Plateau was the bushbuck, found in thick scrub along rivers and also in the swamps and wet places. This animal belongs to a select little coterie of highly prized and rare antelopes, all of which have the distinguishing feature of a spiral horn.

The bushbuck is the smallest, and is found over nearly all of East Africa except upon the open plains and deserts. The females are of a dark chestnut color, and the males dark, almost black, with white markings on the neck and forelegs. A bushbuck with fifteen-inch horns is considered a fine prize, although horns of nineteen inches are on record.

The other members of the same family of spiral-horned antelopes are the kudu, the lesser kudu, the situtunga, the nyala, the bongo, and the lordly eland, king of all antelopes in size. The kudu is largely protected in East Africa, and in my shooting experience I was not in a district where he was to be found. The same was true with respect to the lesser kudu. The nyala is a South African species and is not to be found in British East Africa. The situtunga is a swamp dweller and is found chiefly in Uganda and, to my knowledge, infrequently in the East African protectorate.

The bongo is to the white sportsman what the north pole has been to explorers for centuries. In all records of game shooting there has been, until recently, only one white man who has killed a bongo, although the Wanderobo dwellers of the deep forests have killed many.

The bongo lives in the densest part of dense forests, can drive his way through the worst tangle of vegetation, and has a hearing and eyesight so keen that usually he sees the hunter long before the latter sees him. A hunt after bongo means long hours or even days of hunting the forests, with hardships of travel so disheartening that comparatively few white sportsmen attempt to go in after the elusive antelope. Kermit Roosevelt, however, with the good fortune that has followed his hunting adventures, succeeded in killing a cow and calf bongo after only a few hours of hunting with a Wanderobo.

A few days after I heard of this piece of good luck I was traveling across Victoria Nyanza on one of the little steamers that ply the lake. My cabin mate was a stoical Englishman who told me quite calmly that he had just killed a large bull bongo a few days before. He had been visiting Lord Delamere, and after a few hours in the forest had succeeded in doing what only two white men had done before.

The Englishman who had this good luck was George Grey, a brother of Sir Edward Grey, one of the present cabinet ministers of England.

Eland

The eland is the largest of all antelopes, and we ran across a few on the Tana River and a few on the Guas Ngishu Plateau. Under the old game ordinance the sportsman was allowed to kill one bull eland; under the new ordinance he is allowed to kill none except in certain restricted districts and by special license. The eland is as big as a bull, with spiral horns and beautifully marked skin, and both the male and female carry horns. Those of the latter are usually larger and slenderer, but the skin of the female is not so handsomely marked as that of the male.

It is hard to get near an eland, but as the bull is nearly six feet high at the shoulders it is not especially difficult to hit him at three hundred yards or more. The one I shot was three hundred and sixty-five yards away and carried beautiful horns, twenty-four and one-quarter inches in length. The head of the great bull eland makes a wonderfully imposing trophy when placed in your baronial halls.

In the foregoing list of antelopes I have tried to tell a little about the types of that class of animal that I met in my African travels—in all, sixteen species of antelope. My chief excuse for doing it is to enable people at home to know the difference between a topi and a sun hat and between a sing-sing and a cob. The names of many of the African antelope family are strange and confusing, so that it is little wonder that they mystify people in America. There are a hundred or more kinds, and no one can hope to know them unless he makes a business of it.

I have not seen the grysbok, or the suni, or the dibitag, or the lechwi, or the aoul, or the gerenuk, or the blaauwbok, or the chevrotain, or lots of others, but who in the world could guess what they were or what they looked like, judging only from the names?

CHAPTER XVI
IN THE TALL GRASS OF THE MOUNT ELGON COUNTRY. A NARROW ESCAPE FROM A LONG-HORNED RHINO. A THANKSGIVING DINNER AND A VISIT TO A NATIVE VILLAGE

MOUNT Elgon is one of the four great mountains of Africa. You can find it on the map of the dark continent, standing all alone, just a little bit north of Victoria Nyanza, and surrounded by names that one has never heard of before.

The mountain is distinctly out of the picture-post-card belt—in fact, the only belt that one will find around Elgon is the timber belt that encircles the mountain, and perhaps also a few that the local residents wear on Sundays and national holidays.

The function of the latter class of belt is to keep up a gay appearance. It is worn for looks, not warmth.

The traveler who goes to Mount Elgon will not be distracted by sounds of civilization, except such as he takes with him. He will travel for days without seeing a sign of human life beyond his own following. The country west of the Nzoia River is uninhabited and is abandoned to the elephant and the giraffe and other animals that care not for the madding crowd. Thomas Cook and Son have not yet penetrated that district with schedules and time cards and luggage labels; so if your purpose in traveling is to get a grand assortment of stickers on your trunks and hand-bags, it is useless to include Mount Elgon in your itinerary.

There will be days of marching through high grass, often so deep as almost to bury yourself and your horse; hours of delay at marshy rivers densely choked with a tangle of riotous vegetation, and much groping about in a trackless waste for a suitable course to follow.

Owing to intertribal warfare the Elgon district has been closed for some time and it has only been during the last year or so that hunting parties have again been allowed to enter. Since that time a number of parties have been in, the Duke of Alba among the first, and later Doctor Rainsford, Frederick Selous and, Mr. McMillan, Captain Ashton, the Duke of Peñaranda, Mr. Roosevelt, and a few others. Colonel

Roosevelt went only as far as the Nzoia River, but most of the others crossed and swung up along the northeastern slopes of the mountain where elephants are most frequently found.

Our party decided to take the southern slope, notwithstanding we were warned that we might find the natives troublesome and treacherous. We were also warned that we should be going through an untraveled district where there were no trails and where native guides could not be secured.

A Native Granary

A Chair Is a Sure Sign of Rank

Nevertheless we started and brilliantly blundered into some most diverting adventures.

The first day's march after crossing the Nzoia River was through scrub country and what we considered high grass. The next day we struck *real* high grass! It was so deep that we had to burrow through it. Only the helmets of those on horseback marked where the caravan was passing. The long line of porters carrying their burdens were buried from view. It was a terrible place to meet a rhino and perhaps for that very reason we promptly proceeded to meet one.

We were riding ahead, followed by the cook and the tent boys, and behind them was the long string of a hundred or more porters, askaris, *totos*, and so forth. The end of the line was some hundred yards behind the head. Suddenly there was a wild cry of "*faru!*" (rhino).

It was disconcerting, but after one or two hurried and flurried moments we got our heavy batteries in readiness and prepared to sell his life as cheaply as possible. But no rhino came. The grass was too deep to have seen him if he had come, but we thought it was well to have a reception committee ready just the same.

Then the rear ranks began to telescope into the front ranks. They came forward two or three jumps at a time. They were visibly perturbed, but presently they recovered enough to give expert testimony.

A huge rhino had been in the grass by the trail as we came along and had waited until the whole line had passed. Then he jumped into the trail and charged furiously after the porters. The latter, severally, collectively, and frantically, leaped for their lives, dropping packs and uttering hurried appeals to Allah.

He Estimated the Length at Four Feet

After scattering a few dozen of the rank and file from his line of march the rhino veered off and plunged out of sight in the tall grass. One of the porters whose veracity is unquestioned by those who don't know him estimated the forward horn to be four feet long. He said the rhino charged earnestly and with hostile intent.

A rhino charging a *safari* is always a pleasing diversion—pleasing after it's all over and diverting while it lasts. The cry of "*faru*" is a good deal like "car coming" at an automobile race. Instantly everybody is all attention, with the attention equally divided between the rhino and the nearest tree. If there is no tree the interest in the rhino becomes more acute.

The thought of being impaled *en brochette* on the horn of a rhino is one of the least attractive forms of mental exertion that I know of. It is a close second to the thought of being stepped on by a herd of elephants marching single file.

Well, we survived the charge of the heavy brigade, and then moved onward, ever and anon casting an alert glance at the deep clumps of thicket along the way. Fortunately no more rhinos appeared and the next thing we struck was Thanksgiving Day.

The proper way to celebrate that deservedly popular holiday is not by sitting in tall grass with a can of beans and a bottle of pickles in the foreground. This is said with all respect to the manufacturers of beans and pickles who may advertise in the papers.

For a time, however, beans and pickles seemed to be the nearest outlook for us, but after a while the cook, whose nerves had been shaken by the impetuous advance of the rhino, arose to the demands of the occasion and set up a table upon which soon appeared some hot tea, some bread and honey, some beans and deviled ham, and a few knickknacks in the line of jam and cheese. That was luncheon, and we resolved to do better for dinner.

We told the cook all about Thanksgiving Day and what its chief purpose was. We also told him of the beautiful significance of the occasion, what happy thoughts it inspired, and how much sentiment was attached to it. Then we told him to get busy. We were in a Thanksgiving mood, being grateful that we were not riding around on the bowsprit of the rhino, and also because our relatives and friends at home were well at last reports, two months old.

True, our guide, who had never been over the trail before and who was trying to guess the way by instinct, had got us hopelessly becalmed in a sea of high grass so that we didn't know where we were. But we knew what we were. We were hungry!

In the meantime we planned and carried into brilliant execution a grouse hunt. There were lots of grouse in the country through which we had come and all day long coveys of them had been whirring away from our advancing outposts. It seemed a simple thing to go out and get a few for our Thanksgiving dinner, so we gave orders to make camp and consecrated the afternoon to a grouse quest.

I'll never forget what a formidable looking party it was. When we had spread out to comb the grass by the river side we looked like a skirmish line of an army. There were four of us, supported by seventeen gunbearers and porters. Our battery consisted of four elephant guns, four heavy rifles, three light rifles, and four shotguns. The latter were for grouse and the others were for incidental big game which one must always be prepared for, whether one goes out to shoot grouse or take snapshots with one's camera.

The Grouse Hunt

We spread out and beat two miles of perfect cover. Then we beat it back again and finally, after all our Herculean efforts, one lonely bird flew up and was knocked over. That was the astounding total of our slaughter and when the army marched back into camp with its one little grouse the effect was laughable in the extreme. I took a photograph of the entire group and by good luck the grouse is faintly seen suspended in the middle.

That night, with the camp-fires burning and with our tents almost buried in the tall grass, we celebrated Thanksgiving in a way that must have made old Lucullus fidget in his mausoleum. The wealth of the plains was compelled to yield tribute to our table; eland, grouse and Uganda cob appeared and disappeared as if by magic; the vast storehouses of Europe and America poured their treasures upon our groaning board, and one by one we safely put away succulent lengths of asparagus, cakes and chocolate, wine and olives, pickles and honey, nuts and cheese, plum pudding and coffee, and soup and salad, all in their proper sequence and in sufficient quantities to go round and round.

A soft moon shone down from the velvet sky and the trees of the river bed were bathed in white moonlight as we sat by the great campfire and smoked and talked and dreamed of the folk at home.

It was an unusual occasion, one that called for a special dispensation in the way of late hours, so it was almost nine when we turned in and dreamed of armies of rhinos playing battledore and shuttlecock with our bulging forms. It was a great dinner, and to be on the safe side we complimented the cook before we went to bed.

A Group of Ketosh Ladies

Nearly Buried in Grass

Building a Grass House

A day or two later, after blindly floundering about in a sea of waving grass for miles and miles, and getting more and more hopelessly lost, we stumbled upon signs of human habitation. The first sign was a great stretch of valley in which a number of smoke columns were ascending. Where there's smoke there's folk, we thought, patting ourselves on the back for cleverness. We knew we were approaching fresh eggs and chickens.

A little later we came upon another sign of human agitation. Over a rise in a hill we saw a large spear, and in a few minutes we overhauled a native guarding a herd of cattle. He carried a spear and a shield, and over his shoulders he wore a loose dressing sack that hung down nearly to his armpits. Civilization had touched him lightly, in fact it had barely waved at him as it brushed by.

We tried him with several languages—Swahili, Kikuyu, the language of flowers, American, Masai, and the sign language, none of which he was conversant with. Then we tried a relay system of dialects which established a vague, syncopated kind of intellectual contact. One of our porters spoke Kavirondo, so he held converse with the far from handsome stranger, translated it into Swahili, and this was retranslated into English for our benefit.

The stranger was a Ketosh. We didn't know what a Ketosh was, but it sounded more like something in the imperative mood than anything ethnological. It developed later in the day, however, that a Ketosh is a member of the tribe of that name, and their habitat is on the southern slopes of Elgon.

Lady and Gentleman Ketosh

The Ketoshites, or Ketoshians, as the case may be, are a cattle- and sheep-raising tribe. In other words, a tribe in which the women do all the manual labor while the men folk sit on a hillside with a shield and spear and watch the herds partake of nourishment. They are the standing army.

The Standing Army Sat Around All Day

We followed the man with the spear to a little village hard by. The village, like all the numerous other ones that we came to in the next few days, was inclosed in a zareba, or wall of tangled thorn branches that encircled the village. Within the wall were a number of low houses, six feet high, built of mud and wattle; and within the houses, spilling over plentifully, were large numbers of children and babies and a few women. A gateway of tangled boughs led into the inclosure, while in one part of the village were the curious woven wickerwork granaries in which the community store of kaffir corn is kept. There were no street signs on the lamp posts, probably because there were no streets and no lamp posts.

In the first village all the men were away, evidently waiting to see whether our visit was a hostile or a peaceful one.

We soon established ourselves on a peace footing and after that the warriors began to appear out of the tall grass in large numbers from all points of the compass. They all carried spears and shields, neither of which they would sell for love or money. At least they wouldn't for money. We resolved not to try the other unless the worst came to the worst and we had to fall back on it as a last desperate measure. I suppose they didn't know how soon they might need their weapons, and we heard that the sultan had just sent out a positive order forbidding them to sell their means of defense.

The Ketosh Are Gracefully Nonchalant

Little Shelters of Mud and Sticks

A Family Party

The first procedure when entering a district where the natives may be unfriendly is to send out for the chief, or sultan, as he is known in Africa. There is always a sultan to preside over the destinies of his tribe and to take any money that happens along. So we sent for the sultan, who was off in a neighboring village, so they said. After a long wait, during which we pitched our camp and offered a golden reward for eggs and chickens, a sultan drifted in.

Slowly Being Cremated

We knew he was sultan because he carried a chair—an unfailing sign of rank among a nation of expert sitters. He also wore an old woolen dressing gown that had worked its way from civilization many years before. It was built for arctic regions, but the sultan of all the Ketoshians wore it right straight through the ardent hours when the sun kisses one with the fiery passion of a mustard plaster. He was slowly being cremated and it was fascinating to watch him sizzle.

After the sultan came and seated himself with his retinue of spearmen (dressed in the altogether save for the futile cloth around their shoulders) grouped around him we took our seats and began a *shauri*.

Shauri (rhyming with Bow'ry) is a native word meaning a powwow or a parley and is a word that works overtime. Everything that you do in Africa has to be preceded by a *shauri*. You have a *shauri* if you ask a native which road to take. Other natives hurry up, and then you stand around and talk about it for an hour or so.

If you want to buy a chicken or a cluster of eggs there must first be a prolonged *shauri* with much interchange of views and conversation and aërated persiflage. The native loves his *shauri*, and if he asks you a certain price for a chicken and you give the price without haggling he is greatly disappointed. In fact I have often seen them offer an article for a certain price and then refuse to accept the money if it is at once tendered. Later the native will accept much less if the *shauri* goes with it.

Well, we had *shauris* to burn for a couple of days. As soon as the first sultan had departed with presents and words of good cheer there was a flock of other sultans that hurried in to receive presents and to assist in *shauris*. They came from far and near, and they all carried chairs, thus proving that they were not impostors; and the worst of it was that we couldn't find out exactly which was the real, most exalted sultan of the bunch. Hence we had to give presents to many who perhaps were only amateur or 'prentice sultans, sultans whose domains were only a little village of half a dozen families.

The Camp Was Clogged with Sultans

For two days our camp was clogged with *shauris* and sultans sitting around. We couldn't step out of our tents without stumbling over a sultan or two. When we would take our baths in our tents there would be sultans and warriors peeping in modestly from all sides. There was not a secret of our inner life that remained intact. Even the ladies, from the banana-bellied little girls of five and six up to the leathery-limbed old matrons, inclusive, were not above a feminine curiosity in things which doubtless interested them, but didn't concern them. The standing army of the Ketoshians sat around all day wearing out the grass and being frequently stumbled over.

If we asked a sultan if there were any elephants in the neighborhood it meant at least fifteen minutes of loose conversation through a relay of interpreters, with the final answer boiled down to a "no" in English. For a language that has only a few words like *shauri*, *backsheesh*, *apana*, and *chukula* the native lingo is a most elastic one.

There were two or three things that we had come to Mount Elgon for and about which we desired information. The first was "elephants," and we found, after hours of talk, that there was none in the vicinity. Secondly, we wanted to get food for our men, and thirdly, we wanted guides to take us up to the ancient cave-dwellings in the mountain and more guides to take us up to the top of the mountain itself.

It seemed almost impossible to get satisfactory information upon either of the last two subjects. The natives didn't want to part with their grain, while for their cattle they asked outrageous prices. We were almost tempted to boycott them by stopping eating meat for two months. They also seemed reluctant to let us have guides to take us up to the caves and none of them seemed to know the trails that led up into the forests and the heights of the mountain. It was evident that only a few ever had been up the mountain upon the slopes of which they had spent their lives.

At the Entrance of the Great Cave

There Were Granaries in the Cave

In One of the Elgon Caves

We began to think that they wanted us to stay in their village just so they could have the pleasure of their daily *shauris*.

Finally one sultan promised to get us guides and accepted a generous present on the strength of it; but when the time came he failed to produce them. It was at precisely this point, to be strictly accurate, that we abandoned the polite phraseology of the court and told him with many exclamation points that he would have to guide us himself or we would take steps to dethrone him. Of course, all of this had to be strained through two interpreters, but even then I think he caught the gist of it. He said that he himself would guide us to the nearest and largest cave.

We told him that we would be ready to start immediately after luncheon. Only ourselves and a few men to carry cameras and guns were to constitute our party, the rest of the *safari* remaining in camp, from which certain embassies were sent out to buy grain for the porters' food.

Soon after lunch the sultan arrived and we marched away. Little by little groups of his janissaries, mamelukes, and other members of his official entourage joined us and by the time we reached the slope leading up to the great cave-dwelling we had quite an imposing procession. Most of the natives were armed with spears and knives, and some of them had painted their bodies with red dirt and mutton grease, and when this coating had partly dried they had traced with their fingers many designs in stripes down their arms and legs. Some were a light mauve in color, but most were of a rich chocolate brown. The effect of these designs was rather pretty, but the dripping red oil from their hair was not pretty and on a hot day exuded a strong, overpowering odor.

Above us, nearly a thousand feet from where we stood, boldly visible in the face of the great cliff, was the broad ledge and black opening of the cave. A short distance to the right of it was a bright waterfall, looking like a ribbon, but in reality quite broad and dropping in three stages several hundred feet. An incline of forty-five degrees led up to the cave, while up beyond that was the great stratum of solid rock that extends for miles along the south of Mount Elgon and which is honey-combed with hundreds of prehistoric cave-dwellings. A determined foe stationed at the mouth of any one of the caves could defend it against an enormous attacking force.

It was nearly an hour's climb to the ledge where the cave entrance appeared. Several naked men armed with spears stood upon the rocks, outlined in bold and striking relief against the velvety blackness of the cave entrance. They appeared curious but not unfriendly as we breathlessly panted our way on to the ledge where they stood waiting, spears in hand.

Like a Great Stage

Our first impression was one of gasping wonderment. We seemed to stand upon a great stage of an immensity which words can not describe. It was a stage proportioned for giants. The rock prosscenium arched above us seventy feet and the stage was nearly two hundred feet wide. As an audience chamber one could look out over twenty-five thousand square miles of Central Africa.

The dimensions and the imposing magnitude of the place almost took one's breath away. Two regiments of soldiers could have marched upon that stage. There was even room for a squadron of cavalry to manœuver. Upon the well-beaten floor were the tracks of cattle, showing that from time immemorial the cave people had driven in their herds for shelter or for safety in times of tribal warfare; and in places the solid rock was worn smooth and deep by the bare feet of centuries of naked people.

And yet, in spite of the titanic proportions of the cave, there was something quite homelike about it. It almost suggested a prosperous farm-yard. There were chickens walking about, with little chickens trotting alongside. There were wickerwork graneries standing here and there, while around the inner edge of the great entrance hall were little mud and stick woven houses five feet high, which gave the effect of a small village street.

From the front of the stage back to the row of little houses was a distance of about one hundred feet. By stooping down one could enter one of the little openings, to be surprised to find himself in another little farm-yard where cattle had been housed and where there were many evidences of the thrift and industry of the occupants. Gourds of milk were present in generous numbers, and as one's eyes became accustomed to the semi-darkness all sorts of domestic paraphernalia were revealed.

Little separate inclosures were fenced off for human tenantry, and the glow of embers gave a pleasant, homelike look to the place. Cavern after cavern extended back into the cliff, a network of them, but how far they went would be hard to tell. Perhaps the cave in all its subterranean ramifications has never been entirely explored.

We wandered back through some of the caverns, sometimes stooping to get through and sometimes standing beneath domes thirty and forty feet high. And always that queer, mystical light, with exaggerated shadows and sometimes black darkness ahead, where could be heard the drip, drip, drip of water in invisible lakes. In time of siege the holders of this cave, with granaries filled and with herds of cattle and lakes of water, could hold the place for ever.

The tenants of the place soon became pleasant and hospitable. Perhaps many of them had never seen white people before, but they sat down and watched us with friendly interest. There were many babies and they were all bright-eyed and rugged looking.

While we were there the cattle were out on the open hills grazing, but in the evening the long herds are driven up to their airy stronghold and made snug for the night. And who knows but that a great herd of cattle would add much to the heat of the cave and make its nearly naked tenants forget that they were high on the chilly slopes of one of Africa's greatest mountains?

They certainly do not dress warm. Around their arms and legs are all sorts of brass and nickel wire wound in scores of circles. Chains of wire and necklaces of beads encircle the women's throats and elephant ivory armlets are often clasped about the arms so tight that it would seem that the natural circulation would be hopelessly retarded. But they must be healthy, these people who go about with only a thin sheet of dyed cotton thrown about them, while we northerners shivered with sweaters and warm woolen things about us.

It's all a case of getting used to it, just as it is a case of getting used to seeing people frankly and unconsciously naked, as many of these people are. But after a while one even gets used to seeing them so and regards their nakedness as one would regard the nakedness of animals.

CHAPTER XVII
UP AND DOWN THE MOUNTAIN SIDE FROM THE KETOSH VILLAGE TO THE GREAT CAVE OF BATS. A DRAMATIC EPISODE WITH THE FINDING OF A BLACK BABY AS A CLIMAX

For days we had heard of wonderful places higher up in the mountain. The information had been so vague and uncertain we hardly knew whether to credit the reports or simply put them down as native folk lore or superstition. One night we interviewed Askar, one of the Somali gunbearers.

He said he had been up the mountain a year or two before with a Frenchman who wanted to see the mysterious natural wonders of Mount Elgon. The Frenchman had to threaten to kill his native guides before they would consent to lead him up in the cold heights of the mountain to show him the places that filled the native imagination with such fear and superstitious dread.

There was one place, Askar said, where the water boiled out of the ground far, far up in the mountain heights, and any native who looked at it fell dead. Askar said he went up and looked at it through the glasses, and then ran away.

All this queer information came out at one of our evening camp-fire *shauris*. The great central camp-fire of a *safari* is usually in front of the tents of the *msungu*, or white people, and around it in the evening the *msungu* discuss the adventures of the day and the plans for the morrow. Each night Abdi, the *neapara* or head-man, comes up to get his instructions for the next morning, and soon afterward Abdullah, the cook, appears and waits for his orders for the breakfast hour.

Abdullah is the color of night, and no one ever sees him approach or go away. He simply appears and often stands only a few feet away before any one is aware of his presence. And even after he speaks, one sees only a row of white teeth looming up five feet above the ground. If any important matters are to be adjusted it is usually at the camp-fire that the things are settled. If punishment is to be meted out to a transgressor, it is there that the trial is held and judgment rendered.

Well, on, this night as we sat talking by the camp-fire, Abdi, our head-man, suddenly appeared and squatted down. Soon after up came Askar, who also squatted down, and we knew that we were in for some unusual sort of a *shauri*. It was then that Askar told of the strange mystery of the mountain.

Curious as to Our Home Life

On the Rim of the Crater

A Birthday Dinner

"Askar says," spoke Abdi, interpreting Askar's imperfect English, "that up in the mountain there is a big door and a great cave. He went up with a Frenchman, and the guides refused to go. Then the Frenchman threatened to kill them if they would not go. They were frightened, because all the natives die who go to the big door and see the boiling fountain through the door. Askar say all the natives ran away, but the Frenchman go on."

"Did Askar see the door?"

"Askar says he see the door and he see the fountain through some glasses. Then he ran away."

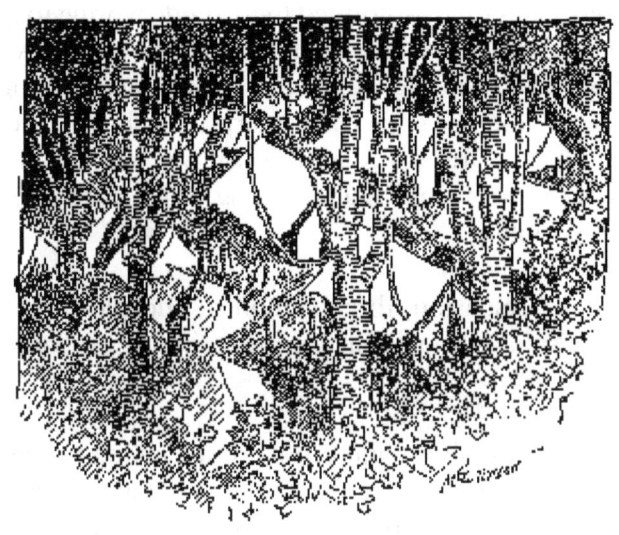

Camp in the Forest

"Can Askar take us up to the cave and the big door?"

There was then a long discussion in Somali between Askar and Abdi, which finally was briefly rendered into English. Askar would show us the way.

We then sent for the sultan of the Ketosh tribe and interviewed him. He was singularly reticent about the subject, and both he and the other natives called in used all their crude intelligence to discourage any attempt to go up into those districts that were so full of strange, forbidding influences. They said there were no trails, and when we said we would go anyway, they said there was a trail, but that it was so tangled with undergrowth and vines that one had to creep through it, like an animal. We still said we would go, and told the sultan to get us guides, for which we would pay well.

All this happened while we were in the Ketosh village that lies on the slope of the mountain just beneath the great rock wall, a thousand feet high, whose upper rim is honeycombed with the ancient caves of the aborigines. For days we had stopped there, endeavoring to get food and guides, and for days the sultan and his people had placed every obstacle in the way of our ascending higher the mysterious and comparatively unknown mountain. The great rock escarpment shut off the view of the peaks beyond, but we felt that if once we could scale the first precipitous slope we would find traveling much easier on the gentle slope of the mountain.

At last, after persuasion, threats, money, and pleading had in turn been tried, the sultan brought his son and said that his son would guide us.

The son was the craftiest and crookedest looking native I had seen in Africa. After one look at him, you were filled with such distrust and suspicion that you would hardly believe him if he said he thought it was going to rain, or that crops were looking up.

With this man as a guide, and with four more who were tempted by the bright red blankets we gave, our caravan started on one of the strangest and perhaps most foolhardy trips that presumably sane people ever made. In the first place, probably fewer than half a dozen white men had ever ascended Mount Elgon. There were no adequate maps of the region, and the one we had was woefully inaccurate. It was made as if from telegraphic description, and the only thing in which it proved trustworthy was that there was a mountain there and that it was about fourteen thousand two hundred feet high, and that the line separating British East Africa from Uganda ran through the crater at the top.

Our delay at the Ketosh village had greatly reduced our food supplies for the porters, and there was only enough left to last six days. In that time we should have to ascend the mountain and descend to some place where food supplies could be procured. It all looked quite quixotic. We bought two bullocks, a sheep, and a goat, and, with our guides ahead, our entire *safari* of over a hundred souls turned toward the grim heights that shot up before us.

Up to the Rim of the Crater

The trail for the first thousand feet of ascent was steep and hard to climb. The rocks high above us were specked with natives, who gazed down in wonder at the strange spectacle. These were the cave-dwellers. After an hour or more we reached the crest of the rim and then continued through elephant grass ten feet high, then dense forest, and finally through miles of clean, cool, shadowy bamboos—always steadily climbing. The trail was fairly good and our progress was encouraging.

In the Belt of Bamboo

Giant Cactus Growth In the Crater

Up Twelve Thousand Feet in the Crater

There were many elephant pits in the bamboo forest, but they were all ancient ones, half-filled with decayed leaves and obviously unused for half a century or more. From some of them fairly large-sized trees had grown. Sometimes in the midst of these great, silent, light-green forests we came upon giant trees, tangled and gnarled, with trunks twenty or thirty feet in circumference. In vain we looked for the impassable trail the natives had warned us to expect.

Late in the afternoon we came to a wonderful cave, over the mouth of which a wonderful fan-shaped waterfall dropped seventy feet or more. My aneroid barometer indicated an elevation of eighty-two hundred feet, showing that we had climbed twenty-seven hundred feet since morning. We found a little clearing in the bamboo forest and pitched our tents on ground that sloped down like the roof of a house. The clearing was barely fifty yards long, yet our twenty or more tents were pitched, our horses tethered in the middle, and the camp-fires crackled merrily as the chill air of night came down upon us. From the forest came the multitude of sounds that told of strange birds and animals that were out on their nocturnal hunt for food.

Early in the morning the *safari* was sent on with the guides while we remained to explore the cave. It was an immense cavern, with an entrance hall, or foyer, about thirty feet high and a hundred feet in length. Along the inner edge were the crumbling remains of little mud and wattle huts that had been occupied by people a long time before. Beyond this great entrance hall were passages that led into other vast, echoing caverns with domes like those of a cathedral.

Countless thousands of bats darted about us as our voices broke the silence of ages, and in places the deposits of bats were two or three feet deep. It staggered one's senses to think how long these creatures had dwelt within the labyrinth of caverns and passageways.

We explored the cave for a quarter of a mile or so, stumbling, stooping, climbing, and sliding down precipitous slopes. Far off in the darkness sounded the steady drip, drip, drip of water, and several times our progress was stopped by black lakes into which a tossed stone would tell of depths that might be almost bottomless. We fired our shotguns and the loosened dirt and rocks and the thunder of thousands of bats' wings were enough to terrify the senses.

There is no telling how many centuries or ages these caverns have stood as they stand to-day. Doubtless the wild tribes of the mountain have occupied them for thousands of years, and doubtless a thousand years from now the descendants of these tribes of people and bats will still be there in the cisternlike caverns with the broad fan of sparkling water spreading like a beautiful curtain across the great archway of an entrance.

That night, after hours of climbing through great forests and across grassy slopes gay with countless varieties of beautiful and strange flowers, we pitched our camp on a wind-swept height eleven thousand feet up. The peaks of the mountain rose high above us only a mile or so farther on.

When the night fell the cold was intense, and we huddled about the camp-fire for warmth. Around each of the porters' camp-fires the humped-up natives crouched and dreamed of the warm valleys far below in the darkness. I suppose the cold made them irritable, for just as we were preparing to turn in there suddenly came a succession of screams from one of the groups—screams of a boy in mortal terror. The sounds breaking out so unexpectedly in the silent night were enough to freeze the blood in one's veins. I never heard such frantic screams—like those that might come from a torture-chamber.

One of the porters had become infuriated by one of the *totos*—small boys who go along to help the porters—and had started in to beat him. The boy was probably more frightened than hurt, but the matter was one demanding instant punitive action. So Abdi immediately inflicted it in a most satisfying manner.

Once more the silence of the mountain fell upon the camp, but it was hours before the shock to one's senses could be forgotten. I never before, nor never again expect to hear screams more harrowing or terrifying.

The next day a Martian sitting upon his planet with a powerful glass might have seen the amazing sight of three horses, one mule, two bullocks, a goat, and a sheep, preceded and followed by over a hundred human beings, painfully creep over the rim of the crater and breathlessly pause before the great panorama of Africa that lay stretched out for hundreds of miles on all sides. It was as though an army had ascended Mont Blanc, and thus Hannibal crossing the Alps was repeated on a small scale.

Leaving our horses on the rim of the crater, a few of us climbed the highest peak, fourteen thousand three hundred and seventy-five feet high, as registered by my aneroid barometer, and stood where very few had stood before. Even the official height of the mountain, as given on the maps, was found to be inaccurate, and illustrated how vaguely the geographers knew the mountain.

That night we camped in the crater, twelve thousand feet up, and washed in a boiling sulphur spring that sprang from the rocks on the Uganda side. Perhaps this was the boiling fountain the superstitious natives feared, for it was the only one we saw. And perhaps the great gorge through which the river Turkwel, or Suam, flowed on its long journey north was the door that Askar had told us about. It was the only door we saw, but Askar said the door he meant was away off somewhere else, and he was so vague and confused in his bearings that we felt his information was unreliable.

The crater of Mount Elgon has long since lost any resemblance to a volcanic crater. It is a great valley, or bowl, surrounded by a lofty rim that in reality is a considerable chain of mountains. The bowl is two or three miles long and as much wide, with tall grass growing on the small hills inside and thousands upon thousands of curious cactus-like trees. Several mountain streams tumble down from the gorges between the peaks and, uniting, flow out of the big gap in one stream, the river Turkwel, which separates Uganda from British East Africa.

In the Crater of Mount Elgon

Mount Elgon is not an imposing mountain and on most occasions there is no snow on its peaks. Only one time during the several weeks that we were in sight of it was its summit capped with snow. A few species of small animals live in the crater, but no human beings. At night ice formed in the little pools where we camped and a furious wind, biting cold, swept down from the peaks and eddied out of the great gap where the Turkwel flows.

To all of our *safari* it was a welcome hour when we struck camp, preparatory to leaving the crater for the lower levels. The guides said there were only two ways out—one by the Turkwel gorge and the other by the route up which we came. The former might lead us far from any sources of food supplies, which by that time were becoming imperatively necessary, and the latter was undesirable unless as a last resort. After some deliberation we resolved to climb over the eastern rim and strike for the Nzoia River. No one had ever been known to take this course, but we felt that we could cut our way out and make trails sufficient to follow.

The guides refused to go, because by doing so they would enter a district where they might encounter tribes that were hostile to their own. On one side of this mountain there was a bitter tribal war even then under way. So we cheerfully said good-by to the Elgonyi guides and slowly climbed the rock rim and started for the unknown.

A Deserted Wanderobo Village

Where We Had Our Thanksgiving Day Lunch

For two days we climbed downward, sometimes along ancient elephant trails and sometimes along the sheep trails made by the flocks of mountain tribes. Several times we came upon deserted Wanderobo villages, and it was evident the natives who occupied them were abandoning their homes in terror before our descending column. Sometimes we groped our way through great forests in which there was no trail to follow, and sometimes we cut our way through dense jungle thickets like a solid wall of vegetation.

Galloping Lions

Upon several occasions we came to impassable places where an abrupt cliff would necessitate a tiresome return and a new attempt. Once we came to a little clearing in the vast forest where the grass was like a lawn and where towering trees rose like the arches of a great cathedral a hundred feet above. It was the most beautiful, serene and majestic spot I have ever seen. Even the religious grandeur of Nikko's cryptomeria aisles was incomparable to this.

One afternoon our column found itself hopelessly lost in a jungle growth so dense that one could penetrate it only by cutting a tunnel through, and for hours we hacked and hacked and made microscopic progress. At last the head of the column came to an abrupt drop of a couple of hundred feet which seemed an effectual bar to all further progress. The cliff fell off at an angle of sixty degrees, with the slope densely matted with heavy scrub and underbrush. It was necessary either to retrace our steps through that long and heart-breaking jungle or else find a way down the cliff. The water was gone and the horses must be got to water before night.

Then, followed the most dramatic episode of our trip. We simply fell over the cliff, plunging, caroming, and ricocheting down through the masses of vegetation. How the horses got down I shall never know and shall always consider as a miracle. And how the burden-bearing porters managed to get their loads down is even more of a mystery.

Somewhere down below we heard the cry of a baby!

That meant that there must be human habitation near and, of course, a mountain stream, and perhaps guides to lead us out of the mountain fastness. A few moments more of falling and sliding and plunging, and the advance guard came into a tiny clearing where a fire was burning. A rude Wanderobo shack, built around the base of a towering tree from which fell great festoons of giant creepers, stood in the center of the clearing. Some food, still hot, was found in the vessels in which it had been cooking. The people had fled and had been swallowed up in the silent depths of the forest.

Coming Down the Mountain

We called and shouted, but no answer came. Some of our porters proceeded to rob the shack of its store of wild honey, but were apprehended in time and were threatened with violent punishment if it continued. Then we prepared to make camp. There was no space for our tents, and trees had to be cut down and a little clearing made. Here the tents were huddled together, clinging to the sloping mountain side. Darkness fell, and then a most wonderful thing happened.

One of the tent boys who was searching for firewood in the darkening forest found a little naked baby, barely three months old. It had been thrown away as its mother, as she thought, fled for her life. The baby was brought into camp, wrapped up, and cared for, and it will never know how near it came to being devoured by a leopard or a forest hog. It was the crying of this baby that we heard, and we assumed that its mother had cast it aside so that its wailing would not betray the hiding-place of the remainder of her family. One can only imagine what her terror must have been to make this sacrifice in the common interest.

Now, a three-months-old baby is a good deal of a problem for a *safari* to handle. In our equipment we had made no provision for the care of infants. We could wrap it up and keep it warm, and feed it canned milk, but I imagine the proper care of a little babe requires even more than that. It was imperative that we find the mother before the baby died.

A Tent Boy Found It

So we first enjoined our mob of porters, who are chronically noisy, to be quiet under penalty of a severe *kiboko* punishment. We then sent out Kavirondo, the big, good-natured porter who always acted as our interpreter when dealing with the natives of the mountain district. He spoke the dialects of the Wanderobo tribes. He was a messenger of peace, and he was told to shout out through the forest that we were friendly, that we had the baby, and that the mother should come and get it. We felt absolutely certain that the sound of his voice would carry to where the mother was hidden.

For an hour or more we heard the strong voice of Kavirondo crying out his message of peace, and yet no answering cry came from the black depths of the forest. It began to look as if we were one little black baby ahead. In the meantime the baby was behaving beautifully. It was wrapped warmly in a bath towel and seemed to enjoy the attention it was receiving. Some one suggested that we leave it in the shack and then all retire so that the mother could creep in and recover it. But this had one objection—a leopard might creep in first.

We cooked our dinner and away off in the forest came the echoing shouts of Kavirondo. The camp settled down to quiet and the campfires twinkled among the towering trees. Then some one rushed in to say that the father and mother had come in.

"Kavirondo"

Outlined Against the Sky

A Reception Committee

Kavirondo had restored the baby! There was an instant impulse to rush down to see the glad reunion, but better counsel prevailed. Such a charge, *en masse*, even though friendly, might frighten the natives away. So Akeley alone went down and assured the father and mother that we were friendly and that nothing would harm them. And when he came back it was to report that the parents and the little baby were peacefully installed in their forest home again.

She Threw Her Baby Away

Early in the morning we went down to see our strange friends. They had greatly increased in number during the night. There were now one man, two of his wives, an old woman, and eight children, and the tiny baby. All fear had vanished, and they seemed certain that no harm was likely to come to them.

The man was a good-looking, strongly built native with fine honest eyes. The women were comely and the children positively handsome. I have never seen such a healthy, fine-eyed, well-built assortment of childhood, ranging all the way from three months up to eight or nine years of age. He was the president of the Anti-Race Suicide Club. We gave them all presents—beads to the children and brass wire to the women. We also made up a little fund of rupees for the baby, although money seemed to mean nothing to any of them. They had never seen white men before and probably knew nothing of metal money. Beads and brass wire were the only currency they knew. We tried to photograph them, but the shades in the forest were deep and the light too was bad for successful pictures.

Little by little we got their story.

There was warfare between the forest people and the savage Kara Mojas to the north. Neither side could ever tell when a band of the foe would swoop down upon them, killing the men, stealing the sheep and seizing the women. Only a few months before one of the Kara Mojas had come in and stolen some sheep and in return our Wanderobo friend had sallied forth, killed the Kara Moja, and captured his wife. It was the latter who was now the mother of the little baby, and she seemed quite reconciled to the change.

The Wanderobos' Home

When, the night before, the little family around the camp-fire heard the crashing of brushes and the hacking of underbrush and the shouts of our porters they thought a great force of the Kara Mojas was upon them. So they fled in terror. The baby cried, and, fearful that its wails would betray their hiding-place, they had cast it away in the bushes. Then they had fled into the depths of the forest and, huddled together in silent fear, waited in the hope that the Kara Mojas would leave.

Finally they heard Kavirondo's shouts and then after hours of indecision they decided to come in.

That is the end of the story. The Wanderobo, grateful to us, led us by secret trails out of the wilderness, or as far as he dared to go. He led us to the edge of the enemy's country and then returned to his forest home.

In a couple of days of hard marching, one of which was through soaking torrents of rain, without food for ten hours, we reached the Nzoia River. Our mountain troubles were overs.

CHAPTER XVIII
ELECTRIC LIGHTS, MOTOR-CARS AND FIFTEEN VARIETIES OF WILD GAME. CHASING LIONS ACROSS COUNTRY IN A CARRIAGE

NAIROBI is a thriving, bustling city, with motor cars, electric lights, clubs, race meets, balls, banquets, and all the frills that constitute an up-to-date community. Carriages and dog-carts and motorcycles rush about, and lords and princes and earls sit upon the veranda of the leading hotel in hunting costumes. Lying out from Nairobi are big grazing farms, many of them fenced in with barbed wire; and the peaceful rows of telegraph poles make exclamation points of civilization across the landscape. It doesn't sound like good hunting in such a district, does it? Yet this is what actually happened:

We had discharged our *safari*, packed up our tents, and were just ready to start to Mombasa to catch a ship for Bombay. A telegram unexpectedly arrived, saying that the boat would not sail until three days later, so we decided to put in two or three more mornings of shooting out beyond the limits of the city.

We got a carriage, a low-necked vehicle drawn by two little mules. It was driven by a young black boy, and we got another boy from the hotel to go along for general utility purposes. Into this vehicle we placed our guns, and at seven o'clock in the morning drove out of the town. In fifteen or twenty minutes we had passed through the streets and had reached the pleasant roads of the open plains. Soon we passed the race-track and then bowled merrily along between peaceful barbed-wire fences. Occasional groups of Kikuyus were tramping along the road, bringing in eggs or milk to Nairobi. A farm-house or two lay off to either side, and once or twice we passed boys herding little bunches of ostriches.

At about a quarter to eight we drove up the tree-lined avenue of a farm-house and a pleasant-faced woman responded to our knock. We asked for permission to shoot on the farm and were told that we were quite welcome to shoot as much as we wished.

Five minutes later, less than an hour's drive from Nairobi, we drove past a herd of nearly sixty impalla. They watched us gravely from a distance of two hundred yards. At this point we left the well-traveled road and drove into the short prairie grass that carpeted, the Athi Plains. The carriage bumped pleasantly along, and as we reached a little rise a few hundred feet away, the great stretch of the plains lay spread out before us.

Mount Kenia, eighty or ninety miles north, was clear and bright with its snow-capped peaks sparkling in the early sunlight. Off to its left rose the Aberdare Range, with the dominating peak of Kinangop; to its right rose the lone bald uplift of Donyo Sabuk, and to the east were the blue Lukenia Hills. The house-tops of Nairobi waved miragically in the valley, with a low range of blue hills beyond. Across the plains ran the row of telegraph poles that marked the course of the railway and a traveling column of smoke indicated the busy course of a railway train. This was the setting within which lay the broad stretches of the Athi Plains, billowing in waves like a grass-covered sea.

A Nest of Ostrich Eggs

A Herd of Ostriches

We Bumped Merrily Along

As we drove along big herds of zebras paused in their grazing to regard the carriage as it merrily bumped across the hills. As long as we remained in the vehicle they showed no alarm, for they had seen many carriages along the neighboring roads. It was only when the carriage stopped that they showed an apprehensive interest. Great numbers of Coke's hartebeest watched us with humorous interest. An eland grazed peacefully upon a distant hill, and a wart-hog trotted away as we approached. Immense numbers of Thompson's gazelle skipped away merrily and then turned to regard us with widespread ears and alert eyes. Two Grant's gazelles were seen, while far off upon a grassy hillside were many wildebeest—the animal that we were seeking. It was impossible to get close enough to shoot effectively, and after a time we gave up our attempts in that direction.

The wildebeest, although living so near Nairobi, are most wild, and with miles of plains stretching out upon all sides it is easy for them to keep several hundred yards of space between themselves and danger. We spent a couple of hours of fruitless stalking and then were obliged to hurry back to town in order to be at the hotel when the tiffin bell rang.

I had not yet secured a Thompson's gazelle, so we stopped and each of us shot one on our way to the road. Then we returned to town. People along the streets regarded us with surprised interest, for there were two gazelles hanging out of the carriage and our four rifles gave the vehicle an incongruously warlike aspect.

Shooting Wildebeest (Cross Marks Location of Wildebeest, Outward Bound)

The next morning at seven o'clock we were again in our carriage. We drove out to the same place and at a few minutes after eight we were amazed to see a wild dog rise from the grass and look at us. We hastily jumped out of the carriage and walked toward him. In a moment a number of others rose from the grass, until we saw seventeen of them. This animal is seldom seen by sportsmen, and I believe it is considered quite rare. In four months only one of our party had previously seen any. Sometimes they savagely attack human beings, and when they do their attack is fierce and hard to repel. They watched us narrowly as we approached them and then moved slowly away. They seemed neither afraid nor ferocious.

We each shot and missed. The pack split, and Stephenson followed one little bunch while I followed another. My course led me toward a shallow, rock-strewn nullah, and once or twice I fired again at the wild dogs. But I couldn't hit them. There was nothing remarkable in my failure to make a good shot, but Stephenson, who is a celebrated rifle shot, seemed to be equally unfortunate in his work. He was some distance away and his bullets would not go where he wanted them to go.

Suddenly my attention was riveted upon three forms that walked slowly out of the nullah and climbed the slope on the other side, about three hundred and fifty yards away. I was transfixed with amazement and could hardly believe my eyes.

They were lions!

One was a female and the other two immense males. They were walking slowly, and once or twice they stopped to look back at me. Then they resumed their stately retreat.

As soon as I recovered from my astonishment I shouted to Stephenson, who had been lured far away by the wild dogs.

"*Simba!*" I yelled, pointing to the three lions.

He seemed not to comprehend, and I saw him reluctantly turn from the dogs and fix his glasses upon the direction I indicated. In no time he was hurrying up to join me, and we hastily formed a plan of campaign. The lions had now disappeared over the brow of the hill. I looked at my watch and the hour was not yet nine o'clock. We were still in sight of the distant house-tops of Nairobi. It seemed unbelievable.

We crossed the nullah and the carriage jolted down and across a few minutes later. We took our seats and studied the plains with our glasses. The lions were not in sight. Then we studied the herds of game and saw that many of them were looking in a certain direction. We drove in that direction and whipped up the mules to a lively trot. In a few minutes Stephenson picked up the three lions far to the left, where they were slowly making their way toward another ravine a mile or so beyond.

Then began one of the strangest lion hunts ever recorded in African sporting annals.

You may have read of the practice of "riding" lions. Doctor Rainsford, in his splendid book on lion hunting, describes this thrilling sport in such vivid words that you shiver as you read them. Mounted men gallop after the lion, bring it to bay, and then hold it there until the white hunter comes up to a close range and shoots it. In the meantime the cornered beast is charging savagely at the horsemen, who trust to the speed and quickness of their mounts to elude the angry rushes of the infuriated animal. It is a most spectacular method of lion hunting and is only eclipsed in danger and daring by the native method of surrounding a lion and spearing it to death.

A Kikuyu Woman Uses Her Head

On the Athi Plains

It Was a Rakish Craft

To my knowledge, no one has ever "galloped" a lion in a carriage drawn by two mules, and probably few hunters have ever galloped three lions at one time under any conditions.

It was a memorable chase. The mules were lashed into a gallop and the carriage rocked like a Channel steamer. We were gaining rapidly and the distance separating us from the lions was quickly diminishing. It seemed as if the three lions were not especially eager to escape, for they moved away slowly, as if half-inclined to turn upon us.

It Rocked Like a Channel Steamer

We hoped to overtake them before they reached the ravine or such uneven ground as would compel us to abandon the carriage.

Five hundred yards! Then four hundred yards, and soon three hundred yards. The mules were doing splendidly, and we knew that we should soon be within good shooting distance. At two hundred and fifty yards the largest of the two males, a great, black-maned lion, stopped and turned toward us. His two companions continued moving away toward the ravine.

Thinking it a good moment to strike, we leaped from the carriage and knelt to fire. Stephenson shot at the big black-mane and I at the male that was retreating. Both shots missed. The black-mane resumed his retreat and we got in a couple more ineffectual shots before the three lions disappeared over the brow of the ravine.

At Two Hundred and Fifty Yards

Once more in the carriage and another wild gallop as far as the vehicle would go. For a few moments we lost sight of the lions, but presently we saw them climbing up the opposite slope, four hundred yards away. It was a long distance to shoot, but we hoped to bring them to bay at least by wounding them into a fighting mood. The large lion turned and swung along the brow of the hill; the others disappeared over the opposite side, but they soon reappeared some distance farther to the right.

Little spurts of dirt showed where our bullets were striking. Once I kicked up the ground just under him and once a shot from Stephenson passed so close to his nose that he ducked his head angrily.

We became frantic with eagerness and continued disappointment. The thought of losing the finest lion we had seen on the whole trip was maddening, yet it seemed impossible to hit him.

Then he disappeared and probably rejoined his companions in a retreat that led down into the ravine where it wound far away from us. There were patches of reeds in the ravine and it was there that I thought they would hide.

Sending the carriage in a wide detour, we climbed across a spur of the ravine and tried to pick up the trail. Once I fell upon the rocks that lined the steep sides of the gully and cut my hand so deeply that the scar will always remain as a reminder of that eventful day. Stephenson kept to the top of the ridge, believing that the lions would continue across the ravine; I went into the ravine, thinking they would take cover in the reeds and might be scared out with a shot or two.

But nothing could be seen of them, and after half an hour we rejoined on the top of the hill, where a wide view of the whole country was revealed.

We sat down in despair. The greatest chance of the whole trip was gone.

"That's the last we'll see of them," said I oracularly as I sat upon a stone. My hand was covered with blood, but alas! it was mine and not the lion's.

The carriage appeared and we held a prolonged consolation meeting. Suddenly our general utility boy, Happy Bill, uttered a low cry of warning. We turned, and there, in the valley ahead of us, the three lions were again seen. They had evidently passed through the reeds without stopping and had continued across only a few yards from where we were now standing.

Fate seemed determined to give us plenty of chances to get these lions. Again we opened fire on them at about four or five hundred yards. My big-gun ammunition was gone, so I fired with my .256.

No result! The distance was too great and our bombardment was fruitless. The black-maned lion was in a bad humor and repeatedly turned as if intent to stop and defend his outraged dignity. In a few moments the three lions disappeared in the tall grass that fringed a big reed bed many acres in extent.

For an hour we raked the reed bed with shot, hoping to drive them from cover. But that was the last we saw of the lions. A little bunch of waterbuck does were scared up, but nothing else. The lions were now safe, for nothing less than fifty beaters could hope to dislodge them from the dense security of the swamp.

It Would Have Been Historic

Talk about dejection! Our ride back to town was as mournful as a ride could be. We thought of the glory of driving through the streets of Nairobi with a lion or two hanging over the back of the carriage. It would have been historic. Citizens would have talked of it for years. It would have taken an honored place in the lion-hunting literature of Africa, for no lion hunters have ever pursued a band of lions in a carriage and brought back a carriage-load of them.

We almost regretted having had the chance that we so heartbreakingly lost.

But we told about it when we struck town, and before the day was over it was the topic in hotels and clubs throughout the whole town of Nairobi. Everybody who had a gun was resolved to go out the next day, and interest was at a fever pitch.

We went out again the following morning, shot at wildebeests at all known ranges, from two hundred yards up to five hundred yards—but our luck was against us. We came back empty-handed, and our chief reward for the morning's work was the great privilege of seeing both Mount Kenia, ninety miles north, and Kilima-Njaro, nearly two hundred miles southeast, as clear as a cameo against the lovely African sky.

The lesson of this story is not so much a review of bad shooting or of bad luck. The thing that seems most noteworthy is that within six or seven miles from Nairobi, nearly all the time within sight of the housetops of that town, we had seen fifteen varieties of wild game, some of which were present in great numbers.

- Wildebeest
- Hartebeest
- Hyena
- Jackal
- Thompson's Gazelle
- Lion
- Rabbit
- Waterbuck
- Impalla
- Giant Bustard
- Ostrich

Wart-hog

Wild Dog

Steinbuck

Grant's Gazelle

Surely there is still some game left in Africa.

CHAPTER XIX
THE LAST WORD IN LION HUNTING. METHODS OF TRAILING, ENSNARING AND OTHERWISE OUTWITTING THE KING OF BEASTS. A CHAPTER OF ADVENTURES

IF some one were to start a correspondence course in lion hunting he would give diagrams and instructions showing how to kill a lion in about six different styles—namely:

> The boma method.
>
> The tall grass method.
>
> The riding method.
>
> The tree method.
>
> The lariat method.
>
> The spear method.

This list does not include the Ananias method, formerly popular.

The tree and boma methods are much esteemed by those sportsmen who wish to reduce personal danger to the least common denominator—the sportsmen who think discretion is the better part of valor and a hunter in a tree is worth two in the bush. The sportsman who confines himself to the tree method is entitled to receive a medal "for conspicuous caution in times of danger," and the loved ones at home need never worry about his safe return. For safe lion hunting the "tree" method would get "first prize," while the "boma" method would receive honorable mention.

The "tall grass" method is less popular in that the lion has some show and often succeeds in getting away to tell about it. It involves danger to all concerned.

Spearing Lions

The "riding" method is also dangerous, for in it the hunter endeavors to "round up" or "herd" a lion by riding him to a standstill. When the lion is fighting mad he stops and turns upon his persecutors. This is when the obituary columns thrive.

The "lariat" method is not as yet in general vogue, but I understand that "Buffalo" Jones, an American, succeeded in roping a lion as they rope cattle out west. It sounds diverting.

A Dead Lion Is a Sign for Jubilation

A Dethroned King of Beasts

The "spear" method is that employed by natives, who, armed with spear and shield, surround a lion and then kill it with their spears. They invariably succeed, but not until a few of the spear-bearers are more or less Fletcherized by the lion. This method does not appeal to those who wish to get home to tell about it, and need not be considered at length in any correspondence course.

The Tree Method

The tree method is comparatively simple. You build a platform in a tree and place a bait near it. Then you wait through the long, silent watches of the night for Felis Leo to appear. The method has few dangers. The chief one lies in falling asleep and tumbling out of the tree, but this is easily obviated by making the platform large enough for two or three men, two of whom may stretch out and sleep while the other one remains awake and keeps guard.

When I went to Africa I resolved never to climb a tree. Later I resolved to try the tree method in order to get experience in a form of lion hunting that has many advocates among the valiant hunters who want lion skins at no expense to their own.

Of course, there are some perils connected with this method of lion slaying. Mosquitoes may bite you, causing a dreadful fever that may later result in death in some lingering and costly form. Also the biting ants may pursue you up to your aery perch and take small but effective bites in many itchable but unscratchable points. These elements of danger are about the only ones encountered in the tree method of lion hunting, but then who could expect to kill lions without some degree of personal discomfort?

My one and only tree experience was not particularly eventful. A large and commodious platform was built in the forks of a great tree in a district where the questing grunt of lions could be heard each night. The platform was comfortable; it only needed hot and cold running water to be a delightful place to spend a tropic night.

I shot a hartebeest and had it dragged beneath the tree. Then my two native gunbearers and I made a satisfactory ascent to the platform. We had a thermos bottle filled with hot tea, and some odds and ends in the way of solid refreshments. We then stretched out in positions that commanded a view of the hartebeest and waited patiently for an obliging lion to come and be shot.

Night came on and soon the landscape became shadowy and indistinct. Trees and bushes fused into vague black masses and the carcass of the bait could be located only because it seemed a shade more opaque than the opaque gloom around it. The more you looked at it the more elusive and shifting it seemed. The sights of the rifle were invisible, and the only way one could find the sight was by aiming at a star and then carefully lowering the direction of the weapon until it approximately pointed at the carcass.

Of course, we were very still; even the stars were not more silent than we. And little by little the noises of an African night were heard, growing in volume until from all sides came the cries of night birds and the songs of insects and tree-toads. It was the apotheosis of loneliness. And thus we sat, with eyes straining to pierce the gloom that hedged us in. We could see no sign of life, yet all about us in those dark shadows there were thousands of creatures moving about on their nightly hunt.

Suddenly there came the soft crescendo of a hyena's howl some place off in the night. It was answered by another, miles away; then another, far off in a still different direction. The scent of the bait was spreading to the far horizon and the keen-scented carrion-eaters had caught it and were hurrying to the feast.

Then, after moments of waiting, the howls came from so near that they startled us. There seemed to be dozens of hyenas—a regular class reunion of them—yet not one could be seen in the "murky gloom." And then, a moment later, we heard the crunching of teeth and the slither of rending flesh, and we knew that a supper party of hyenas was gathered about the festal board below us. I was afraid that they would eat up the carcass and thus keep away the lions, so I fired a shot to scare them away. There was a quick rush of feet—then that dense, expectant silence once more. Soon some little jackals came and were shooed away. Then more hyenas came, were given their congé, and hurried off to the tall grass. And yet no lion. It was quite disappointing.

At midnight, far off to the north, came the grunting voice of a lion. I waited eagerly for the next sound which would indicate whether the lure of the bait was beckoning him on. And soon the sound came, this time much nearer, and after a long silence there was a sharp, snarling grunt of a lion, followed by the panic-stricken rush of a hundred heavy hoofs. The conjunction of sounds told the story as definitely as if the whole scene lay bared to view. The lion had leaped upon a hartebeest, probably instantly breaking its neck, while the rest of the herd had galloped away in terror. And it had all happened within two or three hundred yards of the tree—yet nothing could be seen.

At two o'clock the grunt of a lion was again heard far off to the south. It came steadily toward us, and at last there was no doubt about its destination. It was coming to the bait. How my eyes strained to pierce the darkness and how breathlessly I waited with rifle in readiness! But the lion only paused at the bait, and as I waited for it to settle down to its feast it went grunting away and the chance was gone. Perhaps it had already fed, or perhaps it was an unusually fastidious lion which desired to do its own killing.

An hour or two later, both gunbearers asleep and one snoring peacefully, I became aware of a large animal feeding at the bait.

Although no sound had preceded its coming, I thought it might be a lion, but feared that it was a hyena. I fired at the dark, shifting, black shadow and the roar of the big rifle shattered the silence like a clap of unexpected thunder. Then there was such a dense silence that it seemed to ring in one's ears.

Had I hit or missed? That could not be decided until daybreak, for it is the height of folly to climb down from a tree to feel the pulse of a wounded lion.

When daybreak came we made an investigation. Only the mangled remains of the carcass lay below. Later in the day some members of our party came across the dead body of a hyena lying about a hundred yards from the tree, partly hidden by a little clump of bushes. Its backbone was shattered by a .475 bullet.

Thus ended my first and only adventure in the "tree method."

The boma method is slightly more dangerous and much more exciting. A lot of thorn branches are twisted together in a little circle, within which the hunter sits and waits for his lion. As in the tree method, a bait is placed near the boma, twelve or fifteen yards away, and a little loophole is arranged in the tangle of thorn branches through which the rifle may be trained upon the bait.

The Boma Method

The lion can not get into the boma unless he jumps up and comes in from the top. It is the function of the hunter to prevent this strategic manœuver by killing the lion before he gets in. If he does not, he is likely to find himself engaged in a spirited hand-to-hand fight with an unfriendly lion in a space about as big as the upper berth of a sleeping-car.

My first boma was a meshwork of thorns piled and interwoven together with the architectural simplicity of an Eskimo igloo. When it was finished there didn't seem to be the ghost of a chance of a lion getting in; but at night, as I looked out, it seemed frail indeed. Some dry grass was piled inside, with blankets spread over it to prevent rustling; and when night came we three, myself and two gunbearers, wormed our way in and then pulled some pieces of brush into the opening after us. The rifles were sighted on the bait while it was still daylight and at a spot where the expected lion might appear. Then we waited.

The customary nocturne by birds, beasts and insects began before long, and several times hyenas and jackals came to the bait, but no lions. The boma was on the edge of a great swamp, miles in extent and a great rendezvous for game of many kinds. Theoretically, there couldn't be a better place to expect lions, but nary a lion appeared that night.

Upon a later occasion—Christmas night, it was—I watched from a boma near an elephant we had killed, but except for the distant grunting of lions, there was nothing important to chronicle.

Lion hunting goes by luck. One man may sit in a boma night after night without getting a shot, while another may go out once and bring back a black-mane. I spent two nights in a boma without seeing a lion; Stephenson spent seven nights and saw only a lioness. He held his fire in the expectation that the male was with her and would soon appear. Presently a huge beast appeared, vague in the dark shadows; he thought it was the male lion, shot, and the next morning found a large dead hyena.

Mrs. Akeley went out only once, had a night of thrilling experiences, and killed a large male lion. The lion appeared early in the evening and her first shot just grazed the backbone. An inch higher and it would have missed, but as it was, the mere grazing of the backbone paralyzed the animal, preventing its escape. All night long it crouched helplessly before them, twelve yards away, insane with rage and fury. Its roars were terrifying. A number of times she shot, but in the darkness none of the many hits reached a vital spot. Once in the night two other lions came, but escaped after being fired at.

As soon as daylight appeared and she could see the sights of her rifle she easily killed the lion. It was the largest one of the eleven killed in our hunting trip, and was killed with a little .256 Mannlicher, the same weapon with which she shot her record elephant on Mount Kenia.

In the tall-grass method, native beaters are sent in long skirmish line through swamps and such places as lions like to lay up in during the hours of daylight. The beaters chant a weird and rather musical refrain as they advance and thrash the high reeds with their sticks. Reedbuck, sometimes a bushbuck, frequently hyenas, and many large owls are driven out of nearly every good-sized swamp. The hunters divide, one or more on each side of the swamp and slightly ahead of the line of beaters. As the lion springs out it is up to the hunter nearest to it to meet it with the traditional unerring shot.

The Tree Method of Lion Shooting

Dragged a Zebra to the Boma

The Rifle Was Sighted on the Bait

In our experience we beat dozens of swamps and reed beds. Stephenson would take one side of the swamp, I the other, while Akeley with his moving-picture machine, would take the side best suited to photographic purposes. He got some wonderful results, two of which were records of the death of two lionesses.

Upon the first of these occasions the beaters had worked down a long stretch of swamp and had almost reached the end. Suddenly they showed an agitated interest in something in front of them. They thought it was a lion until an innocent by-stander made an unauthorized guess that it was a hyena. This reassured the beaters and they advanced boldly in the belief that it was a harmless hyena. My valor rose in proportion and for the same reason, and I strolled bravely over to the edge of the reeds where a little opening appeared. It was something of a shock to see two lions stroll suddenly into view. I fired, hitting the last one. Then they both disappeared in the reeds ahead.

It was amazing to note the sudden epidemic of caution upon the part of all concerned. The beaters refused to advance until Stephenson joined them with his big rifle. I moved forward on the side lines and the moving-picture machine reeled off yards of film.

A man has to appear brave when a camera is turned on him, but with two lions a few feet away there was not a tendency to advance with that impetuous dash that one would like to see in a moving picture of oneself. Anyway, I tried to keep up an appearance of advancing without actually covering much territory.

One of my gunbearers suddenly clutched my arm and pointed into the reeds. There, only a few feet away, was the tawny figure of a lion, either lying down or crouching. I fired and nearly blew its head off. It was the one I had wounded a few minutes before.

Photographed in Times of Danger

There was still the other lion in the reeds. So I joined the beaters while Stephenson came out and took a commanding position at the side of the reeds. In a moment or two there was a tawny flash and the lion was seen as it broke from the reeds and sprang away up the hill. It was on the opposite side of the reeds from Stephenson, but his first shot hit it and it stopped and turned angrily. In another instant it would have charged, but a second shot from his rifle killed it instantly. Both of the animals were young lionesses of the same age and nearly full grown.

Sometimes, when a lion is driven to bay in the tall grass at the end of a swamp, the beaters refuse to advance, and it then becomes necessary for the hunter to go in and take the lead. An occasion of this sort was among the most thrilling of my African experiences.

An immense swamp had been beaten out and nothing had developed until the beaters were almost at the end of the swamp. Extending from the end and joining it was a patch of wire-like reeds, eight or ten feet high and covering two or three acres. This high grass was almost impenetrable by a man, and it was only possible to go through it by throwing one's weight forward and crushing down the dense growth. The grass grew from hummocks, between which were deep water channels. An animal could glide through these channels, but a man must batter his way through the stockade of dense grass that spread out above.

It was in this place that the lion was first heard and the beaters refused to follow it in. Guttural grunts and snarls came from that uninviting jungle, and we knew that the only way to force the lion out was to go in and drive it out.

At about this time another lion came out of the swamp behind and loped up the hill. The saises were sent galloping after it to round it up, but they reappeared after a few moments and reported that it had got away in the direction of a huge swamp a mile or so beyond. We began to think we had struck a nest of lions.

Then we went in to drive out that lion in the deep grass. The native beaters, encouraged by seeing armed white men leading the way, came along with renewed enthusiasm. That grass was something terrible. One would hardly care to go through it if he knew that a bag of gold or a fairy princess awaited him beyond; with a lion there, the delight of the job became immeasurably less. We could not see three feet ahead. From time to time we were floundering down into channels of water hidden by the density of the grass. Some of these channels were two feet deep. And with each yard of advance came the realization that we were coming to an inevitable show-down with that lion. Akeley and I were in with the beaters, Stephenson was beyond the patch of grass to intercept the lion should it break forth, from cover.

It was not until we had nearly traversed the entire patch of reeds that the lion was found. It evidently lay silently ahead of us until we were almost upon it. Then, almost beneath my feet, came the angry and ominous growl, and my Somali gunbearer leaped in terror, falling as he did so. I expected to see a long, lean flash of yellow body and to experience the sensation of being mauled by a lion. All was breathlessly silent for a moment. Then a shot from Stephenson's rifle said that the lion had burst from the reeds and into view.

We pushed our way out to see what had happened.

The lion had come out, then turned suddenly back into the cover of reeds, working its way along the front of the beaters. For an instant Stephenson saw it and fired into the grass ahead of it without result.

The track of the lion was followed, but the animal had succeeded in getting around the beaters and back into the swamp. Fires were lighted, but the reeds were too green to burn except in occasional spots.

A few minutes later the saises, posted like sentinels high on the hills that flanked the swamp, saw the lion again and galloped down to head it off. It left the swamp and continued on down the rush-lined banks of a stream, zigzagging its way back and forth. After a pursuit of a couple of miles it was cornered in a small patch of reeds. Further retreat was impossible and it knew that it had to fight.

The moving-picture machine was set up on one side and I was detailed to guard that side. If the lion came out it was to be allowed to charge a certain distance, within forty feet, before I was to fire. If it didn't charge at us, but attempted to escape, it was to be allowed to run across the strip of open ground in front of the camera before I was to shoot.

Stephenson took his place on the other bank, twenty-five or thirty yards from the edge of the reeds. Then the beaters were told to advance, and they moved forward, throwing rocks and sticks into the reeds ahead of them. The lion appeared on Stephenson's side. Like a flash it sprang out. He fired and the lion stopped momentarily under the impact of a heavy ball. Then it sprang a few yards onward, when a second shot laid it out. The last shot was fired at less than twenty yards.

The moving-picture machine recorded the thrilling scene and there was an hour of great rejoicing and jubilation. The animal was an old lioness and the first shot had torn her lower jaw away and had gone into the shoulder. It is amazing that she was not instantly killed—but that's a way lions have. They never know when to quit.

CHAPTER XX
ABDULLAH THE COOK AND SOME INTERESTING GASTRONOMICAL EXPERIENCES. THIRTEEN TRIBES REPRESENTED IN THE SAFARI. ABDI'S STORY OF HIS UNCLE AND THE LIONS

OUR cook was a dark-complexioned man between whom and the ace of spades there was considerable rivalry. He was of that deadly night shade. He was the darkest spot on the Dark Continent. After dark he blended in with the night so that you couldn't tell which was cook and which was night.

His name was Abdullah, his nature was mild and gentle, and his skill in his own particular sphere of action was worthy of honorable mention by all refined eaters. He was about fifty or sixty years of age, five feet tall, with a smile varying from four to six inches from tip to tip. It was a smile that came often, and when really unfurled to its greatest width it gave the pleasing effect of a dark face ambushed behind a row of white tombstones.

When Abdullah joined our *safari* it was freely predicted that he would do well for the first month or so, after which he would fade away to rank mediocrity; but, strangely enough, he became better and better as time went on, and during our last two weeks was springing culinary coups that excited intense interest on our part. He had a way of assembling a few odds and ends together that finally merged into a rice pudding par excellence, while his hot cakes were so good that we spoke of them in rapt, reverential whispers. There wasn't a twinge of indigestion in a "three by six" stack of them, and when flooded with a crown of liquid honey they made one think of paradise and angels' choruses.

Quite naturally, in my wanderings of nine months there were moments when my thoughts dwelt upon such material things as "vittles," and it was instructive to compare the various kinds of food served on a dozen ships, a score of hotels, and a hundred camps. Some were good and some were bad, but as viewed in calm retrospect I think that Abdullah excelled all other chefs, taking him day in and day out.

Upon only three occasions was he vanquished, but these were memorable ones. As food is a pleasant topic, perhaps I may be pardoned if I dwell fondly upon these three red-letter days in my memory.

One was in Paris. The night that we started for Africa a merry little company dined at Henry's. That distinguished master was given *carte blanche* to get up the best dinner known to culinary science, and he had a day's start. Everything was delicious. The dinner was a symphony, starting in a low key and gradually working up in a stirring crescendo until the third course, where it reached supreme heights in climacteric effect. That third course, if done in music, would have sent men cheering to the cannon's mouth or galloping joyously in a desperate cavalry charge.

One of Our Askaris

Hassan Mohammed

The dish was called "poulet archduc," although I should have called it at least poulet archangel. In this divine creation Henry reached the Nirvana of good things to eat. I beseeched him for the recipe, which he cheerfully wrote out, so now I am happy to pass it along that all may try it. It really ought to be dramatized.

I transcribe it in M. Henry's own verbiage:

> The chicken must be well cleaned inside. Next put in it some butter, salt and pepper, a little paprika, and into full of sweet corn, then close the chicken. Next put it in a saucepan with other more sweet corn, against butter, salt, pepper, a little whisky; cook about half of one hour.
>
> The best sweet corn is the California sweet corn in can.

The sauce is done with white of chicken. Squeeze two yolks of eggs and butter like for a sauce mousseline and finish it with a little whisky.

And there you are.

The second occasion came some months later. We had been on *safari* for several weeks and had returned to Nairobi for two or three days. It was the "psychological moment" for something new in the way of food. The stage was all set for it, and it came in the form of a pudding that would have delighted all the gastronomes and epicures of history. We called it the Newland-Tarlton pudding, because it was the joint creation of Mrs. Newland and Mrs. Tarlton. One wrote the poetry in it and the other set it to music. We ate it so thoroughly that the plates looked as clean as new. Cuninghame was there, dressed up for the first time in months, and the way that pudding disappeared behind his burly beard was suggestive of the magic of Kellar or Herrmann.

The recipe of this pudding is worthy of export to the United States, so here it is. It really is a combination of two puddings, served together and eaten at the same time.

THE NEWLAND BANANA CUSTARD

Boil three large cupfuls of milk. Mix a tablespoonful of corn flour with a little cold milk just to make it into a paste. Add four eggs well beaten and mix together with three tablespoonfuls of sugar. Put into the boiled milk and stir until it thickens, but don't let it boil. When taken off add one teaspoonful of vanilla essence. Cut up ten bananas and put in a dish. Pour custard on when cool.

PRUNE SHAPE (A LA TARLTON)

Stew one-half pound prunes until quite soft. Remove stones and cut prunes small. Dissolve one-half ounce gelatin and add to one-quarter pound sugar, prunes, and kernels. Pour into wetted mold to cool, first adding one-half glass of sherry. Must be served with banana cream (the Newland).

The third occasion made memorable by a delicious epoch-making dish I shall not specify, as we have dined with many friends during the last nine months. Let it be sufficient if I say that it was at one of these dinners or luncheons.

In our varied gastronomical experiences we found that the cooking on the English ships was usually bad, while that on the German ships was good, excepting the ship that took us from Naples to Mombasa. The Dutch ships were the best of all and the Dutch hotels in Java were the best we struck outside of Paris and London. In comparison with the Hotel des Indes, in Batavia, all the rest of the hotels of the Orient can be mentioned only in a furtive way. It was a revelation of excellence, in perfect keeping with the charm and beauty of Java as a whole.

But we were speaking of things to eat.

At the Hotel des Indes they served us a modest little dish called rice tafel, or "rijs-tafel." You have to go to luncheon early in order to eat it before dinner time. It was served by twenty-four waiters, marching in single file, the line extending from the kitchen to the table and then returning by a different line of march to the kitchen. It was fifteen minutes passing a given point. Each waiter carried a dish containing one of the fifty-seven ingredients of the grand total of the rice tafel. You helped yourself with one arm until that got tired, then used the other. When you were all ready to begin your plate looked like a rice-covered bunker on a golf course.

The Rice Tafel in Java

Rice tafel is a famous dish in Java. It is served at tiffin, and after you have eaten it you waddle to your room in a congested state and sleep it off. After my first rice tafel I dreamed I was a log jam and that lumber jacks with cant hooks were trying to pry me apart.

As the recipe for rice tafel is not to be found in any cook book on account of its length, we give it here even if you won't believe it. To a large heap of rice add the following:

MEAT AND FISH

>Spiced beef, deviled soup meat, both fried with cocoanut shreds.

>Minced pork, baked.

>Fried fish, soused fish, and baked fish.

>Fried oysters and whitebait.

SPICES

>Red fish.

>Deviled shrimps, chutney.

>Deviled pistachio nuts.

>Deviled onions sliced with pimentos.
>
>Deviled chicken giblets.
>
>Deviled banana tuft.
>
>Pickled cucumbers.
>
>Cucumber plain (to cool the palate after hot ingredients).

FOWL, FRUIT, ETC.

>Roast chicken, plain.
>
>Steamed chicken with chilis.
>
>Monkey nuts fried in paste.
>
>Flour chips with fish lime (called grapak and kripak).
>
>Fried brinjals without the seeds.
>
>Fried bananas.

JUICES

>Yellow—(One) of curry powder with chicken giblets and bouillon.
>
>Brown—(Two) of celery, haricot beans, leeks and young cabbage.

One quart of American pale ale to drink during the "rice tafel."

Our cook Abdullah was not the only interesting type in our *safari*. Among our dusky colleagues there were thirteen different tribes represented. It was a congress of nations and a babel of tongues. Some of the porters became conspicuous figures early in the march, while some were so lacking in individuality that they seemed like new-comers even after four months out.

The "Chantecler" of Our Safari

Of this latter class Hassan Mohammed was not one.

Hassan was my chief gunbearer, and for pious devotion to the Mohammedan faith he was second to none. He was the "Chantecler" of our outfit. Every morning at four o'clock, regardless of the weather, he would crawl out of his tent, drape himself in a white sheet, and cry out his prayers to Mecca. It was his voice that woke the camp, and the immediate answer to his prayers was sometimes quite irreverent, especially from the Wakamba porters, who were accustomed to sit up nearly all night gambling.

Hassan was a Somali, strictly honest and faithful. He had the Somali's love of a rupee, and there was no danger or hardship that he would not undergo in the hope of backsheesh. It is the African custom to backsheesh everybody when a lion is killed, so consequently the Somalis were always looking for lions. Perhaps he also prayed for them each morning.

When we started we had four Somali gunbearers, each of whom rose at dawn to pray. As we got up in the high altitudes, where the mornings were bitter cold, the number of suppliants dwindled down to one, and Hassan was the sole survivor. No cold or rain or early rising could cool the fierce religious ardor that burned within him.

Long before daybreak we would hear his voice raised in a singsong prayer full of strange runs and weird minors. The lions that roared and grunted near the camp would pause in wonder and then steal away as the sound of Hassan's devotions rang out through the chilly, dew-laden dawn. And as if fifteen minutes of morning prayer was not enough to keep him even with his religious obligations, he went through two more long recitals in the afternoon and at night.

I sometimes thought that behind his fervent ardor there was a considerable pride in his voice, for he introduced many interesting by-products of harmony that sounded more or less extraneous to both music and prayer. Nevertheless, Hassan was consistent. He never lied, he never stole, and it was part of his personal creed of honor to stand by his master in case of danger. Somali gunbearers are a good deal of a nuisance about a camp, partly because they are the aristocrats of Africa and demand large salaries, but chiefly because they require certain kinds of food that their religion requires them to eat. This is often difficult to secure when far from sources of supplies, and in consequence the equilibrium of camp harmony is sorely disturbed.

They are avaricious and money loving to a deplorable degree, but there is one thing that can be said for the Somali. He will never desert in time of danger and will cheerfully sacrifice himself for his master. He has the stamina of a higher type of civilization, and in comparison to him the lately reclaimed savage is not nearly so dependable in a crisis.

I sometimes suspected that Hassan was not really a gunbearer, but was merely a "camel man" who was tempted from his flocks by the high pay that African gunbearers receive. Notwithstanding this, he was courageous, faithful, willing, honest, good at skinning, and personally an agreeable companion during the months that we were together. I got to like him and often during our rests after long hours afield we would talk of our travels and adventures.

Jumma, the Tent Boy

Abdullah, the Cook

One day we stopped at the edge of the Molo River. A little bridge crossed the stream and I remembered that the equator is supposed to pass directly across the middle of this bridge. It struck me as being quite noteworthy, so I tried to tell Hassan all about it. I was hampered somewhat because he didn't know that the world was round, but after some time I got him to agree to that fact. Then by many illustrations I endeavored to describe the equator and told him it crossed the bridge. He got up and looked, but seemed unconvinced as well as unimpressed. Then I told him that it was an imaginary line that ran around the world right where it was fullest—half way between the north pole and the south pole. He brightened up at this and hastened to tell me that he had heard of the north pole from a man on a French ship. As I persevered in my geographical lecture he gradually became detached from my point of view, and when we finished I was talking equator and he was talking about a friend of his who had once been to Rotterdam.

The lecture was a "draw." But I noticed with satisfaction that when we walked across the bridge he looked furtively between each crack as if expecting to see something.

It was rather a curious thing, speaking of Hassan, to observe the respect with which the other natives treated his daily religious devotions. He was the only one in camp who prayed—at least openly—and as he knelt and bowed and went through the customary form of a Mohammedan prayer there was never the slightest disposition to make fun of him. In a camp of one hundred white men I feel sure that one of them who prayed aloud three times a day would hardly have escaped a good deal of irreverent ridicule from those about him. The natives in our camp never dreamed of questioning Hassan's right to worship in any way he pleased and the life and activities of the camp flowed along smoothly as if unconscious of the white-robed figure whose voice sang out his praises of Allah. The whole camp seemed to have a deep respect for Hassan.

Abdi, our head-man, was also a Somali, but of a different tribe. He was from Jubaland and had lived many years with white men. In all save color he was more white than black. He was handsome, good-tempered, efficient, and so kind to his men that sometimes the discipline of the camp suffered because of it. It was Abdi's duty to direct the porters in their work of moving camp, distributing loads, pitching camp, getting wood for the big camp-fires, punishing delinquents and, in fact, to see that the work of the *safari* was done.

One night after we had been most successful in a big lion hunt during the day Abdi came to the mess tent, where we were lingering over a particularly good dinner. Abdi asked for his orders for the following day and then, seeing that we were in a talkative mood, he stopped a while to join in the stories of lion hunting.

After a time he told two of his own that he had brought from his boyhood home in Jubaland. They were so remarkable that you don't have to believe them unless you want to.

Abdi's Uncle and the Man-Eaters

ABDI'S STORY ABOUT HIS UNCLE AND THE LIONS

"Once upon a time my uncle, who was a great runner, encountered six man-eating lions sitting in the road. He took his spear and tried to kill them, but they divided, three on each side of the road. So he took to his heels. To the next town it was twelve hours' march, but he ran it in ten hours, the lions in hot pursuit every minute of the time. When he reached the town he jumped over the thorn bush zareba, and the lions, close behind him, jumped over after him and were killed by his spear, one after the other."

ABDI'S STORY ABOUT THE WILY SOMALI AND THE LION

"Once upon a time there was a Somali who was warned not to go down a certain road on account of the man-eating lions. But he started out, armed with knife and spear. For a week he marched, sleeping in the trees at night and marching during the day. One day he suddenly came upon a big lion sitting in the road. He stopped, sharpening a little stick which he held in his left hand. Then he wrapped his 'tobe' or blanket around his left hand and arm. He then advanced to the lion and when it opened its mouth to bite him he thrust the sharp stick inside, up and down, thus gagging the lion. Then with his two hands he held the lion by its ears for three days. He couldn't let go because the lion would maul him with its heavy paws. He was thus in quite a fix.

He Hastily Cut a Stick

"Finally another Somali came along and he asked the newcomer to hold the lion while he killed it with his spear. The other Somali consented and seized the lion by the ears. Then the first Somali laughed long and loud and said, 'I've held him three days, now you hold him three days.' Then he strolled down the road and disappeared. For seven days the second

Somali held the lion and then by the same subterfuge turned it over to a third Somali. By this time the lion was pretty tired, so after one day the Somali shook the lion hard and then took out his knife and stabbed it to death."

Sulimani was my second gunbearer. His name wasn't Sulimani, but some one gave him that name because his own Kikuyu name was too hard to pronounce and impossible to remember. Sulimani was quite a study. He had the savage's love of snuff, and when not eating or sleeping he was taking pinches of that narcotic from an old kodak tin. In consequence he had the chronic appearance of being full of dope. He walked along as though in a trance. He never seemed to be looking anywhere except at the stretch of trail directly in front of him. His thoughts were far away, or else there were no thoughts at all. I often watched him and wondered what he was thinking about.

Sulimani was really one of the best natural hunters in the whole *safari*. He had a native instinct for tracking that was wonderful; he had courage that was fatalistic, and he seemed to know what an animal would do and where it would go under certain conditions. Beneath that dopy somnolence of manner his senses were alert and his eyes were usually the first to see distant game.

He had originally been a porter when we started out, but I gave him a new suit of khaki and promoted him to the position of second gunbearer. As long as we were in touch with civilization he kept that khaki suit in a condition of spotlessness, but when we got out in the wilds, away from the girls, it soon became stiff with blood-stains and dirt. The natural savage instinct became predominant; he reverted to type.

His jaunty red fez was replaced by a headgear made of the beautiful skin of a Uganda cob. Ostrich and maribou feathers stuck out from the top, while upon his feet were sandals made from the thick skin of a waterbuck. A zebra tail was fashioned into a sheath for his skinning-knife, so that, little by little, he resolved himself back into a condition of savage splendor. He usually did most of my skinning, and that being dirty work, I was disposed to be tolerant with the disgraceful condition of his khaki suit.

Finally we approached civilization once more, and I told Sulimani that he'd have to clean up, otherwise the girls wouldn't like him. I gave him half a day off to wash his clothes, and he dutifully disappeared from society for that period. When he once more turned up he was resplendent in his clean clothes. As we marched along toward Nairobi he broke his long silence by bursting into song. For a day or two it was the wonder of the camp, but he was quite unconscious of it. Music was in his soul and the germ of love was churning it up. And so he sang as he marched along, and his thoughts were racing ahead of him to the "sing sing" girls who wait in Nairobi for returning porters with rupees to spend.

The general average of health in the *safari* was high. Only one porter died in the four months or more that we were out. But in spite of the low mortality there were many cases that came up for treatment. Akeley, with his long experience as a hunter and explorer, acted as the health department of the camp. His three or four remedies for all ills were quinine, calomel, witch-hazel, and zinc oxide adhesive plaster. And it was simply amazing what those four things could do when applied to the naturally healthy constitutions of the blacks. He cured a bowed tendon with witch-hazel and adhesive plaster in three or four days. A white man would have gone to a hospital for weeks.

There were two common complaints. One was fever, but the fiercest fever took to its heels when charged by General Quinine and General Calomel. The other and more common complaint rose from abrasions and cuts. There was always a string of porters lined up for treatment and each went away happy with large pieces of adhesive plaster decorating his ebony skin. A simple piece of this plaster cured the worst and most inflamed cut, and it was seldom that a man came back for a second treatment. The plaster remained on until, weeks afterward, it fell off from sheer weariness.

And once in a while there would be knife wounds, for whenever we killed a zebra as meat for the porters there would be a frenzied fight over the body. Each man, with knife out, was fighting for the choice pieces. It was like a scrimmage of human vultures—fighting, clawing, slashing and rending, with blood and meat flying about in a horrifying manner. I used to marvel that many were not killed, because each one was armed with a knife and each one was frenzied with savage greed. However, only once in a while did we have to treat the injured from this cause. Two men could fight for ten minutes over a piece of meat or a bone, but when finally the ownership was settled the victor could toss his meat to the ground with the certainty that no one else would take it.

Jumma was my tent boy—a Wakamba with filed teeth. Jumma is the Swahili word for Friday and is about as common a name in East Africa as John is in white communities. I suppose I ought to call him "my man Friday," but he was so dignified that no one would dream of taking such a liberty with him. Jumma's thoughts ran to clothes. He wore a neat khaki suit—blouse and "shorts," a pair of blue puttees, a pair of stout shoes, and a dazzling red fez, from which sprang a long waving ostrich feather. My key ring hung at his belt, while around his wrist a neat watch was fastened. The longest march, through mud and rain and wind and sun, would find him as trim and clean at the finish as though he had just stepped out of a bandbox. Jumma had the happy faculty of never looking rumpled, a trick which I tried hard to learn, but all in vain. He was as black as ebony, yet his features were like those of a Caucasian; in fact, he strikingly resembled an old Chicago friend.

Sulimani—Second Gunbearer

The Mess Tent

Where the Equator Crosses the Molo

Among our porters there were many types of features, and in a curious way many of them resembled people we had known at home. One porter had the eyes and expression of a young north-side girl; another had the walk and features of a prominent young Chicago man; and so on.

Saa Sitaa was one of our brightest porters. His name means "Six O'clock" in Swahili, six o'clock in the native reckoning being our noon and our midnight. Just why he was given this significant name I never discovered. Perhaps he was born at that hour. It always used to amuse me to hear Abdi calling out, "*Enjani hapa, Saa Sitaa*"—"Come here, Six O'clock."

Baa Baa was a porter who always used to sing a queer native chant in which those words were predominant. He would sing it by the hour while on the march, and before long his real name was replaced by the new one. Henceforth he will, no doubt, continue to be Baa Baa. He was promoted from porter to camera-bearer, but one day he could not be found when most needed, and he was reduced back to the ranks. I never heard him sing again. His heart was broken.

CHAPTER XXI
BACK HOME FROM AFRICA. NINETY DAYS ON THE WAY THROUGH INDIA, JAVA, CHINA, MANILA AND JAPAN. THREE CHOW DOGS AND A FINAL SERIES OF AMUSING ADVENTURES

AT last the day came for us to say good-by to the happy hunting grounds and return to the perils and dangers of civilization. Occasional newspapers had filtered into the wild places and in the peaceful security of our tents we had read of frightful mining disasters in America, of unparalleled floods in France, of the clash and jangle of rival polar explorers, of disasters at sea, of rioting and lynching in Illinois. Automobile accidents were chronicled with staggering frequency, and there were murmurs of impending rebellions in India, political crises in England, feverish war talk in Germany, volcanic threats from Mount Etna, and a bewildering lot of other dreadful things.

In contrast to this dire picture of life in civilized places, our pleasant days among the lions and wild beasts of Africa seemed curiously peaceful and orderly. Now we were to leave—to go back into the maelstrom of the busy places and bid farewell to our friendly savages and genial camp-fires. The Akeleys were remaining some months longer, but Stephenson and I were scheduled to leave.

Just Before Saying Good-by to My Horse

Manila Bay

The Boro Boedoer Ruins

There were a few busy days in Nairobi. The horses were sold, the porters were paid off, the trophies were prepared for shipment, and our camp outfits and guns were either sold or packed for their journey homeward. There were affectionate and rather tearful partings from good friends, then a quick railway trip to the coast and a day or two of waiting in Mombasa. The hunting was over. Now it was a mere matter of getting home in ninety days, and for variety's sake we elected to go home through India, Java, China, and Japan. I was curious to note the changes that those countries had undergone since I had last seen them years before.

We had some mild adventures. The first occurred in Mombasa, and concerns the strange conduct of two little white dogs that flashed in and out of our lives.

One day when I returned to my room in the hotel at Mombasa I was surprised to find that two small dogs had established themselves therein. The room boy knew nothing about them; the people around the hotel did not remember having ever seen them before. No clue to their owner was obtainable, and we regarded their advent as something of a mild kind of miracle. They played about the room as if they had long been there. When we went out they were at our heels and in the course of our wanderings through the old streets of the town the two dogs were always close at hand, or, rather, close at feet. When I worked in the room at the hotel they lay on the floor or played near my table and made no effort to rush away to the many temptations of the warm sunshine outside. I became much attached to them. Such steadfast devotion from strange dogs is always flattering.

Then our ship, the *Umzumbi*, South Africa to Bombay, came into the harbor and anchored a quarter of a mile out from the custom-house dock. We decided to go out and visit her and accordingly shut the door to prevent the two little dogs from joining us. Before we reached the dock they were with us, however, having escaped some way or other. And when we got into the rowboat to go out they looked appealingly after us from the dripping steps of the boat landing. We were sorry, but really we couldn't take them to the ship.

The Two Dogs of Mombasa

Suddenly there was a splash, and one of the little dogs was bravely swimming after us. He wasn't built for swimming, but he was making a gallant effort. We stopped and picked him up, a drippy but grateful little creature. Then we had to row back to get the other one. By much strategy we succeeded in getting on board the *Umzumbi* without taking them with us, but as we were not sailing until the afternoon we stayed on board only long enough to see that our state-room arrangements were satisfactory and to meet the chief steward.

On our way back through the town the dogs got lost from us, but when we reached the room at the hotel they were comfortably installed in the square of sunshine that streamed through the window. They refused to break home ties. Several more times that day we executed elaborate manœuvers to lose them without the painful formality of saying good-by. But all in vain. We tried to give them away and finally succeeded in persuading one woman from up Uganda way that they would be useful to her.

She was considering the matter when we, feeling like heartless criminals, stole away from the room, leaving it locked, and leaving two trustful and trusting little dogs incarcerated within. We told the proprietor of our dastardly conduct, but cautioned him not to liberate the captives until the steamer was hull down on the horizon. So by this time I suppose there are two little white dogs searching Mombasa for two missing Americans and wondering at the duplicity of human nature.

We imagined that the ship from Mombasa to Bombay would be nearly uninhabited by passengers. Few people are supposed to cross that part of the Indian Ocean. But when we embarked on the *Umzumbi* on February first we found the ship full. There were British army officers bound for India, rich Parsees bound from Zanzibar to Bombay, two elderly American churchmen bound from the missionary fields of Rhodesia to inspect the missionary fields of India; two or three traveling men, a South African legislator bound for India on recreation bent, and a few others.

After leaving Mombasa our travels were upon crowded ships, on crowded trains, and from one crowded hotel to another crowded hotel. It seemed as if the whole world had suddenly decided to see the rest of the world.

Bombay was crowded and we barely succeeded in getting rooms at the Taj Mahal. There were swarms of Americans outward bound and inward bound. You couldn't go down a street without encountering scores of new sun hats and red-bound "Murrays." The taxicabs were full of eager faces peering out inquiringly at the monuments and points of interest that flashed past.

The train to Agra was crowded and we succeeded in getting reservations only by the skin of our teeth. Also the hotels at Agra were jammed and many people were being turned away, while the procession of carriages jogging out toward the Taj Mahal was like an endless chain. Upon all sides as you paused in spellbound rapture before the most beautiful building in the world, you heard the voice of the tourist explaining the beauties of the structure.

During the Tourist Rush

The Taj Mahal is justly called the most beautiful edifice in the world. It is so exquisite in its architecture and its ornamentation that one may believe the story that it was designed by a poet and constructed by a jeweler. It was built by Shah Jehan as a memorial to his wife and for centuries it has stood as a token of his great love for her.

When I visited it this year I was surprised to find that Lord Curzon had placed within the great marble dome a hanging lamp as a memorial to his own wife. It seemed like a shocking piece of presumption—much as if the president of France should hang a memorial to one of his own family over the sarcophagus of Napoleon, or a president of the United States should do the same at Washington's tomb at Mount Vernon. It seemed like an inexpensive way of diverting the most beautiful structure of the world to personal uses.

And yet later I was compelled to modify this opinion when I saw how much excellent work Lord Curzon did toward restoring the old palaces of Agra and preserving them for future generations. As a reward for this work, perhaps, there may have been some justification in placing a memorial lamp in the dome of the Taj, especially as the lamp is exquisite in workmanship and adds rather than detracts from the stately beauty of the interior. But just the same the first verdict of the spectator is that Lord Curzon displayed a colossal egotism in so doing.

The tourist's beaten track in India was as thronged with American sightseers as the château country in France. Lucknow was crowded, Benares was crowded, Calcutta was crowded, and the trains that ran in all directions were crowded. A traveler wore a look of perpetual anxiety lest he should fail to get hotel or railway accommodations.

The India of one's imagination—the somber land of mystery, of untold riches, of eastern enchantment, of far-away romance—was gone, buried under picture post-cards, hustling tourists, and all the commonplaces of a popular tourist track. It was distinctly disappointing from one point of view, and yet, I suppose, one should rejoice that his fellow countrymen have cash and energy enough to travel in distant places, even though they destroy the romantic charm of those places by so doing.

Tourists in India

The rush of Americans through India was as brisk as was the rush of Americans through Europe ten years ago. Age was no handicap. There were old couples, sixty, seventy, and eighty years old, jogging along as eagerly and excitedly as young bridal couples. The conversation one encountered was always pretty much the same—how such a train was crowded, how accommodations could not be secured at such a hotel, how poor the hotels were, and how long they would have to wait to get a berth on some outgoing ship. There were many people hung up in

Bombay and Calcutta vainly trying to get away, but the boats were booked full for two or more voyages ahead.

One of the peculiarities of Indian travel has been the fact that most tourists plan to be in India during December, January and February. Hence they arrive in bunches, and try to get away in a bunch, which is impossible owing to the limited capacity of the steamships. This year the swarms of tourists have been so great that many of them could not get out of the country until late in March and along in April.

The Americans have become the great travelers of the world. In India there are two American tourists for one of all other nationalities. The hotel registers bristle with U.S.A. addresses and the shops and hotels regard the American trade as being the most profitable. One desirable result of the American tendency to fare afield has been the steady improvement in hotel and railway accommodations in the Far East.

We said good-by to India without much regret; in fact, we were elated to secure accommodations on a small Indo-China boat that made the run to Penang and Singapore in about eight days. No berths could be secured on the ships that go by the way of Burma. Those ships were booked full for several trips ahead. So we settled down comfortably on the good ship Lai Sang and droned lazily down through the Bay of Bengal. There were accommodations for only twelve first-class passengers, and there were only six on board. We had elbow room for the first time since leaving Africa.

When we stopped at Penang there were two distinct sensations. One was that Georgetown, the capital of the Island of Penang, is the prettiest tropical city I have ever seen; and the other was the first shock of the rubber craze. From that time on we were constantly in a seething roar of rubber talk; everybody was buying rubber shares and everybody else was talking about starting rubber plantations. The fever was epidemic. Planters were destroying profitable cocoanut groves in order to replace them with rubber trees. Nearly every local resident was putting his last cent in rubber shares and the tales of suddenly increased wealth inflamed the imaginations and cupidity of every one who heard them.

I mentally jotted down the names of one or two companies that are going to declare enormous dividends soon, but that's as far as I've got in my rubber investments.

Penang, like Hongkong, is an island. The city on the island is Georgetown, while the city on Hongkong is Victoria; but you will never hear any one speak of Georgetown or Victoria. It is just Penang and Hongkong, and the other names are useless incumbrances.

Singapore was crowded with Americans fighting for accommodations on the China and Japan steamers; other Americans fighting to get reservations on the Java steamers; still other Americans who, in despair, were going to Hongkong by way of Borneo and the Philippines. They were willing to go first, second or third class—any way at all to get on a ship.

At Raffles' Hotel

The Singapore hotels were crowded and we got the last room in the Raffles Hotel. The great and stately veranda, which serves the double purpose of a bar and an out-of-door reception-room, was usually crowded. That veranda is the redeeming feature of Raffles Hotel. In other respects this great hotel, situated at the cross-roads where East and West and North and South meet, is not up to what a good hotel should be.

We got the last state-room on a steamer to Java, and to our great surprise we found the ship to be the nicest we had traveled on, and the cooking to rival that of the great restaurants of Paris.

Cholera was rampant in certain parts of Java, but that didn't stop the sightseers. Nothing less than an earthquake or a lost letter of credit could have stopped them.

Our adventures in Java were a repetition of "crowds." The Hotel des Indes in Batavia was crowded and we got the last room. The railways were crowded, but not so much as the ones in India, and the carriages are most comfortable.

For a week we did volcanoes and gorgeous scenery, and realized what a delightful place Java is. It is even nicer than Japan, and the hotels are the best in the East.

My chief purpose in going to Java was to get a Javanese waterwheel. They had one at the world's fair in Chicago, and I have remembered it ever since as one of the most musical things I have ever heard. A friend of mine wanted me to get him one and I volunteered to do so. I supposed that we would hear waterwheels just as soon as we got off the ship. But I was evidently mistaken.

Nobody in Java, so far as I could discover, had ever seen or heard of a Javanese waterwheel. I inquired of dozens of people—people who had lived there all their lives—but they looked blank when I spoke of waterwheels. I drew pictures of it, but that didn't enlighten them.

Finally in despair, after a week of vain searching, I drew the plans for a waterwheel and had it made. And I am taking it home with me, hoping that it may make music. Next year, owing to the demand I created for waterwheels, I suppose the Javanese will start making them for the tourist trade.

Java in a State of High Cultivation

Just as Russia is the land of "nitchevo," Spain the land of "mañana," and China the land of "maskee," so Java is the land of "never mind." You will hear the expression dozens of times in the course of a talk between residents of Java—at the beginning, in the middle, and at the end of sentences.

"I think it will rain to-morrow, but—never mind."

"I missed the train, but—never mind."

"I'm not feeling well, but—never mind."

You hear it all the time, all through Java.

In Java we had the best coffee we had struck since leaving Paris, in fact, the first real good coffee we had found. Even worthy Abdullah, our camp cook, was considerable of a failure at coffee making. The

Boro Boedoer ruins are among the most stupendous in the world; the volcanoes of Java are like chimneys in Pittsburg, the terraced rice fields are beautiful beyond belief, but—never mind. I think I shall remember Java chiefly for its delicious coffee and for my house-to-house hunt for a waterwheel.

I was sitting one day in the Singapore club talking to Colonel Glover of the British army, when a hand tapped me on my shoulder. I looked around and there stood the King of Christmas Island. I no more expected to see him than I did the great Emperor Charlemagne, for it had been many years since we were college mates at Purdue University. His story is romantic. He is the nephew of Sir John Murray, who owns immense phosphate deposits in Christmas Island, two hundred miles south of Java Head. Years ago he went out to help work these great deposits and has climbed up until now he is the virtual head of the island. His authority is absolute and he has come to be called the King of Christmas Island. His every-day name is that of his distinguished uncle, Sir John, but his Sunday name is "King."

For a day or two we motored around Singapore and it was worth seeing to note how the tourists stared when I casually said, "Well, King, let's have a bamboo." In a day or two he was going to meet his wife, who was just coming from England with a little three-months-old crown prince whom he had not yet seen. Then, together, the royal family was going back to Christmas Island on one of the king's ships.

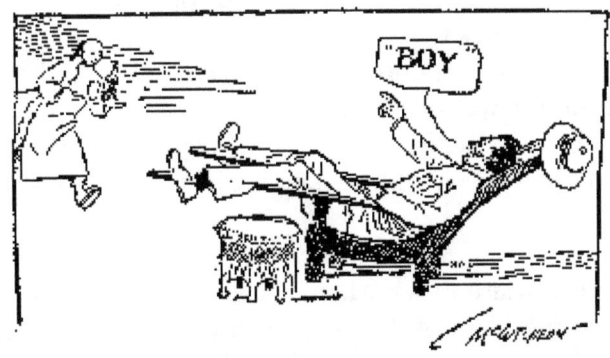

The Call of the East

The China coast is distinguished for its excellent United States consular officials. And it hasn't been so for many years. Our representative in Singapore, Mr. Dubois, is one of the best men I have yet encountered in one of our consulates. He is a new-comer in Singapore and yet in his few months he has added more prestige to our consulate general than all the former men put together. One can not but wonder why he is not a minister or an ambassador, instead of only a consul general.

Hongkong has been fortunate in having an excellent representative in Mr. Rublee, and his recent untimely death is a distinct loss to the country. Mr. Wilder is in Shanghai and he is decidedly a man of the best mental and temperamental equipment. So now an American traveler may go up and down the China coast and "point with pride" to his nation's representatives. How different it was ten or twelve years ago!

We barely managed to get on board the *Prinz Ludwig*–Singapore to Hongkong. It is one of the N.D. Lloyd's crack ships and everybody tries to take it. We got the last cabin, as usual, and spent hours thanking our lucky stars.

The China Sea is chronically disposed to be disagreeable, but on this occasion it was quite well behaved. There were three days of delightful sunshine and then a sudden blighting chill in the air. We landed in Hongkong with overcoats buttoned up and with garments drenched by the rains and mist clouds that battled around the great peaks of this little island. The hotels were jammed to the sidewalks and we got the last room at the Hongkong Hotel, while throngs were turned away; the steamers for the States were booked full for several voyages ahead and tourists were rushing around in despair. The *Asia* had been booked up to the limit for weeks and it seemed as if we might have to wait a long time before getting berths on any ship. But some one unexpectedly had to give up a state-room and we were fortunate in getting it.

I had a great desire to see Manila again. It had been ten years since I left there in the "days of the empire" and everything in me quivered with longing to revisit the place where I spent my golden period of adventure. We booked on the old *Yuen Sang*, a friend of former days, and the skipper, Captain Percy Rolfe, handsome, cultured, and capable, was still in command. He loves the China Sea and has steadfastly refused to be lured away by offers of greater ships and more important commands. When we engaged our passage the agent warned us that the vessel was carrying a cargo of naphtha and kerosene and that we might not wish to risk it; but we went. A Jap and a Chinaman were the only two other passengers, and they were invisible during the sixty hours to cross.

We steamed out of Hongkong in a chilling wind and at once plunged into a fog, but the next morning we ran into smooth seas and warm weather. A full moon hung over the empty waste of waters and the nights were gorgeous.

As we neared the coast of Luzon I became much excited, for in my memory were those vivid, expectant days of old when our little American fleet crossed this selfsame stretch of sea to find and destroy the Spanish ships. I lived over again those boding days when the air was electric with impending danger.

It was long before daylight when the *Yuen Sang*, at half-speed, arrived at Corregidor. The captain wished to report his number to the signal station, and we had to wait until light had come before the ship could enter. So the engines were stopped and for an hour we drifted on under the ship's momentum. The silencing of the engines on a ship is always ominous, and just now, with the dim bulk of Corregidor looming grimly before us, it seemed as if there was something particularly sinister about our stealthy approach.

From five o'clock onward we stood on the bridge, our voices unconsciously hushed as we spoke. Here was where the *Baltimore* had dropped a Greek fire life preserver and for a long time it had bobbed about on the tumbling sea, weird and terrifying to those who didn't know what it was. There was where the soot in the McCulloch's funnel had suddenly blazed up like the chimney of a blast furnace. And over there on the lower edge of the black bulk of the island was where a little signal light had flared up and then died out, leaving every man on our ships tense with expectant dread, and all about us here had reigned a silence so penetrating that it in itself was harder to bear than the thunder and flash of guns.

And still we drifted on, nearer and nearer to Boca Chica, the northern passage into Manila Bay. Dawn and light came slowly. In poetry the dawn of the tropics may come up like thunder and the transition of darkness to light may be startling and sudden, but in my own experience the tropic dawn comes slowly and pervadingly. First a faint grayness, gradually growing brighter until the sun shoots up joyous and golden in its glory, painting the skies with flaming banners and penciling the tips and edges of clouds with the fires of morning. When we lazily drifted in toward Corregidor from the China Sea that morning, it was light enough to see distinctly for nearly an hour before the sun rose.

Presently a fluttering string of signal flags appeared on the top of the island, and a moment later our engines resumed their throbbing and we headed boldly into Boca Chica. Here on the left was Mariveles Bay, the scene of the famous German ship, *Irene*, incident, which electrified the world.

Every point that rose before my eyes was pregnant with historic memories and suggestions. I was thrilled and yet I half-dreaded my return to Manila, for fear that the peace and commercialism of the present days would be disappointing to one who knew it when each day was filled with trouble and threats of trouble; when the city lay always as if under an impending cloud and when the borders of the bay rang with the thunder of guns and the sputter of musketry.

As the *Yuen Sang* steamed across the twenty-five miles of the bay it seemed as if it were only yesterday that I had been there. The waters were glassy and smooth, just as the bay used to be every morning of the long blockade, when the air was still and the broad glistening water was tranquil and at rest.

The surprises came in Manila. Great changes had taken place in the harbor, new breakwaters were where there had been none before, new buildings were up, and still more were building. Big electric cars rushed along where formerly the snail-like horse cars crept painfully by. The city was unbelievably clean and the main streets were full of busy life.

I visited the old houses where we had once lived in economical splendor, with servants and carriages and expenses that were microscopic as compared to those of the present day. Upon all sides were the visible evidences that some day Manila will be the finest city of the Orient if the time ever comes when capital may feel assured that our occupation has some prospect of permanence.

In my old days I used to know a beautiful Mestiza girl in Manila. She was very pretty and very nice. I used to draw pictures of her and struggle bravely with the Spanish language. And she was kind and patient with my efforts to learn. Her name was Victoria and she kept a little shop where she and her ancestors for generations before had sold silk jusi and piña cloth. I visited her often there and sometimes went out to her home, a beautiful big Spanish house in Calle Zarigoza.

I determined to find her and went over to her shop. Fatal mistake! Ten years and the tropics work many changes in the soft-eyed daughters south of the fifteenth degree of latitude.

I once read a story by Pierre Loti, a sad and haunting story of how he sought, after years of absence, to find an old-time sweetheart in Stamboul. He didn't find her and he should be grateful for his failure.

Ten Years After

I found Victoria. She recognized me at once, although I hardly knew in her the slender, pretty Victoria of old. Her eyes were soft and nice, but smallpox had pitted her nose and cheeks and the deadly incubus of flesh had upholstered her in many soft and cushiony folds. I asked her if she had married and she said she never had, which information I matched with promptness. She spoke English quite well and seemed prosperous and—yes, motherly. There's no other word for it, although she is now hardly thirty.

It was a terrible disappointment, a collapse of delightful memories, and as I walked away from her little silk shop with a vague promise to call again I knew perfectly well that I should never go back.

I left Manila after less than two days and rolled and plunged and tumbled back across the China Sea to Hongkong. I bought a little chow dog puppy from the Chinese steward on board, but I suppose it will grow up and get fat one of these days, too. Allison Armour and his nephew, Norman Armour, were with us and in Hongkong the latter bought two chow dog puppies to send home. They looked exactly like teddy bears. Later he resolved that the trouble and risk were too great, inasmuch as he was not returning by the Pacific, so he gave them to me. And with three chow dogs and my friend Stephenson I embarked on the *Asia* for the twenty-eight day trip to Frisco.

The ship was jammed and we found a little fat man consigned to the sofa in our state-room. He was pleasant looking, but we little realized what hours of nocturnal horror were in store for us. He was the champion snorist of the five continents. He could snore in all keys, all languages, all directions, and it was like trying to sleep in the same room with a fog-horn. Nothing could waken him and he went to sleep before he struck the bed. And from that moment on through the night he tried the acoustic properties of that end of the ship to the utmost. After two or three nights of sleeplessness we resolved to rebel, mutiny, revolt, and if necessary joyfully to commit justifiable homicide.

Never an American Flag

One night Stephenson turned on the light and reached for his cane. "What are you going to do? Kill him?" I asked eagerly. But he only poked at the quivering form to awaken it, and merely succeeded in changing the key from B flat to a discord of minors.

At Yokohama somebody got off and by buying an extra berth we moved into another state-room and slept for twenty-four hours. We called him "Snoring Cupid," because of his cherubic appearance and proficiency in snoring.

It was the cherry blossom season in Japan. Through the constant rain we saw the hillsides pink with loveliness. But it was cold and disheartening and after five days in Japan we turned with relief to the voyage homeward. And it was very pleasant. Lots of pleasant things happened, but nothing more.

It is good to be back where the American flag is a familiar sight and not a curiosity. We saw thousands and thousands of merchant ships, but except in Manila and Honolulu we never saw a solitary American flag on one of them.

And that's the end of our hunting trip. We are now back where we have to pay two or three times as much for things as we did in the Orient. A cigar that costs three cents gold in Manila costs twelve and one-half cents gold in San Francisco! But—never mind. A pleasant time was had.

CHAPTER XXII
WAYS AND MEANS. WHAT TO TAKE AND WHAT NOT TO TAKE, INFORMATION FOR THOSE THAT WISH, INTEND OR HOPE TO HUNT IN THE AFRICAN HIGHLANDS

WHEN one returns to America after some time in the African game country, he is assailed by many questions from others who wish, intend, or hope to make a similar trip. Almost without variation the questioner will ask about the cost, about the danger from fever and sickness, about snakes and insects, about the tempers of the tribes one encounters, and then, if he be a specialist, he will ask about the rifles and the camp equipment. As these familiar and oft repeated inquiries have been made by friends who had read my African letters, I must assume that the features of an African hunting trip, about which people are most curious, were very imperfectly answered in the preceding chapters. Hence, this supplementary chapter, dealing briefly with the ways and means of such a trip, is added for the enlightenment of such readers as may be planning a journey into those fascinating regions of Africa where I have so recently been.

As to the cost of a trip of three or more months in the field I should say that about one thousand dollars a month would amply cover the total expenses from New York back to New York. This amount would include passage money, guns, ammunition, landing charges, commissions, camera expenses on a reasonable scale, tents, customs—in fact all the incidental items which are not customarily included in the estimate given by the Nairobi outfitters. These firms, chief of which are the Newland, Tarlton and Company, Limited, which directed Colonel Roosevelt's *safari*, and the Boma Trading Company, which directed the Duke of Connaught's hunt, agree to outfit a party at a cost of about five-hundred dollars a month for each white man. For this amount they furnish everything except your ammunition, clothes, medicines, camera supplies, export and import duties, mounting of trophies, passage money to and from Africa, and such items. To particularize, they agree to supply for this amount, a complete outfit of tents, foods, porters, camp attendants, gunbearers, horses, mules or ox teams, as may be required, and a native head-man or overseer.

One who wished to do so could telegraph ahead to have one of the Nairobi outfitting firms prepare a one, two or three months' hunt, or *safari*, and then, with only a suit-case he could arrive, with the certainty that everything would be in readiness. There would be no worry or concern about any feature of that part of the work. He would be relieved of the anxiety of preparation, and it is hardly likely that he would ever regret having taken this course. The dealings of our *safari* with Messrs. Newland and Tarlton were most satisfactory in all respects and the charges they made were entirely reasonable. To the one who desires to make this trip in this, the simplest way, there is the need of giving only one suggestion: Let him write to one of the outfitting firms, stating the length of time that he can spend in the field, the class of game that he chiefly wishes to get, the number of white men in his party, and the season of the year that he plans to be in Africa. The outfitters will then answer, giving all the particulars of cost and equipment. This is the course that I should recommend for the average hunter who has had no previous experience in Africa. It will save him the trouble of making an endless amount of preparation, much of which will be useless because of his ignorance of conditions in that field of sport.

In the case of our own *safari*, we bought our guns, tents, ammunition, foods and entire equipment in London and had it shipped to Nairobi. This equipment contemplated a trip of six months in the field, and included sixty-five "chop boxes" of sixty pounds each, containing foods. These chop boxes were of wood, with lids and locks, twenty of which were tin lined for use in packing specimens later in the trip, and all marked with bands of various colors to identify their contents. The boxes contained the following supplies:

TWENTY CASES (RED BAND)

    Two tins imperial cheese.

    One pound Ceylon tea.

    One three-quarter pound tin ground coffee.

    One four-pound tin granulated sugar.

    Two tins ox tongue.

One tin oxford sausage.

Two tins sardines.

Two tins kippered herrings.

Three tins deviled ham (Underwood's).

Two tins jam (assorted).

Two tins marmalade (Dundee).

Three half-pound tins butter.

Three half-pound tins dripping.

Ten half-pound tins ideal milk.

Two tins small captain biscuit.

Two tins baked beans, Heinz (tomato sauce).

One half-pound tin salt.

One two-pound tin chocolate (Army and Navy).

Two parchment skins pea soup.

One one and one-half pound tin Scotch oatmeal.

TWENTY CASES (BLUE BAND)

Two tins baked beans (Heinz) (tomato sauce).

One tin bologna sausage.

One tin sardines.

One tin sardines, smoked.

Two one-pound tins camp, pie.

Five tins jam, assorted.

Two tins marmalade (Dundee).

Five half-pound tins butter.

Three half-pound tins dripping.

Ten half-pound tins ideal milk.

Two tins imperial cheese.

One one and one-quarter pound tin Ceylon tea.

One three-quarter pound tin ground coffee.

One four pound tin granulated sugar.

One quarter-pound tin cocoa.

Two tins camp biscuit.

One half-pound tin salt.

One one and one-half tin Scotch oatmeal.

One one-pound tin lentils.

One tin mixed vegetables (dried).

One two-pound tin German prunes.

Six soup squares.

One ounce W. pepper.

Two sponge cloths.

One-half quire kitchen paper.

One two-pound tin chocolate (Army and Navy).

SIXTEEN CASES (GREEN BAND)

Three fourteen-pound tins self-raising flour.

Two cases (black band) containing fifteen bottles lime juice (plain) Montserrat.

Two cases, each containing one dozen Scotch whisky.

Two cases (red and blue band) thirty pounds bacon, well packed in salt.

Two cases (yellow and black band) five ten-pound tins plaster of Paris for making casts of animals.

One case (red and green band) fifty pounds sperm candles—large size (carriage).

Four folding lanterns.

The following items to be equally divided into as many lots as necessary to make sixty-pound cases:

Eight Edam cheeses.

Twenty tins bovril.

Twenty two-pound tins sultana raisins.

Ten two-pound tins currants.

Ten one-pound tins macaroni.

Thirty tins Underwood deviled ham.

Eighty tablets carbolic soap.

Eighty packets toilet paper.

Ten bottles Enos' fruit salt.

Twenty one-pound tins plum pudding.

Six tins curry powder.

Twenty one-pound tins yellow Dubbin.

Six one-pound tins veterinary vaseline.

Six one-pound tins powdered sugar.

Six tin openers.

Twelve tins asparagus tips.

Twelve tins black mushrooms.

Six large bottles Pond's extract.

Twelve ten-yard spools zinc oxide surgeon's tape one inch wide.

Two small bottles Worcestershire sauce.

In addition to the foregoing we added the following equipment of table ware:

Eight white enamel soup plates—light weight.

Eight white enamel dinner plates—light weight.

Three white enamel vegetable dishes—medium size.

Six one-pint cups.

Eight knives and forks.

Twelve teaspoons.

Six soup spoons.

Six large table-spoons.

One carving knife and fork.

Six white enamel oatmeal dishes.

As our tent equipment and some of the miscellanies necessary to our expedition, the subjoined articles were procured:

Four double roof ridge tents 10 by 8—4 feet walls, in valises.

One extra fly of above size, with poles, ropes, etc, complete.

Five ground sheets for above, one foot larger each way, *i.e.,* 11 by 9.

Four mosquito nets for one-half tents, 9 feet long.

Four circular canvas baths.

Twelve green, round-bottom bags 43 by 30.

Four hold-all bags with padlocks.

Two fifty-yard coils 1 1-4 Manila rope.

One pair wood blocks for 1 1-4 brass sheaves, strapped with tails.

Four four-quart tin water bottles.

Two eight-quart Uganda water bottles.

Four large canvas water buckets.

One gross No. 1 circlets.

One punch and die.

The foregoing lot of supplies were ordered through Newland, Tarlton and Company's agent at 166 Piccadilly, London, and were ready when we reached London.

MEDICINES AND SURGICAL EQUIPMENT

It is well to provide a good store of medicines and some instruments, even though, as in our case, we had little occasion to use any of it. One of the Burroughs and Wellcome medicine cases "for East Africa" is compact and well selected. In addition there should be plenty of zinc oxide adhesive plaster, some bandages and some hypodermic syringes for use in case of wounds which might lead to blood poisoning. In our first experience with lions we always went prepared for wounds of this sort, but later we took no precautions whatever and fortunately had no occasion for heroic measures. At the same time, it is far wiser always to be prepared.

We were also well supplied with tick medicines, but in spite of the fact that we encountered millions of ticks, they gave us no concern and no tick preventatives were used. Quinine and calomel are essentials and may be bought in Nairobi.

RIFLES

It is important that each hunter include in his battery one heavy double-barreled cordite rifle for use at close quarters where a shocking impact is desirable. Each of our party had a .475 Jeffery, which we found to be entirely satisfactory, and which served us as well as though we had used the more expensive Holland and Holland's .450. I do not presume to know much about the relative merits of rifles, but after an experience of four and a half months with the Jeffery's .475, I feel justified in saying that this type would meet all requirements reliably. These rifles cost thirty-five guineas each.

Mr. Akeley and I each had a nine millimeter Mannlicher, which we found to be unsatisfactory, either through fault of our own or of the rifle. We had a feeling that the weight of the ball was too great for the charge of powder. Others may favor it, but I should not include it in my battery if I were to go again. This type costs twelve guineas.

Mr. Stephenson used a .318 Mauser, which he found most satisfactory. We also had three .256 Mannlichers, which in my experience is a type for which too much praise can not be given. It is also a twelve guinea rifle.

In mentioning these three rifles of foreign make, I do not wish to imply that they are superior to our own American guns. Colonel Roosevelt used a Winchester .405 and a Springfield, both of which he considered most desirable. I think if I were to go again I should take a .405 as my second gun, heavy enough for all purposes except the close-quarter work where the big cordite double-barrels are necessary.

The matter of a battery is one which each sportsman should determine for himself. There are many good types and a man is naturally inclined to favor those with which he is familiar.

We also carried shot guns, one ten-gauge which, with buck shot, makes a formidable weapon for stopping charges of soft-skinned animals at close range; and two twenty-gauge Parkers for bird shooting.

In addition, we included revolvers, none of which we fired or needed at any time in Africa. Perhaps a heavy six-shooter might some time be a valuable reserve, but our experience leads me to think that it would generally repose quietly in camp at all times.

In the way of ammunition for a six-months' shoot, we took for each cordite rifle, 200 full mantle, 200 soft nose and 100 split cartridges. For the 9 millimeter, we took for each rifle 450 solids, 500 splits and 500 soft-nosed bullets, and practically the same for the .256 Mannlichers. We found that we had far more ammunition than we required, especially the solids for the smaller rifles, but it is better to have too much than to have the fear of running short. One should not forget that he is likely to shoot more than in his wildest dreams he supposed possible and the meanest feeling on a hunt is to have constantly to economize cartridges.

None of us used telescope sights but by many sportsmen they are considered highly desirable in African shooting where often the range is great and the light confusing.

PERSONAL EQUIPMENT

When we stopped in New York on our way to Africa, we talked with Mr. Bayard Dominick, who had just returned from such a trip as we had in mind, and from him secured a list of articles which he found to be sufficient and equal to all needs. We used this list to guide us and except in minor details, assembled a similar equipment:

    Two suits—coat and breeches—gabardine or khaki.

One belt.

Two knives—one hunting-knife, one jack-knife.

Three pair cloth putties.

Three flannel shirts (I actually only used two).

Six suits summer flannels, merino, long drawers.

Three pair Abercrombie lightest shoes (one pair rubber soles).

Three colored silk handkerchiefs.

Two face towels—two bath towels.

Three khaki cartridge holders to put on shirts to hold big cartridges, one for each shirt.

One pair long trousers to put on at night, khaki.

Two suits flannel pajamas.

Eight pair socks (I used gray Jaeger socks, fine).

One light west sweater.

One Mackinaw coat (not absolutely necessary).

One rubber coat.

One pair mosquito boots (Lawn and Alder, London).

Soft leather top boots for evening wear in camp.

Five leather pockets to hold cartridges to go on belt.

Three whetstones (one for self and two for gunbearers).

One helmet (we used Gyppy pattern Army and Navy stores).

One double terai hat, brown (Army and Navy stores).

One six-_or_eight-foot pocket tape of steel to measure horns.

One compass.

One diary.

Writing materials.

Toilet articles.

Articles for personal use, however, may be determined by the wishes and experiences of the individual.

We each had good Zeiss glasses, which are essential, and later, in Nairobi, were able to obtain a satisfactory replenishment of hunting clothes and shoes.

Cameras

Everybody who goes shooting will want at least one camera if only for the purpose of having his picture taken with his first lion, if he is successful in getting one. Mr. Akeley made special preparations for taking fine photographs, and for this reason carried a complete outfit, even to a dark-room equipment for developing negatives and moving picture films in the field. He carried a naturalist's graflex, a small hand camera and a moving-picture machine. Mr. Stephenson had a 3A Kodak, I had the same and also a Verascope stereoscopic camera. We used films and plates and found no deterioration in them even after several months in the field. Films and camera supplies may be purchased in Nairobi; and also the developing and printing may be done most satisfactorily in the town.

Fevers and Sickness

It is my belief that the dangers of this sort are magnified in the imaginations of those who contemplate a trip to East Africa. Very little of the hunting is done in jungles—in fact there are few jungles except on the slopes of the mountains and along the course of streams.

Our *safari* went into the Athi Plains, along the Athi River down the Tana River, up on Mount Kenia and later on the Guas Ngishu Plateau, along the Nzoia River, and up Mount Elgon. Coming out of this district, we passed through the Rift Valley and part of our *safari* went up to Lake Hannington. So, from personal experience, I can speak with knowledge of only these sections. Along the Tana we were in fever country, the altitude being only about thirty-five hundred feet. And yet only two of our party had touches of fever, so light that they readily yielded to quinine. This was tick country, and we had been led to believe that we should be fearfully pestered with these insects. But there was almost no annoyance from them, due, perhaps, to a good deal of care in keeping them out of our clothes. There were many mosquitoes in this section, but effective mosquito nets over our cots protected us from them.

On Mount Kenia, the high Guas Ngishu Plateau and Mount Elgon, the thought of sickness was entirely absent. These districts were found to be salubrious and free from ticks and mosquitoes.

SNAKES

Before going to Africa, I must admit that the thought of serpents occasioned much anxiety. I didn't like the idea of tramping around through grass and reeds where poisonous snakes might be found. And yet, after a few days in the field, I never seriously thought of snakes as a possible, or rather probable, source of danger. In four and a half months, in all kinds of country, much of the time on foot, I saw only six live snakes. They were all small and only two, a puff adder and a little viper, were known to be venomous. Our porters, with bare feet and legs, penetrated all kinds of snaky-looking spots and yet not one was bitten. In fact, I have never heard of any one being bitten by snakes in East Africa, and for this reason I can not avoid the conclusion that the fear of snakes need not be seriously considered as an element of danger in the country.

The Natives

So many hunting parties have gone over the game fields that the natives are familiar with white men and are not at all likely to be hostile or troublesome. Our *safari* at one time went into a district where we were warned to expect trouble, but there was none and I think there never need be any if the white men are considerate and fair. If a district is known to be particularly troublesome, the government authorities would not permit a hunting party to go into it, so for that reason the hunters need apprehend no dangers from that source.

Game

Game is found in varying degrees of abundance in most parts of the East African highlands. Within two hours of Nairobi the sportsman may find twelve or fifteen species, while within the space of four weeks a lucky hunter might secure elephant, lion, rhinoceros, buffalo, eland and hippopotamus. It is hardly *likely* that he would, but it is quite within the range of possibilities. It all depends upon luck. The hunter is allowed under his two hundred and fifty dollar license, about one hundred and ninety-five animals, comprising thirty-five species, and not including lion, leopard, wart-hog and hyena. There is no restriction on the number of these last-named species that one is allowed to shoot, but there is on the number that he gets the opportunity of shooting.

The success of an expedition should not be measured by the number of trophies, but rather by the quality of them. For example, the new license allows twenty zebras, but no one would want to kill more than two unless as food for the porters. The same is true of many other species, and a temperate sportsman should have no desire to kill more than a couple of each species, say sixty or eighty head in all, unless, of course, he is making collections for museums or for other scientific purposes.

The gunbearers are usually fairly good skinners and if carefully watched and directed can treat the heads and skins so that they may be safely got in to Nairobi. Here they should be overhauled carefully and packed in brine for shipment out of the country. The agents in Nairobi should be consulted about these details and will give competent instructions covering this phase of the work.

GAME LAWS

These are of necessity under frequent revision, but the latest available information allows the holder of a fifty-pound license, which lasts for one year from date of issue, to kill or capture the following:

Buffalo (Bull), 2; [A]Rhinoceros, 2; [A]Hippopotamus, 2; [A]Eland, 1; Zebra (Grevey's), 2; Zebra, (Common), 20; Oryx callotis, 2; Oryx beisa, 4; Waterbuck (of each species), 2; Sable antelope (male), 1; [A]Roan antelope (male), 1; [A]Greater Kudu (male), 1; Lesser Kudu, 4; Topi, 2; Topi (in Jubaland, Tanaland and Loita Plains), 8; Coke's Hartebeest, 20; [A]Neumann's Hartebeest, 2; Jackson's Hartebeest, 4; Hunter's Antelope, 6; Thomas' Kob, 4; Bongo, 2; Impalla, 4; Sitatunga, 2; Wildebeest, 3; Grant's Gazelle (Typica, Notata Bright's, Robertsi), each, 3; Gerenuk, 4; Duiker (Harvey's, Isaac's, and Blue), each, 10; Dik-dik (Kirk's, Guenther's, Hinde's, Cavendish's), each, 10; Oribi (Abyssinian, Haggard's, Kenia), each, 10; Suni (Nesotragus Moschatus), 10; Klipspringer, 10; Reedbuck (Ward's, Chanler's), each, 10; Gazelle (Thompson's, Peter's, Soemmering's), each, 10; Bushbuck (Common, Haywood's), each, 10; Colobi Monkeys, of each species, 6; Marabou, 4; Egret, of each species, 4.

[Footnote A: Can not be killed in certain districts.]

SPECIAL LICENSES

These can be taken out for ten pounds each and entitle the holder to kill or capture:

Elephant with tusks over thirty pounds, each, 1; Bull Giraffe in certain districts, 1.

A second elephant is allowed on payment of a further fee of twenty pounds, this fee being returnable in the event of the elephant not being obtained.

Lions and leopards are classed as vermin, and consequently no license to kill them is required.

The Season for Shooting

"Practically any time of the year will do for shooting in British East Africa, but the season of the 'big rains' from the end of January to the end of April, is not one to choose willingly from the point of view of comfort. There is also a short spell of rainy weather about October and November which, however, is not looked upon as an obstacle to a *safari*, and we may say that from May to February constitutes the shooting season."

The foregoing is quoted from a pamphlet on East Africa game shooting. In our own experience the weather between September and February was perfectly delightful and I judge, from reading accounts of Colonel Roosevelt's trip, that his operations between April and December were never seriously hampered by bad weather. From the experiences of these two *safaris*, one might reasonably conclude that any time is good except February, March and April, the season of the "big rains."

Heat

On the Athi Plains in September, we found the heat in the middle of the day to be very ardent, to say the least. But with the exception of fewer than a dozen days in all, we never were obliged to consider this phase of the hunting experience as an objectionable feature. We found the cold of the high altitudes to be severe in the evenings and in contrast to it, the warm days were most welcome. Along the coast, of course, the heat is intense, but all of the shooting is done at altitudes exceeding thirty-five hundred feet and one merely pauses at the coast town long enough to catch his train. In September even Mombasa was delightful, but in January it was very hot.

In conclusion, I might say that all one needs for an African hunting trip is sufficient time, sufficient money, and a fair degree of health. Also the services of a reliable outfitting firm which will furnish enlightenment upon all subjects not specifically included in the foregoing chapter of advice and information.

With the exception of the photographs, all of which are here reproduced for the first time, a great part of this material appeared originally in The Chicago Tribune, and is now published in book form by the courtesy of that paper.

www.ingramcontent.com/pod-product-compliance
Lightning Source LLC
Chambersburg PA
CBHW051707160426
43209CB00004B/1052